DATE			

THE
ASEAN
STATES

Coping with Dependence

Donald K. Crone

PRAEGER SPECIAL STUDIES • PRAEGER SCIENTIFIC

Library of Congress Cataloging in Publication Data

Crone, Donald K.
    The ASEAN states.

    Bibliography: p.
    Includes index.
    1. Asia, Southeastern—Economic policy. 2. Asia,
Southeastern—Foreign economic relations. 3. Asia,
Southeastern—Dependency on foreign countries. 4. ASEAN.
I. Title.   II. Title: A.S.E.A.N. states.
HC441.C76 1983   337'.0959   83-2433
ISBN 0-03-062911-X

Published in 1983 by Praeger Publishers
CBS Educational and Professional Publishing
a Division of CBS Inc.
521 Fifth Avenue, New York, NY 10175 USA

    456789   052   98765432

Printed in the United States of America
on acid-free paper.

CONTENTS

LIST OF TABLES

ACKNOWLEDGMENTS

I have incurred many debts of gratitude during the preparation of this book. A major one is to the several institutions that provided financial support and assistance: the Institute of International Relations of the University of British Columbia, the Institute of Southeast Asian Studies in Singapore, the Killam Foundation of Canada, and the Donnor Foundation of Canada. Numerous, busy scholars took time to read all or parts of the manuscript. These include Peter Busch, Michael Haas, Kal Holsti, Frank Langdon, Terry McGee, Stephen Milne, Michael Schechter, Sheldon Simon, and Mark Zacher. My gain from their insights is major, whether or not I satisfied their specific suggestions. Patricia Morison converted sloppy drafts into a respectable manuscript. Others have provided moral support and understanding, particularly my wife, Nukhet Kardam, and daughter, Maya Jenny. The remaining shortcomings are surely mine.

I wish to give credit to two sources that have granted me permission to reprint materials I contributed to them: "Regional Mobilization and Transnational Associations in ASEAN," in The Southeast Asian Environment, ed. Douglas Webster (Ottawa: Canadian Council of Southeast Asian Studies, 1982); and "Emerging Trends in the Control of Foreign Investments in ASEAN," © April 1981 by the Regents of the University of California, reprinted from Asian Survey, vol. 21, no. 4, pp. 417-36, by permission of the Regents.

1

DIVERSIFICATION, DEPENDENCE, AND REGIONALISM

> Politics is for most of us a passing parade of abstract
> symbols, yet a parade which our experience teaches us
> to be a benevolent or malevolent force that can be close
> to omnipotent.
>
> Murray Edelman[1]

A "New International Economic Order" has become the symbol
of hope for most of the Third World states, holding out a promise of
redistribution of global economic power to the less advantaged. Thus,
the focus of "development" has shifted from an emphasis in the 1960s
on the domestic blockages that prevent Third World states from equal-
ing the political power and wealth of the West to a scrutiny of the
structure of the international economic system as an element hindering greater progress in closing the gap between rich and poor states.
Yet, despite the efforts of a Third World coalition to change the international system, such as in the United Nations Conference on Trade
and Development (UNCTAD) series and the North-South Conferences,
little progress is evident.[2] An economic order in which Third World
states remain dependent on those major global powers that manage
the global system remains a symbol, abstract rather than concrete,
of the malevolent force of international politics.

Many writers have addressed the issue of dependence, with
little consensus on its existence or effects.[3] Others have provided
case studies focusing on single countries and their interactions with
particular global economic actors, mostly multinational corporations.[4]
All of these studies have a common assumption that economic and
political factors are intertwined in the analysis of international politics. Yet, as Nazli Choucri has pointed out, the field of international political economy is largely an emerging one, with relation-

ships between economics and politics yet to be systematically delineated.[5] Dependence is certainly central to development: a lack of autonomy over economic and political elements of policy frustrates attempts to adapt growth to local circumstances. But this type of political economy is as uncharted as the rest.

This book takes a rather different approach to the topic. No effort is made to prove that dependence has had negative (or positive) effects or to describe the details of interactions between dependent countries and strong actors attempting to dominate them. Instead, what follows is an analysis of the position of a group of Third World states in the international political-economic system and a description of the policies undertaken to cope with economic dependence and penetration. What is of interest here are changes in the patterns of dependence, with dependence taken simply as relational inequality. Since the existence of a pattern implies a corresponding structure,[6] this is an examination of structural change as it is affected by economic interactions. It is, therefore, neither a study of exclusively systemic factors, as is the case with most dependency studies, nor of exclusively actor interactions, as with the case studies of multinational corporations. The focus here is on how, and to what degree, Third World states can change the structure of the system that has allocated them dependent roles and how their policy affects the structure.

The perspective developed here is that dependence is a phenomenon of power relations between developed and developing states. Stronger states exercise their capabilities by molding the structure of international political and economic relations to their advantage.[7] In the sense that structures reflect power, dependence is also, as James Caporaso maintains,[8] a structural phenomenon. As developing states learn to make more effective use of their power capabilities, the structure of the system will be changed. The appropriate point to study dependence, then, is at the level of structures. As structures are relatively enduring patterns, dependence is not likely to disappear quickly, but it is significant if these structures are changing toward less dependence, indicating a shift in the pattern of power relations.

THE ASEAN MEMBERS

The states chosen for this analysis are the five members of the Association of Southeast Asian Nations (ASEAN). These are Indonesia, Malaysia, the Philippines, Singapore, and Thailand. The members vary widely in certain respects: Singapore is almost a city-state with slightly more than 2 million residents, while Indonesia spans 3,000 miles of the equator with a correspondingly large popula-

TABLE 1.1

ASEAN Members: Selected Statistics, 1978

	Population (millions)	Gross Domestic Product (GDP) Total[b]	Gross Domestic Product (GDP) Per Capita	Exports Total[b]	Exports Percent GDP	Foreign Investment[a] Total[b]	Foreign Investment[a] Percent GDP
Indonesia	145.1	49,289	340	11,643	23.6	5,760	11.7
Malaysia	12.3	15,472	1,258	7,413	47.9	2,880	18.6
Philippines	46.4	23,438	505	3,384	14.4	1,820	7.8
Singapore	2.3	7,726	3,359	10,132	131.1	1,700	22.0
Thailand	45.1	21,843	484	4,054	18.6	445	2.0

[a]Stock of foreign direct investment of Organization for Economic Cooperation and Development countries, end 1978.

[b]Millions of U.S. dollars.

Sources: Population: United Nations, Demographic Yearbook, 1979 (New York: United Nations, 1979); GDP: United Nations, Yearbook of National Accounts Statistics, 1979, vol. 2 (New York: United Nations, 1980); Exports: International Monetary Fund, Directions of Trade: Yearbook (Washington, D.C.: IMF, 1979); Foreign Investment: Organization for Economic Cooperation and Development, Development Cooperation: 1980 Review (Paris: OECD, 1980), p. 165.

tion; Singapore can hardly be classified "poor" by the standard of per capita gross domestic product (GDP), but Indonesia certainly can (see Table 1.1); the Philippines and Thailand are relatively homogeneous in the ethnic composition of their populations, while Malaysia and Indonesia are quite fragmented; three different colonial powers had, or still have to some degree, decisive influence in shaping the modern states. Still, the five states share two things that make this book worthwhile: a relatively similar vision of future economic growth and a regional organization to assist in their objectives.

The shared economic vision revolves around growth through export-led development. Each of the five states is committed to some version of an open economy, although with a large measure of state control and involvement. They have developed a high degree of involvement with the international economic system through trade and investment ties, and they depend on interaction with the outside world for a substantial degree of their wealth, both earned and capital. Together, they exported more than $36 billion worth of goods and services in 1978, more than 31 percent of their collective GDP. The Organization for Economic Cooperation and Development (OECD) countries report more than $12 billion of direct foreign investment in the ASEAN countries, almost 11 percent of the ASEAN GDP. In addition, they are all, with the exception of Singapore, consumers of loans from foreign banks; the Philippines, Indonesia, and Thailand are among the most heavily in debt of all developing countries. [9] The international economic system is clearly of vast importance to them all. With their large exports and more than 250 million combined population, they are of some importance to the international economic system, too, but not equally so. They may hold investment and loans hostage or withhold some commodities important to their trade partners, but the effect would be disastrous for them and only inconvenient to their far-larger economic partners. A part of their shared economic vision, then, is a substantial degree of dependence.

Coping with dependence is part of their common bond. To a large degree, the five ASEAN states also agree on a common strategy to maximize their ability to participate in the international economic system and to minimize their dependence. They have focused on diversification of their economic partners as a means of controlling the political influence of any one. Through this strategy they are attempting to foster economic growth while increasing their political independence. A large part of this book is devoted to describing how the ASEAN states have gone about implementing this strategy and to assessing the results. If it can be effective in reducing the degree of dependence, diversification will be of interest to other similarly situated countries, although no claim of universal panacea is made here. Attaining greater independence through diversification is an important part of the shared ASEAN economic vision.

While this work is not specifically a theoretical one but rather a case study of the experience of a group of states in coping with dependence, it is informed by theoretical considerations. Insofar as the particular strategy of the ASEAN states is based on a set of assumptions about the nature of the international political system, it has a conceptual basis that can be approached as a theory and tested. Briefly stated, the underlying basis of the ASEAN strategy is the hypothesis that policies of individual states that focus on structural diversification will lead to reductions in important aspects of dependence on outside powers. As applied in their foreign policies, this amounts to stipulating a change in power relationships in an advantageous direction for the ASEAN states as a result of diversifying the geographical basis of ties in trade relations, investment relations and foreign-policy orientation as expressed through international organizations.

This hypothesis on the relationship between diversification and dependence is based on a number of assumptions. Few of these are explicitly addressed by the states under consideration, but they must be considered here. First, it is assumed that dependence is a structural situation characterized by concentration of linkages; in the most extreme form of dependence, linkages are concentrated on a single foreign partner. This structural interpretation of dependence is consistent with several theorists' formulations. Caporaso, for example, casts dependence as a relatively enduring, asymmetrical pattern of interactions that are also central aspects of dependency, constraining the behavior of dependent states and distorting their development. [10] Johan Galtung also casts his theory of imperialism as a structural situation characterized by concentrated economic relations, a feudal center-periphery structure, where the center dominates the economic transactions of the periphery through an exclusive relationship. [11] Hirschman gives a vivid account of the process whereby one state (Germany before World War II) consciously created dependence on the part of other states (in southeastern Europe) by acting to concentrate economic relations, specifically in order to dominate them. [12] Thus, the assumption of a structural character to dependence finds support in international political theory and practice. However, this observation of the nature of the phenomenon of dependence merely describes it; it does not explain it.

A second assumption offers at least a partial explanation of the link between the structure of relations and dependence. A network of concentrated relations is assumed to produce a power differential unfavorable to the dependent state. This assumption finds support in the political anthropology literature, particularly in the analysis of patron-client systems and in social-network theory. The key to maintaining the subordination of a client is partly through channeling

all contact through a single patron, rather than allowing some differentiation of ties to various, alternate partners; this system of undifferentiated ties allows the patron's authority to spill from one area
to another in a reinforcing manner.[13] Exclusiveness prevents the
client from playing one patron off against another or even from seeking
help from other clients.[14] This insight into the results of concentrated
relations is reinforced by social-network theory, where centrality
within a network of social relations is thought to produce an advantage
in control over the network;[15] concentration of linkages on the dominant power gives that actor the advantage of centrality, the ability to
control and mediate transactions within the network. This assumption
on the relationship between structure and power potential helps to
explain how dominance relations are maintained once they are established.

Further support for the propagation of unequal influence through
the structure of relations is derived from the interdependence literature. In this literature, the structure of international relations is
seen as multistranded, transnational linkages in which each particular
linkage can reflect inequality of bargaining resources, based in each
case on the importance of the linkage to each state and on the alternatives available in the case of disruption of the existing relationship.[16] "Asymmetrical interdependence" is said to exist when the
aggregate of linkages favors one of the partners. In the case of relatively small developing countries, both the relative importance of
linkages concentrated on a larger foreign partner and the general
lack of domestic alternatives would be expected to generate inequality
in favor of the larger foreign partner through the overall asymmetry
of the relationship. Thus, the relative size of the partners, as well
as the concentrated structure of relationships, can be expected to
generate inequality. One partner is more "vulnerable" than the other,
simply from the structure of the relationship. This vulnerability is
based on an anticipation that disruption of the relationship would be
highly costly to the dependent partner and less so to the dominant
partner, which then deters the dependent partner from pursuing a
particular course of action that would likely incur costly responses.
In short, the structure of relations generates a psychology of dependence that is based on anticipated results in the event of confrontation.
Manipulation of the symbols of vulnerability, rather than concrete
acts, transforms the structure of relationships into actual influence.
In order to change the distribution of influence, the structure itself
must be altered.

This line of reasoning leads to the conclusion that altering the
structure of relations can lead to reductions in power inequalities.
Specifically, the differentiation of ties, or diversification, eases the
psychology of dependence that formerly deterred the dependent part-

ner from pursuing an independent course of action. Implementation of a strategy based on this conclusion, however, rests on a further assumption, namely that policies of dependent states can be effective in attaining structural change. If the condition of dependence itself constrains the dependent state from acting in its own interests when they are in conflict with those of the dominant partner, any strategy based on the action or policies of the dependent state, however theoretically valid it may be, is practically unobtainable and therefore meaningless. Certain characteristics of Third World countries do, indeed, lead to this conclusion. Among the stereotypes of Third World states is that they are administratively "soft states," unable to implement many of their preferred policy programs due to bureaucratic disorganization, factional conflict, or dissipation of resources. Another frequently argued characteristic is that the interests of the faction in control of the regime are identical to the interests of the elites in the dominant country, which militates against reducing dependence and, in fact, results in behavior that deepens it. A third example is the generalization from the apparent condition of dependence on the part of Third World states to the conclusion that because they are dominated, their behavior is controlled by the dominant power, and they will not be allowed to act against its interests—a realist power assumption. If these characteristics accurately portray the constraints under which Third World states operate, a conscious policy of structural manipulation to reduce dependence is unlikely to obtain the desired results, even if adopted.

However, the Third World is not an undifferentiated mass of more than 100 states; some may correspond to the dismal paradigm given above and others not. Some may, in fact, exist in an environment quite different from the generalized notion of constraints. Policy articulation can be followed up with concrete behavior to attain the stipulated goals; that is, the state may be "hard" rather than "soft." The process of building stronger states than existed in the immediate postcolonial world has generated a considerable amount of scholarship focused on the "relative autonomy" of the state in developing societies;[17] this autonomy may lead to more effective control over international as well as domestic policy. Similarly, economic nationalism has become almost characteristic of developing countries, with the frequent result that local elites act in contradiction to the interests of foreign elites. Finally, the nature of the international system has changed from one dominated by only a few "superpowers" to one much more characterized by competition among a larger number of powers, significant for economic collaboration, and security issues have become less intensive determinants of dominant-power policy in some areas of the world. These changes in the system are favorable to a more permissive policy on the part of the dominant powers toward the dependent ones. In short, there are also sets of conditions that may make dependence less "tight," providing the dependent states with the opportunity to manuever in their own interests. As will be discussed, it is the latter set of circumstances that seems to prevail in the case of the ASEAN countries; whether these conditions are prerequisite to policy effectiveness is an impossible question to answer with certainty, but they may be.

The question of conditions for policy effectiveness is an important one, but the existence of effective policy is easier to address. Ultimately, it is an empirical proposition. It is this question of policy effectiveness in an important area of domestic and international policy that is the focus of this book: the question here is not whether it is possible to follow a program of dependence reduction, but rather what have the ASEAN states done in this area?

The original hypothesis, that policies of states that focus on structural diversification will lead to reductions in important aspects of dependence on outside powers, has generated a series of questions that can be researched. First, do policies of diversification exist in appropriate areas of linkage? This can be observed and described through an examination of government policies; here the sectors of trade, investment and international organizations are examined. Second, has the structure of relations actually changed? Statistical analysis can answer this question in each policy domain. Third, has there been, as a result, a reduction in important aspects of dependence on outside powers? The degree to which this is true for each state can be assessed from the collected evidence.

Together these questions address the results of individual attempts to cope with dependence within the common ASEAN strategy of participation in the international economy in order to achieve growth more quickly. This is the first component of the common ASEAN bond, conceptually distinct from, but closely interrelated to, the entire strategy.

The ASEAN organization itself is the second major component of the shared Southeast Asian strategy of development. ASEAN was formed in 1967 as a developmental regional association, in the pattern of many other Third World regional organizations. But while most of these organizations appear to limit their objectives to regional economic rationalization in order to permit greater growth of transactions among themselves, ASEAN has become an important instrument of its members' international economic bargaining. Large parts of this book take the founding date of ASEAN as the starting point for analysis of structural change as a matter of convenience— although seeking explanation in earlier periods where necessary— even though ASEAN did not become central to the members' economic diplomacy until the early 1970s. In a sense, this is a study of regionalism and its uses in Southeast Asia.

At the same time, this is not strictly a study of regionalism. Asian regionalism has attracted its share of academic attention in the last few years. Kegley and Howell have constructed a typology of the dimensions of regional integration in Southeast Asia and suggest that societal interdependence, attitudinal integration, and intergovernmental cooperation are the major distinct types of integration emerging from their factor analysis.[18] Howell and Solidum have each studied elite attitudes in ASEAN as an element contributing to the development of regional policy.[19] Hill, following the transactionalist tradition, was unable to detect signs of increasing integration, comparing the mutual exchanges of ASEAN with their external exchanges.[20] James Schubert has applied the functionalist approach to Asian regionalism and has found that the ASEAN members are quite integrated compared with their Asian neighbors.[21] While all of these studies are informative, they largely share the teleological loading of the regional integration literature[22] and are bound by the failure of that literature's logic.[23] "Regionalism" in this book is simply used to describe observable cooperation in domestic and international policy, rather than carrying an implication of ultimate economic and political unification. ASEAN is seen as part of a strategy of foreign policy that responds to the situation of its members in a global society.

ASEAN is important, but in many ways it is a peak organization of the five members, rather than a separate actor. The main characters are the five member states themselves, which created a regional organization to serve their interests and which will maintain that organization as long as it continues to serve their interests. The driving forces behind the organization's activities are the policies of the members; rather than detracting from the importance of the organization, this affirms it. ASEAN itself is treated both as an essential part of the members' strategy of development and as simply the sixth actor in the cast.

ORGANIZATION OF THE STUDY

While the units analyzed are the five states plus their common regional organization, the discussion is organized around several major issues of particular importance to the general topic of dependence and its reduction.

Chapter 2 examines the general strategy of diversification as a theoretical method of reducing dependence. Based on a survey of the major streams of literature in the international, political-economy tradition, a composite strategy of diversification is advanced, drawing on insights from a broad range of writers as their work applies to the situation of developing countries. This discussion isolates three major domains for the application of policies of diversification: trade relations, foreign investment relations, and memberships in various types of international organizations. In each case, a pattern of concentration of relations, particularly where that concentration is on large economic powers, is identified as contributing to continued weakness, while a pattern of greater diversification is more likely to strengthen the structural position of the developing country. Methods of inquiry for each issue area are stipulated. Finally, the role of regionalism is brought into the discussion, and the limitations of a strategy of diversification are considered.

Chapter 3 returns to the topic of regionalism and sets the context of the ASEAN organization in Southeast Asian politics. The origins and development of the organization are described, leading to the conclusion that, at the present time, the major value of the regional organization is in enhancing the members' external economic diplomacy. The major economic programs of ASEAN are described, both those focusing on economic cooperation among the members and those coordinating economic cooperation with external states, in order to provide a basis for later discussion of ASEAN activities in particular domains of diversification effort. The extensive involvement of the ASEAN organization in the economic affairs of its members is apparent, giving content to regionalism in Southeast Asia.

Chapters 4, 5, and 6 examine the three substantive domains of diversification. Chapter 4 describes the evolution of policies on trade for each state and the activities of ASEAN in this area, drawing together the reasons each state turned to a policy of diversification at a particular time. Actual trade patterns are analyzed with simple descriptive statistics to determine the extent of diversification and its timing, and the effectiveness of the states' policies is assessed. The various factors inhibiting diversification of trade partners are discussed.

Chapter 5 examines the topic of foreign investment. Policies of each state are presented as they relate to the control of foreign investment, to domestic concerns over foreign domination of local productive assets, and to the necessity of preserving an adequate flow of capital from without to supplement local finance. The tension between fearing foreign domination and achieving adequate domestic economic growth is related to the adoption of a policy of diversification. ASEAN's financial activities are described. Data on the sources of foreign investment for each state are analyzed to determine the extent and type of diversification actually achieved, and this is related to the policies of the states. Economic and political limitations to diversification in the domain of investment are considered.

Chapter 6 returns to the realm of international organizations. It looks at the patterns of the ASEAN states' participation, through

membership, in intergovernmental organizations since 1967 to determine whether and to what degree they have become a bloc in the community of nations. Since the methodology of this chapter differs from those preceding it, the approach is explained. The transnational organizations having an ASEAN membership, both those involving the ASEAN members with outside participants and those within the region, are described in some detail. The structure of the ASEAN members' participation in international organizations is related to the theme of diversification, although with a slightly different emphasis from trade and investment diversification.

Chapter 7 concludes the study. A framework for the comparison of the various international, economic-policy orientations is presented, and the strategy of the ASEAN states is placed in this wider context. The ASEAN states are held to be pursuing a policy best described as defensive regionalism. The major findings of the study are reviewed and integrated. Finally, this study is discussed in the context of structural power and dependence.

The theme of this book, controlling dependence through diversification and regionalism, is central to the interests of many Third World states. As criticism of the exploitative nature of the international economic system mounts and as attempts to redress the grievances of the Third World continue, all possible options need to be systematically explored. It does not appear that the richer states are likely to concede to the demands of the south as they are articulated in UNCTAD or the North-South Conferences. If the strategy of the ASEAN states is effective in reducing dependence, it may have wider applicability. Although all strategies have their limitations, the one elaborated here has the singular advantage that it does not rely on the largesse of the industrial states for its implementation.

This study explores a novel strategy. So far as I am aware, no other study has addressed the same problems seriously, in Southeast Asia or elsewhere. Studies of Third World regionalism abound, but not from the perspective of instruments of foreign policy; debate over what dependence is and how to reduce it continues, but it is not focused on specific states or groups of states. This study should advance both the study of regionalism in the Third World and consideration of concrete methods of reducing dependence. In a narrower context, much of the research on ASEAN and its members is drawn together, supplemented, and focused on a broad theme. The subjects of Southeast Asian politics and the Third World in the international system are limitless, but this study should add something to each.

This is not a study or "proof" of dependency, but rather an exploration of some aspects of dependence. The dependency school asks questions about how the international system affects the structure of domestic politics in the Third World, and it answers them through historical-sociological analysis. Dependence as construed here, on the other hand, asks questions about the structure of international relationships and how that influences the interactions of states, in particular whether the pattern of these relationships has become more equal/less dependent and how, through the effects of Third World domestic and foreign policies. The answers certainly draw on aspects of domestic politics but as sources of foreign policies, the major focus of dependence analysis. While dependency looks at the effects of the system on the Third World, this book examines the pressures of the Third World on the system.

NOTES

1. Murray Edelman, The Symbolic Uses of Politics (Urbana: University of Illinois Press, 1964), p. 5.
2. See Robert Mortimer, The Third World Coalition in International Politics (New York: Praeger, 1980), and Robert Rothstein, Global Bargaining: UNCTAD and the Quest for a New International Economic Order (Princeton: Princeton University Press, 1979).
3. For a thorough, if not disinterested, review, see R. Dan Walleri, "The Political Economy Literature on North-South Relations," International Studies Quarterly 22 (December 1978): 587-624.
4. For a review of many of these studies, see H. Jeffery Leonard, "Multinational Corporations and Politics in Developing Countries," World Politics 32 (April 1980): 454-83; Robert T. Snow, "Southeast Asia in the World System: Origins and Extent of Export Oriented Industrialization in the ASEAN Countries," paper, Association for Asian Studies, Washington, D.C., 1980.
5. Nazli Choucri, "International Political Economy: A Theoretical Perspective," in Change in the International System, ed. Ole Holsti, Randolph Siverson, and Alexander George (Boulder, Colo.: Westview Press, 1980), pp. 103-29.
6. See Kenneth Waltz, Theory of International Politics (Reading, Mass.: Addison-Wesley, 1979), pp. 79-101, on political structures.
7. For examples, see Robert O. Keohane and Joseph S. Nye, Power and Independence: World Politics in Transition (Boston: Little, Brown, 1977), especially Part II.
8. James Caporaso, "Dependence, Dependency, and Power in the Global System: A Structural and Behavioral Analysis," International Organization 32 (Winter 1978): 22.
9. See Organization for Economic Cooperation and Development, Development Cooperation, 1980 Review (Paris: OECD, 1980), p. 221; and Far Eastern Economic Review, March 20, 1981, pp. 46-47.

10. Caporaso, "Dependence, Dependency, and Power," p. 22f.

11. Johan Galtung, "A Structural Theory of Imperialism," Journal of Peace Research 13 (1971): 81-94.

12. Albert O. Hirschman, National Power and the Structure of Foreign Trade (Berkeley: University of California Press, 1945).

13. Steffan Schmidt, James Scott, Carl Landé, and Laura Guasti, eds., Friends, Followers and Factions (Berkeley: University of California Press, 1977).

14. See Joel Migdal, Peasants, Politics and Revolution (Princeton: Princeton University Press, 1974), pp. 34-37.

15. Jeremy Boissevain, Friends of Friends: Networks, Manipulators and Coalitions (Oxford: Basil Blackwell, 1974).

16. Keohane and Nye, Power and Independence.

17. See Alfred Stepan, The State and Society (Princeton: Princeton University Press, 1978), pp. xi-xiv; Theda Skocpol, States and Social Revolutions (Cambridge: At the University Press, 1979), pp. 24-28.

18. Charles Kegley, Jr., and Llewellyn Howell, Jr., "The Dimensionality of Regional Integration: Construct Validation in the Southeast Asian Context," International Organization 29 (Autumn 1975): 997-1020.

19. Llewellyn Howell, Jr., "Attitudinal Distance in Southeast Asia: Social and Political Ingredients in Integration," Southeast Asia 11 (Winter 1974): 577-608; Estrella Solidum, "The Nature of Cooperation among the ASEAN States as Perceived through Elite Attitudes— A Factor for Regionalism," Ph.D. diss., University of Kentucky, 1970.

20. H. Monte Hill, "Community Formation within ASEAN," International Organization 32 (1978): 569-75.

21. James N. Schubert, "Toward a 'Working Peace System' in Asia: Organizational Growth and State Participation in Asian Regionalism," International Organization 32 (1978): 425-62.

22. Ernst B. Haas, "On System and International Regimes," World Politics 37 (1975): 147-74.

23. Ernst B. Haas, "Turbulent Fields and the Theory of Regional Integration," International Organization 30 (1976): 173-212.

2

INTERNATIONAL THEORY AND THE STRATEGY OF DIVERSIFICATION

None of the states in Southeast Asia is, or likely ever will be, a significant power in the global system. They are, therefore, confronted with a dilemma arising from their relative weakness. If they participate in the global system, especially in economic matters, they must interact with the more powerful states and with their strong interests and must lose some degree of independence and autonomy in adapting to the needs of these powerful agents. If they withdraw from the global system, their likely fate is stagnation rather than more rapid economic growth, which is required to improve material welfare and to contribute to social stability. Dependence or destitution would appear to be the choice, neither of which is particularly attractive.

The ASEAN states have chosen to link themselves to the global system. They invite foreign investment; they seek to expand foreign trade; they choose to become involved in a wide range of international organizations. Yet, in an age of strong nationalism, none of these states wishes to sacrifice any autonomy to greater dependence. They invite the vehicles of dependence, but hope to avoid the worst of the consequences.

Diversification is the apparent means by which the ASEAN states hope to minimize their dependence on their larger, more influential economic partners. Later chapters will examine the details of this strategy in specific areas. The goals of this chapter are to examine the major bodies of writing on international political economy for insights on diversification and to provide the conceptual basis for analysis of its effectiveness and limitations as a strategy.

There are, of course, several meanings of the term diversification. The one that comes most immediately to mind is economic diversification, or the widening of the base of the economy through

15

the production of a larger variety of goods and services. A second
meaning is the defensive balancing of investments, based on the assumption that a given amount of investment spread over a number of
different types of securities is safer than concentrating on a single
type. Both of these meanings are to be found in dictionary definitions,
but neither is exactly what is meant here.

The particular conception of diversification used here concerns
the geographical concentration of foreign ties, or the pattern of economic relations with foreign states. This is indirectly related to the
first type of diversification previously mentioned in that the more different types of product a given nation produces, the greater the possibility of exporting to a wider variety of customers in the world.
And the same would be true the wider the variety of imports required.
But this type of diversification is essentially an economic problem
(although with political linkages), and it is not the focus of this work.
The second meaning of diversification previously mentioned is actually closer to the type examined here, as portfolio diversification
is a defensive strategy to reduce possible losses. Investment losses
are, of course, economic ones, and so are some of the losses being
insured against by geographical diversification; disruption of trade
relations with an important foreign market, for example, would have
significant economic consequences. However, it is the primary purpose to examine geographical diversification as a political strategy
to reduce the potential consequences of economic relations, by limiting the magnitude of influence any foreign actor derives from its economic ties with a given state. Geographical diversification is a political strategy to reduce the degree of dependence.

Although diversification is treated here as a political strategy,
it should be clear that it is not the only one for controlling dependence.
Others are producer cartels, withdrawal from foreign economic contacts, regional pacts, nationalization of foreign assets, pursuit of a
new international economic order, and exploitation of a great power's
local strategic interests.[1] Each of these strategies has, at one time
or another, been followed by some Southeast Asian state: Indonesia
is an Organization of Petroleum Exporting Countries (OPEC) member; ASEAN is a regional pact; Burma kept itself largely isolated;
foreign assets have been, on occasion, nationalized; the New Industrial Economic Order (NIEO) is supported; and U.S. strategic interests have been held hostage to more lucrative support. Although
these other strategies also come into play, diversification appears
to be a fundamental part of the strategy of the ASEAN states and to
be largely unexamined to date. Diversification offers several potential advantages as a strategy, which may help explain its appeal in
Southeast Asia. In contrast to cartels, nationalization, or the NIEO,
it is not easily interpreted by its objects as an aggressive, confrontive

policy, which makes diversification stylistically more compatible with a general Asian preference for preserving the appearance of harmony and nonaggressiveness. Further, it offers a flexible formula for reconciling the interest of some sectors of the elite in growth with that of others in protection, a significant advantage in societies generally oriented toward consensus in important policy matters. Finally, diversification is a policy that can easily be pursued incrementally, an especially valuable characteristic for dependent states that may have to tack to the shifting winds of dominant powers.

In the following sections, the three major approaches to international political economy—economic nationalism, dependency, and interdependence—will be examined as to their views on the strategy of diversification. The assumptions about the nature of the international economic system of each approach are summarized, the explicit or implicit avenues to strengthen a particular state's position in the international system are explored, and conclusions for diversification are drawn. The perspective developed is that the strategy of diversification is supported by each of these theoretical policy approaches and that each approach offers unique yet overlapping rationales for a redirection of economic ties.

THREE SCHOOLS OF INTERNATIONAL POLITICAL ECONOMY

Economic Nationalism

Economic nationalism, harking back to mercantilism, is the oldest school of political economy. One might also observe that, as a basis for actual practice by developed as well as developing countries, it is also the most widely adhered to of the economic doctrines. Its appeal derives from a firmly realistic conception of the nature of the international economic system and from prescriptions designed for the maximum short-term benefit to national economic actors.

The mercantilists, and more modern neomercantilists and economic nationalists alike, cast the international economic system in static terms, where the gain by one is at the expense of a loss by another. The goal of all nations is to gain strength through economic growth, led by a strong state that intervenes to produce desirable results. In the age of mercantilism, this was construed to be a surplus of exports over imports, thus accumulating wealth. However, the German Historical School, led by Friedrich List, saw the economy in more sophisticated terms and aimed at organic development to produce a strong national economy.[2] This was a process of national competition as seen by Alexander Hamilton, which justified protectionism to spur the development of manufacturing in the U.S. economy. Or consider List's rationale for mercantilism as the route to German unification:

> Nations are thus the victims of each other, and selfish policy is continually disturbing and delaying the economical development of nations. To preserve, to develop, and to improve itself as a nation is consequently, at present, and ever must be, the principal object of a nation's efforts. But some of them, favored by circumstances . . . have adopted and still persevere in a policy so well adapted to give them the monopoly of manufactures, of industry and of commerce, and to impede the progress of less advanced nations. [3]

This has a thoroughly contemporary ring about it, despite the archaic style. A developed economy is the basis of a strong state, and this must be achieved at the expense of others—in the early mercantilist version, by exporting more than importing, but in the later economic nationalist version, by displacing those states occupying the more industrialized niches. As Gilpin contends, mercantilism seeks for security through economic means,[4] and the concern for security is the basis of a realist worldview.

The prescriptions of the mercantilists and economic nationalists were designed to contribute to the building of a strong national economy through manipulation of foreign trade by the state. A surplus of exports over imports was to be achieved by state control over valuable export commodities and high tariffs to reduce imports. This was supplemented in the nineteenth century by a concern to foster the development of manufacturing industries with tariff policies, the "infant industry" argument. In contemporary terms, dependence on foreign imports, particularly those that could serve as the basis of military power, was to be avoided, while the national economy grew equal in strength to others. Gilpin observes that, in part, the attraction of economic nationalism as a doctrine derives from a sensitivity within governments to the dangers inherent in becoming overly dependent on the global economy.[5] Economic nationalism is the preferred doctrine of the weak and of politicians seeking domestic support.

However, not just the weak concern themselves with increasing state power through the manipulation of trade relations. Albert O. Hirschman's analysis of the policies of German trade practices during the interwar period clearly indicates that state power can be enhanced by creating dependence, particularly with smaller states, by encouraging concentrated trade on a bilateral basis.[6] The "influence effect" of foreign trade, as he terms it, derives from the power to disrupt exports and imports with the smaller partner, creating a situation where the threat of economic loss encourages political compliance. Although German practices were informed by the Historical School of economic nationalists, this was an extension of the central concern over state power rather than an application of the existing economic doctrine. The doctrine of the weak was converted to use by the strong.

The strategic implication for the weak is obvious. As Hirschman points out, the small state should avoid having too large a share of its trade with any one large country.[7] This is the root of a strategy of geographical diversification as a means of avoiding, or minimizing, dependence. Thus, the implicit conclusion of the doctrine of mercantilism and economic nationalism recommends the sort of diversification examined here. Diversification properly becomes a part of the doctrine of economic nationalism for the weak.

Dependency

Dependency as a body of writing has a relatively more recent origin in the experience of new states, largely in Latin America. The verbiage of dependency has come to characterize a wide range of critiques of industrialized-state behavior, by more moderate Third World states as well as by the more radical. Its appeal as an international, political-economic doctrine has at least two bases. First, by clearly polarizing the world into industrial-state oppressors and developing-state oppressed, it attributes many of the ills of the latter to the historical role of the former, which must appeal to elites struggling to cope with the problems of modernization. Second, many of the prescriptions are entirely compatible with the nationalistic feelings of formerly colonial populations and therefore have strong domestic appeal.

Dependency frames the contemporary international economic system in its historical context, as a stage of development following the colonial era.[8] Because of extensive economic penetration of the colonies (and other subordinate territories) by the metropolitan powers during the colonial era and after, developmental choice has been limited by the structure of relations resulting from that penetration. Past economic development in the Third World was directed to meet the needs of the industrializing nations, which resulted in emphasis on the exploitation of the colonies' resources for export to the manufacturing sectors abroad and in repression of manufacturing in the Third World. The basic economic infrastructure was set by this pattern. For example, rail and road networks were built from export ports to relevant resource areas, making it difficult after decolonization to reorient the economy from trade to production activities. This pattern of economic development was facilitated by foreign ownership and investment, which frustrated the growth of a domestic

entrepreneurial class and removed whole sectors of the economy from
effective national control. National policy elites lost a significant degree of influence over domestic economic and political affairs, as those
who were aware of the locus of real economic power became more externally oriented and responsive to the social and economic needs of
the metropolitan countries. Economic, social, and political growth
patterns were distorted from what would have occurred in the absence
of the intrusion of the colonial powers, and the decolonized territories
were linked to the needs of the international capitalist system.

Extensive linkage to foreign economic systems, then, has the
effect of tying the dependent economy to an external frame of reference. As Theotonio Dos Santos defines the situation:

> By dependence we mean a situation in which the economy
> of certain countries is conditioned by the development
> and expansion of another economy to which the former is
> subjected. The relations of interdependence between two
> or more economies, and between those and world trade,
> assumes the form of dependence when some countries
> (the dominant ones) can expand and can be self-sustain-
> ing, while other countries (the dependent ones) can do
> this only as a reflection of that expansion, which can
> have either a positive or a negative effect on their
> immediate development. [9]

The smaller economic size and less advanced character of the dependent economy make it peripheral to the developed economy and, thus,
both more subject to dislocations arising from changes in the dominant
economy and unable to alter the pattern of relations through independent
action. Because of the historical development of economic roles in the
international economy, reinforced by contemporary disparities in power, the Third World states are confined to a peripheral and unequal set
of relations within the international economic system. Even under the
most favorable circumstances, the best that can be achieved is a measure of "associated-dependent" development within the existing system, [10] which allows economic growth without political autonomy.

The prescriptions of dependency writers are designed to alter
this situation in its entirety. Perhaps as a result of the Marxist assumptions of early dependency writing, the question of relations between states was given only cursory attention in favor of relations
among classes within the state. A socialist revolution to displace the
comprador class and to lead to internal equality and withdrawal from
the capitalist world system were the only solutions advanced. This
outlook assumed the nationalization of foreign assets, which struck a
responsive note in many developing countries. However, as the option
of joining the socialist international system began to lose its gloss with
charges of socialist imperialism and reactions against developments in

Cuba, more detailed consideration was given to alternative patterns of relations between states. "Delinking" and "self-reliance" are the elements of an emerging prescriptive strategy that sets out a systematic restructuring of relations between Third World and industrialized states. [11]

The first element, delinking, involves severing most, if not all, of the previous relations with the industrial countries. Trade, aid, investment and technology transfers, employment of foreign nationals, and relations with international bodies that might compromise a state's autonomy are all targets for elimination. This might be selective, doing away with the worst offenders first, or wholesale, as part of the national revolution that changes the domestic pattern of class relations perpetuating external dependence. The goal is less to eliminate transactions with foreign actors completely than to reduce the magnitude to a level easily controlled by the state for national purposes. Although aid and finance linkages are to be avoided, exports necessary to pay for absolutely required imports and carefully controlled, small foreign projects, as parts of larger state projects, are seen as relatively uncompromising. In this way, the state regains control over foreign influences and can proceed with autogenic development.

The second element, self-reliance, is directed toward replacing the previously foreign activities with locally sustained ones of a non-exploitative nature. The major focus is the development of domestic capabilities, but selective relinking with international actors is also recognized as necessary. Since all relations between unequal partners are seen as inherently exploitative, relations with the industrialized nations are to be kept to a minimum in favor of exchanges with other developing countries. Thus, exports channeled through multinational corporations (MNCs) are to be avoided in favor of free-market exchange; "appropriate" technologies are to be adopted over MNC packages; and exports should be carefully diversified to insulate the national economy from powerful partners. Since other developing countries are also relatively weak and therefore likely to be more equal partners, relations with them should be expanded. More trade, more exchange of technology and information, common institutions, and regional integration schemes as vehicles for negotiating accords with developed countries should all be sought as part of "collective self-reliance." With these changes, a new international economic order of a less exploitative nature can be achieved, and relations between industrial and developing countries can be reduced and controlled. This is balanced by expanded relations among developing countries, to be established on the principle of mutual advantage rather than exploitation.

The strategy of diversification is explicitly advocated by dependency writers in several forms. As with economic nationalism, diversifying trade, particularly exports, among a large number of nations is recommended. Furthermore, trade in general should be diversified away from the industrial nations, especially to avoid control by MNCs, and toward other developing countries. In addition, the institutional basis of international political interaction is to be diversified to give greater weight to organizations of developing countries, both regional and global in scope. The rationale for diversification in the writings on dependency is slightly different from that of economic nationalism in that the goals of greater state autonomy and "organic development" are steps to attain domestic economic justice, a distinction more important to domestic politics than foreign policy. Diversification is a central element of a foreign policy program to erase dependency.

Interdependence

Interdependence, grounded in the assumptions of classical liberalism, is the dominant approach to international political economy in the developed West. This doctrine finds strong appeal in arguments of economic rationality, which offers concrete advantages to the dominant states in the international economic system. At least to some degree, the other two doctrines previously discussed are reactions to the results of the practice of liberalism.

The classical school of economic liberalism viewed the world economy in terms analogous to advocates of domestic laissez-faire policies. The ideal situation was unobstructed trade based on comparative advantage and the free flow of all factors of production across national borders. All restrictions placed on economic interactions by governments were undesirable, distorting the operation of the open market and decreasing general economic welfare. [12] Furthermore, it was thought that mutual dependence induced by free and open trade would lead to international peace.

Interdependence is an attempt to describe and analyze the effects of a world economy that, at least among Western nations and their associated economic partners, is characterized by liberalism as modified by the rise of the welfare state. Basing its analysis on an unprecedented growth in world exchange and interconnectedness resulting from a political structure established and supported by the United States after World War II, the growth and spread of multinational business enterprise, and the increasing involvement of a widened range of public and private actors in the international economy, [13] the interdependence literature points to a substantial erosion in the ability of governments to exercise sufficient control over their economic policies, domestic as well as international. Governments, although still sovereign in the legal sense, are thought to have lost autonomy due to interpenetration in the global economic system. More accurately, the prices of autonomy and independence are judged to have been substantially raised.

Prodded by increasingly active, domestic interest groups and the requirements of a welfare state, governments must intervene to adjust for the dislocations arising from international transactions with a reduced assortment of effective policy instruments. The result is policy interdependence over a wide range of economic and political issues. [14] Policy is set not so much by states acting in their own interests (as in the mercantilist world), but by networks of governmental and private actors, international in scope, concerned to further their separate interests through cooperation. Economic policy has become internationalized, both in the sense of being directly influenced by events originating beyond a state's borders and in the sense that foreign actors frequently participate. None of this would surprise economic nationalists or dependistas, as their view of the nature of the global economic system assumes that inequities arise from the operation of an open international economy and that state intervention is required to preserve national interests. [15] There is at least some convergence in world views among the major contending approaches.

There are also some similarities of analytical approach, but not of prescriptions. The interdependence school presents a framework to analyze the effects of interconnection among the various parts of the global economy that has two major parts to it. First, the primary result of systemic interdependence is an increased sensitivity of a given national economy to the surrounding international system. The greater the degree of interconnectedness, the more rapidly and completely are impulses from the international system transmitted to domestic economies. A country drawing on the international petroleum market for its energy requirements has little buffer when OPEC raises prices. Sensitivity has costs, but some states have more alternatives than others in adjusting to these costs. A state with adequate domestic resources to adjust to the effects of sensitivity—for example, a surplus of coal—may be only marginally affected by sensitivity. A state not having these resources is said to be vulnerable, the second dimension of analysis of interdependence. [16] Sensitivity imposes short-term costs, while vulnerability imposes longer-term costs. Since the states with fewer underlying capabilities suffer both short- and long-term costs, a system of interdependence benefits the economically more powerful roughly in proportion to the degree of asymmetry of interdependence. This parallels the argument made by economic nationalists and dependency writers speaking on behalf of the weaker and developing states.

The prescriptions of interdependence analysts are almost precisely the opposite of dependency. The basic orientation of classical liberal economics is toward expanding the degree of freedom in the international economic system and the integration of individual economies within it. Thus nations should reduce tariff barriers to trade while attempting to expand those exports in which they have a natural advantage, free the movement of factors of production such as capi-

relations insofar as possible, and they recommend that those remaining be either nationalized or subjected to state control in a careful manner. Foreign aid should be rejected entirely. Absolutely necessary foreign technology should preferably come from other developing countries, and that allowed from developed countries should be from diverse sources. Interdependence writers reject limitations on volumes of investment (or loans), but they do support diversification of sources to control vulnerability. The common thread is diversification of sources, and from a Third World standpoint, this would include at least careful state control. Economic nationalists would probably also support extensive controls. The composite strategy, then, is to diversify investment at least among the major developed countries, to shift as much as possible to other developing countries, and to impose domestic controls.

One last area, membership in international organizations, remains. The dependency school advocates disengagement from potentially compromising international organizations, such as financial institutions and peacekeeping forces, and the building of regional and global institutions among developing countries, with the goal of enhancing bargaining power vis-à-vis the developed states. Since the institutional ties of many developing countries are with universal organizations and their former colonial powers, this implies another arena of geographical diversification. A benefit implied by the structural approach to dependency would be breaking the elite ties to the industrial nations and replacing them with ties focused on local interests.[21] The interdependence literature supports changes in organizational relationships, too, specifically creating or joining institutional forums to manage the effects of interdependence ("regimes"); for most developing countries, this too would represent diversification. A composite strategy includes regional organization where possible, expanded organizational ties to other developing countries, and joint mechanisms to bargain over the effects of interdependence with the industrial states.

In each of these three areas—trade, financial ties, and international organizations—there is a strategy to defend the weak based on diversification. For the most part, the form of diversification is to reduce ties to the stronger industrial nations and to expand relations with other weaker developing nations. Those ties remaining with strong nations should be balanced among several of them and in common with other developing nations.

Methods of Inquiry

A defensive strategy of diversification finds theoretical support in the body of international, political-economy writings. Using this theoretical framework, the body of this work explores how this strategy works in practice. The conceptual framework needs to be translated into an operational method of inquiry before case studies can be analyzed.

The major analytical focus is the strategy of diversification. It is studied in three specific policy areas: trade, financial ties, and international organizations. In the case of trade, statistics are available for both exports and imports between all (or almost all) nations for the entire postwar period. These can be aggregated in various ways for analysis. In the case of financial relations, reliable statistics are more difficult to obtain. Figures for public and private debt are not available in reliable form with debtor and creditor nations identified for any substantial period of time; furthermore, with the practice of handling debt through consortia of banks becoming more common, it is difficult to determine which nations are the creditors and in what amounts. Therefore, debt is not considered, even given its increasing importance to developing countries. Much of the foreign aid extended has also been multilateralized through country consortia and international institutions, and it is also omitted. Perhaps the most important form of financial tie is direct foreign investment; figures for this form of economic relation have been gathered. Foreign investment provides the basis of analysis of financial ties. Data on memberships in international organizations are available, and these are used to develop the theme of organizational diversity, especially among the five ASEAN members; additional descriptive material is provided on the development of transnational organizations under the ASEAN umbrella. In the cases of trade and investment, descriptive material examining the development of policy precedes the statistical sections, allowing the comparison of policies with results.

The concept of diversification has little analytical meaning in a static sense. Diversification is something that occurs over time; therefore, the study must be secular. Since one informing aspect of the study is the role of regional organizations among developing countries, the formation of ASEAN in 1967 marks the initial point for statistical analysis. In the case of trade, the period extends up to 1979, the most recent year for which data are available. Foreign investment statistics are not collected by any international agency for a sufficient time span, and coverage extends to the most recent date for which data were available from each of the five countries. Information on memberships in international organizations is likewise available up through 1979. This choice of a time period allows for at least a 10-year period for patterns to show change.

The statistical analysis of geographical diversification for trade and investment is straightforward. Data can be presented for various geographic regions in terms of percentages of the total for the year under consideration. This allows direct comparison over time. In addition, Hirschman's index of geographical concentration is presented, which allows for analysis of trends that might not be obvious on inspection.[22]

Analyzing organizational memberships requires a somewhat different approach, as the data do not lend themselves to an identical treatment, and the focus is slightly different from that of trade and investment. What has been adopted here is a modified version of social-network theory, which has been used as the basis of descriptive studies of transnational and domestic coalitions and groups.[23] Network theory casts a social system as a structured set of relationships that may vary over a number of measures (range, density, and centrality) of relative closeness, which can change over time. It is used to indicate the structured nature of relationships in the social system of international organizations among the ASEAN countries. Conclusions as to the nature and extent of diversification and commonality in organized memberships are then drawn.

The framework of interdependence theories has been adopted for use in the analysis of trade and investment issues as a matter of convenience. Dependency research is basically historical-sociological, although there have been numerous attempts to use quantitative techniques to validate some of the theses, mainly those to do with the effects of dependency on growth of the economy;[24] most of these have been criticized for their inappropriateness.[25] Sensitivity and vulnerability seem to capture the major effects of interconnectedness among nations quite well, and the latter term has been used in a similar sense by at least one dependency writer.[26] In using these terms, I define their meanings a bit more rigorously than do their originators, however, in order to apply them to the statistical base. Sensitivity is taken as the degree to which a country is connected to the subsystem of the major industrial nations in its economic relations (trade and investment). This should indicate the ease with which extraneous costs can be transmitted to the weaker country. Reducing sensitivity, then, involves diversifying away from those major industrial nations. Vulnerability is taken as the degree to which economic relations are concentrated with any particular country; this indicates the potential cost of disruption of relations and the degree of inequality of potential political influence. Reducing vulnerability, then, involves diversifying relations so that the relative position of a formerly dominant partner is reduced. For diversification to be an effective strategy to counter dependence, both sensitivity and vulnerability should be lessened. Of the two, vulnerability is the more important, as it is translated into influence in bargaining contexts, while sensitivity is a more general indicator of the degree of interconnection.

As with many social science terms, there is no clear definition of dependence. It obviously implies something less than independence, but the conceptual waters have become muddied with competing claims and definitions of dependence, dependency, and asymmetrical interdependence; all have some bearing on a structure of relations characterized by a degree of inequality.[27] It does seem useful to follow Caporaso's suggestion that dependence should be used to refer to inequalities in foreign-policy capabilities and that dependency be reserved for reference to the more encompassing domestic distortions from developmental ideals argued primarily by the Latin American school of analysts.[28] The label "asymmetrical interdependence" is in itself a semantical contradiction. Although there is an obvious continuum of possibilities between equal and unequal, two nations either share the mutuality of interdependence, or they do not, and one of them is dependent.[29]

Dependence here refers to a situation of relational inequality, generally between advanced industrial states and the Third World states, but not exclusively so; dependence may also characterize relations between large and small industrial states or between large and small Third World states. The criterion of dependence is relational inequality, which may lead to political domination. As a condition, dependence can be observed in an unequal pattern of relations and can be reversed by altering that pattern in the direction of more equality.

That patterns of relations are significant resources of power is supported by recent attempts to assay the role of power in the international system. It has been suggested that the ability to set the structure of relations between two countries is in itself a significant power resource. This leads to a distinction between two levels of influence analysis, "decisional power," which is manifested in a specific instance of bargaining, and "structural power" flowing from the pattern of relations between the interacting parties.[30] These two levels are clearly mutually contingent; a specific bargain may include alterations to the overall structure, or the structure may constrain the particular bargain. Methods of research therefore differ. Investigating differences in decisional power would necessarily focus on the range of factors that determine the outcome of particular negotiations; a "bureaucratic politics" approach would probably be most appropriate. Examining structural power requires a focus on the longer-term patterns of economic and political relations; that is the focus of this study. Other studies have focused on the general foreign policy behavior of nations under conditions of dependence;[31] this one concentrates on a strategy of changing structural power on the part of dependent nations.

This study, then, neither addresses the domestic issues raised by the dependency school nor makes predictive claims about the outcomes of particular negotiating situations for the ASEAN states. It is quite possible that the ASEAN states will continue to exhibit the symptoms of domestic social and economic distortion pointed to by the dependency school, despite the success of a strategy of diversification. It is equally possible that they will conclude bad bargains with stronger (or weaker) states, in foreign relations or in areas with direct domestic consequence, even if diversification leads to a lessening of inequality in structural power. It does seem possible that reducing dependence through a process of effective diversification would eventually result in more equal bargaining situations and in more favorable outcomes to the formerly dependent states; it also seems possible that in the long term better bargains would allow a measure of autogenic development to emerge, erasing the symptoms of dependency. But these are future scenarios, and they rely on the will and choices of leaders in those dependent countries analyzed here as those leaders attempt to cope with the technological and political forces of the global economy.

REGIONALISM AND THE LIMITS
OF DIVERSIFICATION

Six political entities are the subjects of this study, five states in Southeast Asia and ASEAN, their common organization. The patterns of relations for the five states are analyzed through application of the framework previously set out, but analysis of a regional organization is somewhat more difficult. The development and activities of ASEAN are described and further discussed in each chapter. But perhaps the most important aspect of ASEAN is simply its existence. In the same sense that a union reduces the vulnerability of each employee toward the employer, a regional organization, by increasing the size of the bargaining unit, reduces the vulnerability of its members toward outside states. It automatically changes the structure of relations between its members and others in a favorable manner if it is active and effective in becoming an alternate forum for external policy on behalf of its members; it must be both used and accepted. Thus, while evidence on the effectiveness of states' policies can be presented, evidence that a regional organization is contributing to reductions in dependence is more limited to the existence of a continuous high level of activities that binds the members together and serves their common purposes. A "paper organization" will limit, rather than further, attempts to reduce dependence.

Diversification also has its limits. It may reduce the degree of inequality between particular states, and it may reduce the sensitivity of a particular state to the larger industrial nations, but it is unlikely to erase dependence. A cynic might say that nothing, short of a massive and dramatic change in the distribution of economic capabilities and military power, will erase the dependence of smaller, economically less developed states on the major industrial powers. As long as some states exercise vastly more influence on world affairs than others do, they are capable of changing the "rules" to preserve their relative position. Since diversification assumes continued interaction with these powers, it is contingent on their permission, on their willingness to perpetuate the existing system. Perhaps more immediately important, diversification addresses the political influence of particular states but not the collective influence of all foreign states. Without some restrictions on the magnitude of foreign influences, a strategy of diversification could win the battle but lose the war.

It is suggested that a strategy of diversification can reduce dependence on particular foreign states. If pursued systematically, it can also reduce the magnitude of inequality of influence with many of the more important states. But this is a marginal strategy in the sense that it reduces the degree of disparity. Used by a weak state, it will not convert weakness into strength or change lead into gold. Diversification may simply make the most of endemic weakness.

NOTES

1. For discussion of various alternatives, see David Blake and Robert Walters, The Politics of Global Economic Relations (Englewood Cliffs, N.J.: Prentice-Hall, 1976), pp. 168-96; W. Howard Wriggins, "Third-World Strategies for Change: The Political Context of North-South Interdependence," ed. W. H. Wriggins and Gunnar Adler-Karlsson in Reducing Global Inequities (New York: McGraw-Hill, 1978), pp. 21-120.

2. Useful discussions of mercantilism and economic nationalism are to be found in Robert Gilpin, "Economic Interdependence and National Security in Historical Perspective," in Economic Issues and National Security, ed. Klaus Knorr and Frank Trager (Lawrence, Kan.: Regents Press of Kansas, 1977); R. Dan Walleri, "The Political Economy Literature on North-South Relations," International Studies Quarterly 22 (December 1978): 596-99; Harry Johnson, "A Theoretical Model of Economic Nationalism in New and Developing States," Political Science Quarterly 80 (June 1965): 169-85.

3. Quoted in Jacob Oser and William Blanchfield, The Evolution of Economic Thought, 3rd ed. (New York: Harcourt, Brace, Jovanovich, 1975), p. 206.

4. Gilpin, "Economic Interdependence," p. 28.

5. Ibid., p. 50.

6. Albert O. Hirschman, National Power and the Structure of Foreign Trade (Berkeley: University of California Press, 1945), pp. 13-52.

7. Ibid., pp. 31, 85.

8. For discussions of dependency theories, see Ronald Chilcote, "Dependency: A Critical Synthesis of the Literature," Latin American Perspectives 1 (1974): 4-29; Charles K. Wilbur, ed., The Political Economy of Development and Underdevelopment (New York: Random House, 1973); Heraldo Munoz, ed., From Dependency to Development (Boulder, Colo.: Westview, 1981).

9. Quoted in Wilbur, The Political Economy of Development, p. 109.

10. Fernando Cardoso, "Associated-Dependent Development: Theoretical and Practical Implications," in Authoritarian Brazil, ed. Alfred Stepan (New Haven, Conn.: Yale University Press, 1973), pp. 142-76.

11. See Carlos Diaz-Alejandro, "Delinking North and South: Unshackled or Unhinged?" in Rich and Poor Nations in the World Economy, ed. Diaz-Alejandro (New York: McGraw-Hill, 1978), pp. 87-162; Thomas Biersteker, "Self-Reliance in Theory and Practice in Tanzanian Trade Relations," International Organization 34 (Spring 1980): 229-64; Johan Galtung, "The Politics of Self-Reliance," in From Dependency to Development, ed. Heraldo Munoz (Boulder, Colo.: Westview, 1981).

12. For discussion of the various theorists and their policies, see Oser and Blanchfield, The Evolution of Economic Thought, pp. 42-142.

13. Richard Rosecrance and Arthur Stein, "Interdependence: Myth or Reality?" World Politics 26 (October 1973): 1-27; Alex Inkeles, "The Emerging Social Structure of the World," World Politics 27 (July 1975): 467-95; Richard Cooper, The Economics of Interdependence: Economic Policy in the Atlantic Community (New York: McGraw-Hill, 1968); and idem, "Economic Interdependence and Foreign Policy in the Seventies," World Politics 24 (1972): 159-81.

14. Robert Keohane and Joseph S. Nye, Power and Interdependence: World Politics in Transition (Boston: Little, Brown, 1977); Edward Morse, Modernization and the Transformation of International Relations (New York: Free Press, 1976); Karl Kaiser, "Transnational Politics: Toward a Theory of Multinational Politics," International Organization 25 (1971): 790-817; and Richard Cooper, "Trade Policy Is Foreign Policy," Foreign Policy 9 (1972): 18-36.

15. Interesting support for this view is provided by John Gallagher and Ronald Robinson, "The Imperialism of Free Trade," Economic History Review, 2d series, 6 (1953): 1-15; and by Jeanne Laux,

"Global Interdependence and State Intervention," in Canada's Foreign Policy, ed. Brian Tomlin (Toronto: Methuen, 1978).

16. I am following the definitions of Keohane and Nye, Power and Interdependence. As I argue later, the more logical division is to define sensitivity as the degree of connection and vulnerability as the costs (or potential costs) of connection with a particular actor.

17. Keohane and Nye, Power and Interdependence, p. 21; Robert Keohane, "The Theory of Hegemonic Stability and Changes in Intertional Economic Regimes, 1967-1977," in Change in the International System, ed. Ole Holsti, Randolph Siverson, and Alexander George (Boulder, Colo: Westview Press, 1980).

18. Keohane and Nye, Power and Interdependence, pp. 16-18.

19. Edward Morse, "Crisis Diplomacy, Interdependence and the Politics of International Economic Relations," World Politics 24 (Spring supplement 1972): 123-50.

20. Cooper, "Foreign Policy," p. 169.

21. Johan Galtung, "A Structural Theory of Integration," Journal of Peace Research 4 (1968): 375-95.

22. Details on the index are discussed in Hirschman, National Power, especially Index A, pp. 155-62, and in James Caporaso, "Methodological Issues in the Measurement of Inequality, Dependence, and Exploitation," in Testing Theories of Economic Imperialism, ed. Steven Rosen and James Kurth (Toronto: Lexington, 1974), pp. 87-114.

23. For the basic theory, see Jeremy Boissevain, Friends of Friends: Networks, Manipulators and Coalitions (Oxford: Basil Blackwell, 1974), and J. Clyde Mitchell, ed., Social Networks in Urban Situations (Manchester: Manchester University Press, 1969); applications include William Averyt, "Eurogroups, Clientela, and the European Community," International Organization 29 (1975): 949-72; Peter Busch and Donald Puchala, "Interests, Influence and Integration," Comparative Political Studies 9 (1976): 235-54; Peter Busch, "Germany in the European Economic Community: Theory and Case Study," Canadian Journal of Political Science 11 (1978): 545-74; Glenda Rosenthal, The Men behind the Decisions (Lexington, Mass.: D. C. Heath, 1975); Steffan Schmidt, James Scott, Carl Landé, and Laura Guasti, eds., Friends, Followers and Factions: A Reader in Political Clientelism (Berkeley: University of California Press, 1977); and Hellen Wallace, William Wallace, and Carole Webb, eds., Policy Making in the European Communities (New York: Wiley, 1977).

24. Walleri, "The Political Economy Literature," pp. 613-19, surveys the results of these.

25. Raymond Duvall, "Dependence and Dependencia Theory: Notes toward Precision of Concept and Argument," International Organization 32 (1978): 51-78.

26. Dennis Goulet, The Cruel Choice (New York: Atheneon, 1971).

27. For an argument that all have the same origins and roughly the same meaning, see David Baldwin, "Interdependence and Power: A Conceptual Analysis," International Organization 34 (1980): 471-506.

28. James Caporaso, "Dependence, Dependency, and Power in the Global System: A Structural and Behavioral Analysis," International Organization 32 (Winter 1978): 13-44.

29. The confusion here is a likely result of the developed-country focus of interdependence studies, which yields a range of cases narrower than if developing countries had been included. Keohane and Nye, Power and Interdependence, argue that weak states are frequently able to manipulate the vulnerabilities of stronger states to advantageous ends, conjuring up a problematical vision of the erosion of stronger-state dominance of the international system. See K. J. Holsti, "A New International Politics? Diplomacy in Complex Interdependence," International Organization 32 (1978): 513-30; and Stanley Michalak, Jr., "Theoretical Perspectives for Understanding International Interdependence," World Politics 32 (1979): 136-50.

30. See Caporaso, "Dependence, Dependency, and Power," pp. 27-31; Robert Keohane and Joseph Nye, "World Politics and the International Economic System, in The Future of the International Economic Order, ed. C. Fred Bergsten (Lexington, Mass.: D. C. Heath, 1973); and Thomas Baumgartner and Thomas Burns, "The Structuring of International Economic Relations, " International Studies Quarterly 19 (1975): 126-59.

31. Neil Richardson, Foreign Policy and Economic Dependence (Austin: University of Texas Press, 1978); Neil Richardson and Charles Kegley, Jr., "Trade Dependence and Foreign Policy Compliance: A Longitudinal Analysis," International Studies Quarterly 24 (June 1980): 191-222; and Michael Dolan, Brian Tomlin, Maureen Appel Molot, and Harald Von Riekhoff, "Foreign Policies of African States in Asymmetrical Dyads," International Studies Quarterly 24 (September 1980): 415-49.

3

ASEAN: BUILDING
AND USING A
REGIONAL ORGANIZATION

The Association of Southeast Asian Nations (ASEAN) is a relative newcomer to the international political environment of Asia. It has developed slowly, but surely, to become a central feature in Southeast Asian politics, particularly in the foreign policies of its five members. Although each of the members conducts much of its foreign policy independently, and each is ultimately responsible for domestic development policies, the regional organization has become progressively more important as the vehicle for joint efforts in foreign policy and development. ASEAN has been woven into the fabric of national policies and strategies, particularly those examined here.

The regional organization itself is an excellent starting point for a study of the changing role of its members in the international political system. Its very existence is a signal that these states are more actively attempting to shape the nature of their international environment. As discussed in Chapter 2, the evolution of ASEAN into a regular part of the international economic diplomacy of the members has a direct bearing on their ability to pursue courses of action designed to reduce dependence on larger states. This chapter surveys the origins and development of ASEAN and then focuses on the economic programs pursued through the regional organization, both those designed for the members only and those directed toward outside states. Not all of the discussion of ASEAN and its programs is contained here. Some of the activities and programs of ASEAN are reserved for following chapters, where they are better understood in the context of the policy problems raised there; this chapter frames those later references to ASEAN. Regionalism is suggested as an element of a program to reduce dependence between small, less developed states and larger, more developed states. It is this aspect of ASEAN that is the focus of discussion in this chapter.

ORIGINS AND DEVELOPMENT

ASEAN is the latest stage in an evolutionary process of international community formation in Southeast Asia. It is a culmination of previous attempts at regionalism as well as the accumulated experience of the association itself. The pace of cooperation has been determined in part by domestic political concerns of the members and in part by responses to international stimuli; it is where these two elements coincide that ASEAN has made its greatest progress. At the same time, there have been factors of a divisive nature that have militated against faster collaboration. In order to understand the present level of development of ASEAN programs, one must first look briefly at the origins of regionalism, at the domestic and international factors promoting and retarding regionalism, and at the interests of the members in developing a regional association.

ASEAN, formed in 1967, is essentially an extension and amalgamation of prior attempts to create regional institutions. Following World War II, a number of regional associations were grafted onto the Asian system by external powers. These were largely functional organizations in the economic sphere, such as the UN Economic Commission for Asia and the Far East (now the UN Economic and Social Commission for Asia and the Pacific [ESCAP]) and the Colombo Plan or security organizations such as the Southeast Asia Treaty Organization (SEATO) and the Anglo-Malayan Defense Agreement.[1] The major effect on regional cooperation would appear to be that these early ventures exposed the new states to various forms of cooperation, creating an environment of experience conducive to later cooperative efforts.[2]

A different set of regional initiatives emerged in the 1960s, characterized by several attempts to create organizations at the behest of local states. The Association of Southeast Asia (ASA) was established in 1961 by Thailand, the Philippines, and Malaya, foreshadowing in many respects the later structure and purpose of ASEAN. In 1963 Maphilindo, a "Greater Malayan Confederation," was set up by Malaysia, the Philippines, and Indonesia, only to die the following year under the weight of conflict among the three members. The Asian and Pacific Council (ASPAC) attempted to bind Japan, Taiwan, Malaysia, Thailand, the Philippines, South Vietnam, South Korea, Australia, and New Zealand together in 1966, but the political disabilities of its anticommunist stance became too onerous for the Philippines, Malaysia, and Thailand; as China emerged in the 1970s to be a major Asian power, it was not to be so blatantly affronted.[3] Though none of these organizations survived in Southeast Asia, their formation indicates the desire to create the basis for increased regional interaction among Southeast Asian states in political and economic affairs, through local sponsorship of loosely structured associations. Along with the proliferation of functional international organizations, which included some of the Southeast Asian states, these provided experience in organizing regional interests for mutual benefit.

ASEAN itself is seen by many as an extension and enlargement of ASA, as the parallels in organizational structure, goals, and membership interests are striking.[4] Even much of ASEAN's early business was essentially that set by ASA and simply carried over to the larger forum.[5] However, the similarity with ASA should not be overemphasized, as both organizations are extremely vague in self-definition, and ASA in fact accomplished little, leaving its organizational structure as the major bequest. Had it in fact done much, there is some likelihood that this would have discredited its inheritance, as Indonesia was convinced that it was a front for SEATO and had refused to join on those grounds.[6] Nevertheless, it seems to be the case that ASA, as well as ASPAC and Maphilindo, did contribute to an increase in communication among the states of the region and added to their experience in initiating cooperative behavior. ASEAN, then, did not spring from uncultivated soil but, rather, emerged as the dominant hybrid of numerous crossbreedings.

Much has been made of the factors inhibiting the development of regionalism in Southeast Asia. In fact, one is moved to sympathize with Indonesian President Suharto's lament:

> I feel that it is a pity that so many foreign analysts place far too much emphasis upon noting the differences between member-countries and then proceed from these observations to conclude that ASEAN is an impossibility.[7]

The litany of problems cited is long: diplomatic disputes such as the boundary debate between the Philippines and Malaysia and the hostilities initiated by Indonesia after the creation of the state of Malaysia;[8] competitive rather than complementary economies;[9] mutual attitudes of "distrust, suspicion, fears and even animosity";[10] the colonial legacy of political and economic isolation;[11] the neocolonial legacy of independence;[12] ethnonationalism;[13] nationalism and the conflict of national interests.[14] In short, "Southeast Asian regionalism has been inhibited by a broad array of political, economic, and cultural factors."[15] Despite this apparently insurmountable environment, regionalism and ASEAN have survived and, to a degree, have prospered.

The degree to which ASEAN has prospered is, however, another contentious issue. On top of the previously listed factors curtailing regionalism there are numerous critical evaluations of the performance of the association itself. If regional cooperation is in part a matter of building experience, some would argue that this experience has contributed little to setting the agenda for further cooperation. Several analysts point to the excruciatingly slow pace of accomplishment as measured by the implementation of ASEAN recommendations, many of which are in themselves of little consequence.[16] The primary cause of this lack of performance is seen to be defects in the institutional structure, itself a reflection of hesitance on the part of the members in accelerating regionalism: too highly decentralized and loosely coordinated; constantly changing venues and turnover of personnel, inhibiting the development of a transnational outlook; an overloaded bureaucratic structure.[17] In addition, general uncertainty owing to a narrow base of support limited to top elites and the real possibility of changes in these elites damaging commitment produce a deliberately slow pace.[18] One analyst concludes ambiguously: "ASEAN's survival is in itself an achievement that might be said to counterbalance the organization's relatively slow pace of action."[19]

ASEAN's survival, however, is not simply a matter of inertia. There are positive contributing factors. One is a degree of commonality in the perception of major problems. The five states share concerns regarding threats to their independence, stability, and security—internal as well as external.[20] Furthermore, their perceptions of security and social stability are linked together as a set, and approaches to the issue of economic development are identical, creating a core of preconditions for regional cooperation;[21] these conclusions, interestingly, were based on a study conducted in the same time period (1959-69) as many of the previously cited works that came to precisely the opposite conclusion. That this commonality of perception continues and is having some effect in forging political will to act as a region is noted in more recent evaluations.[22] Common motivations and perceptions in the ASEAN area have served to create a bond among the members.

A major set of stimuli to regionalism is derived from the international system and appears to be a domestic response to perceptions of common external threats. External threats are accorded a prominent role in the formation and continuation of ASEAN but, at the same time, act as restraints to the pace of cooperation in isolated instances.[23] The theme of weakness in the face of a hostile international system is recurrent; for example, the remarks of Thanat Khoman, then foreign minister of Thailand, at ASEAN's inception: through ASEAN, "individual weakness and impotence will gradually be replaced by a greater combined strength. . . . It becomes increasingly necessary for the small and weak nations to close their ranks and pool their limited means and potential."[24] In the same line, ASEAN is seen as a "product of a combination of common fears and weaknesses, not of common strength," and as a case of "collective political will" imposed by a "common concern with external exploitation of internal weaknesses."[25]

The first of these external threats is a result of changes in the balance of power among the major international actors in the Asian arena. The announced withdrawal of the United Kingdom, along with fears of Chinese dominance, were instrumental in the initiation of ASEAN; one author goes so far as to suggest that ASEAN was an attempt to avoid being included in the Chinese sphere of influence.[26] U. S. withdrawal and the reunification of Vietnam were certainly key stimuli to the timing of ASEAN's more active phase set out at the Bali Summit in 1976. Again in 1979, Vietnam's invasion of Kampuchea elicited common perceptions of danger[27] and joint action, for example, in the United Nations. The major response to these security threats has been to accept and promote the earlier Malaysian concept of a Southeast Asian "Zone of Peace, Freedom, and Neutrality" in order to encourage an equilibrium of the major powers in the region, which would allow all to be active to varying degrees but none to dominate.[28] Secondarily, there has been increasing coordination of military and intelligence activities, although this is kept strictly bilateral and formally outside of ASEAN auspices,[29] possibly to allay Chinese suspicions that military security is a core to ASEAN. To the degree that ASEAN is seen as strong and stable, so the thinking goes, outside powers will not have an incentive to intervene.[30]

The second of these threats is externally linked but internal in effect. Domestic political and economic stability, referred to as resilience by the Indonesians, is menaced by potential revolutions. Economic development as a route to domestic stability is, as van der Kroef puts it, the leitmotiv of ASEAN security policy.[31] Domestic challenges from insurgent and potentially revolutionary peasants must be defused by rapid economic growth that allows wider distribution of wealth. Since all five states are heavily penetrated by external economic actors, expectations are focused on growth led by international trade and investment and are more easily realized as a regional group that supplements the bargaining strength of any single member.

It would appear that the balance between those forces inhibiting and those forces impelling regional cooperation reached a decisive point in the early 1970s. As expressed by the Malaysian deputy prime minister in 1971:

> Regional cooperation is now widely recognized . . . as an important instrument, if not an imperative in the development of nations, particularly those that are small. That way only can we rise effectively to challenge and provide an alternative to the threat of domination by the big countries with their powerful economies.[32]

For reasons linked to economics but derived from security considerations as well as wealth, ASEAN moved into a more active period, marked by burgeoning programs over a wide spectrum of affairs.

It is a commonplace observation that little of substance was undertaken by ASEAN prior to 1976, when the second decade was launched with fanfare and more substantive programs. Yet, the first decade was hardly wasted. ASEAN was largely concerned with less political, less dramatic, less visible programs that contributed an infrastructure for, and experience at, cooperation. By 1975 official committees existed for food and agriculture, shipping, communications, transportation, tourism, finance, commerce, science and technology, mass media, and sociocultural activities. Each was engaged in modest cooperative ventures, which brought responsible officials from all five countries together, something that is unlikely to have happened without ASEAN. In addition, a parallel set of nongovernmental organizations was springing up to link private citizens in each of the countries, covering almost every conceivable type of activity: the Committee for ASEAN Youth Cooperation, the ASEAN Federation of Women, the ASEAN Motion Picture Producers' Association, the ASEAN Cardiologists' Federation, and the ASEAN Consumers' Protection Agency (this subject is further discussed in Chapter 6). These organizations laid the groundwork for wider cooperation. By the end of the 1970s, any casual traveler through the region could hardly avoid exposure to the idea that there were extensive bonds among the ASEAN members through such publicized items as ASEAN book fairs, special ASEAN airfares, and ASEAN sports fairs.

Despite the "nonpolitical" image of the early years of ASEAN, there was, in fact, some degree of political cooperation before 1975. As early as 1971, ministerial meetings included discussions of the need for consultation in preparation for international forums.[33] By 1973 there were several efforts undertaken in this direction, including joint strategy sessions for the General Agreement on Tariffs and Trade (GATT),[34] joint approaches toward modification of the European Economic Community (EEC) trade-preference system for developing countries,[35] and common policy agreements for UN conferences and the General Assembly.[36] In addition, from 1971 on, the foreign ministers met yearly to discuss political problems of joint concern. Nominally, this was outside the ASEAN framework in order to protect the image of limited economic and sociocultural cooperation as set out in original definitions of the organization.[37] But starting in 1973, ASEAN took a joint stand in opposing Japan's increased production of synthetic rubber, which was seen as threatening the market for natural rubber; this was eventually resolved in ASEAN's favor through extensive joint diplomacy, aided by increases in petroleum prices that made the Japanese industry less viable.[38] The utility of

ASEAN as an instrument of international economic diplomacy was being actively explored in this period.

These initial successes, allowing the Ministerial Conference in
1974 to report the first concrete achievements,[39] were given a fillip
by the unification of Vietnam. Prime Minister Lee of Singapore reported that the regional international situation in early 1975 drew the
ASEAN members closer together in the economic, diplomatic, and
political fields.[40] By the end of the year, the economic ministers
met and approved a program of economic cooperation, setting the
agenda for the first summit in February 1976 at Bali.[41] This summit
brought the heads of government together under ASEAN auspices for
the first time and was followed by another the next year (1977) in Kuala
Lumpur. Not only did these summits forcus world attention on the
ASEAN organization, they also publicly marked the transition of
ASEAN from limited, informal cooperation to a wide-ranging program
of formal projects, for the most part economic in nature. According
to the final communiqué of the Bali meeting, it became "essential for
the members to move to higher levels of cooperation, especially in
political, economic, social, cultural, scientific, and technological
fields."[42] One might search for fields not included. ASEAN was no
longer wary of attracting international attention; that was precisely
what was required for the future.

ASEAN, then, is the culmination of regionalist efforts in Southeast Asia. It exists in an environment marked by both negative and
positive factors, and it has developed at a relatively slow pace. At
the same time, the challenges of economic development, stability,
and international security are of such gravity as to impel the members
to continue their efforts toward more unity. Its activities range across
a wide spectrum of social and cultural interests, but they have become
focused on economic and political affairs. ASEAN is an open-ended
association of convenience, designed to meet the needs of the members
through concerted international action.

ASEAN ECONOMIC PROGRAMS

The programs initiated at the Bali Summit and the follow-up in
Kuala Lumpur the next year form the basis of ASEAN economic cooperation. For convenience, these can be divided into those programs
directed at increasing the scope of economic activity among ASEAN
members, or internal programs, and those aimed at increasing the
level of coordination of international economic diplomacy, or external
programs. The major points of these programs are outlined below.
However, it should be kept in mind that the division is an artificial
one created for ease of discussion; it is my contention that the major

purpose of all ASEAN economic programs is to increase ASEAN leverage in the international system.

Internal Economic Programs

The Declaration of ASEAN Concord signed at the Bali Summit is generally seen as the initiation of ASEAN economic cooperation, as it identifies the major areas of future effort and directs the economic ministers to consider the means of implementation. However, the blueprint for the internal economic programs has much earlier origins. At the Second Ministerial Meeting of ASEAN in 1968, a proposal for a study of potential ASEAN economic cooperation by the United Nations was accepted.[43] The result was returned to the ASEAN governments two years later and was kept confidential for another two years; eventually it was published by the United Nations.[44] The study was done under the supervision of a Cambridge economist, Austin Robinson, with a great deal of consultation with a wide variety of ASEAN economists, government officials, and other figures in the region. According to one of the participants, the emphasis was on working out pragmatic areas of cooperation that were most likely to win acceptance among the governments rather than laying out the academic possibilities.[45] The study was again considered by the ASEAN ministers in 1972 and 1973 and by an expert group appointed to consider implementation in 1974; by 1975 the report was being reformulated for the Bali Summit.[46] The major techniques of cooperation were identified as selective trade liberalization, package deals of major industrial projects, and industrial complementation schemes.[47] These remain the main programs of ASEAN internal economic cooperation.

The Preferential Trade Agreement (PTA), signed in Manila at the end of February 1977, took effect January 1, 1978.[48] The general purpose is gradually to free intraregional trade from widely divergent tariff barriers. The key dispute is how gradual this is to be, reflected in the selection of means for implementation. Singapore and the Philippines initially advocated a formula whereby tariffs would be lowered by some set amount on all items, across the board; the suggested amounts varied from 10 to 15 percent.[49] This would lead directly to a free-trade zone. Indonesia alone found this unacceptable, as the existing inequality among the members might rebound to Indonesia's ultimate disadvantage if exaggerated by free trade.[50] Notwithstanding some criticism from other ASEAN members, notably the Philippines,[51] the typical ASEAN pattern was followed, and Indonesia as the least flexible member was left to present the working paper on the trade program.[52] The result was the item-by-item approach advocated by the UN report.

Although Singapore dropped the more ambitious, across-the-board approach at the Bali Summit,[53] the government went ahead with the idea on a separate basis with Thailand and with the Philippines in early 1977,[54] leaving it open to accession by the other members as they saw fit. This attempt at acceleration elicited a hostile response from Indonesia, and the arrangements were suspended in the interests of ASEAN solidarity.[55] Singapore indicated its early enthusiasm for economic cooperation but, as was to happen often, it was restrained. Nevertheless, the pace of implementation of the PTA has since increased from the initial list of 71 products, first, to 2,000 a year and, most recently, to 8,530 products a year, with each to be "significantly traded" in the region.[56] Indonesia's continuing reluctance to be dragged into a free-trade area is perhaps indicated by a unilateral increase of tariffs on some 400 items in early 1979,[57] but the program is progressing more to the satisfaction of the other members.

The economic effects of the PTA are subject to some dispute. In addition to the trade provisions previously outlined, there are arrangements to encourage long-term quantity contracts financed at preferential rates among ASEAN purchasers, stipulations for ASEAN preferences in the sources of governmental purchases, and the inclusion of any ASEAN industrial products in preferential tariff arrangements. These provisions are largely unused to date, leaving the trade area the only significant one. However, the relatively small cuts in tariffs, mostly 10 percent of existing levels, and the extremely large number of items to be individually negotiated under the scheme (a potential of several million) have brought its effectiveness into question.[58] In addition, bureaucratic procedures, including port administration and paperwork requirements, are so cumbersome that many regional business managers comment that the small benefits offered by the PTA are not enough of an incentive to get them to use the system. The apparent lack of real economic impact raises the credibility of early reports that the free-trade proposal was designed to give a boost to outside perceptions of the seriousness of ASEAN regionalism.[59]

The Declaration of ASEAN Concord sets out that "member states shall cooperate to establish large-scale ASEAN industrial plants, particularly to meet regional requirements of essential commodities." These are the showcase projects of ASEAN—the high-visibility, regional, import-substitution, manufacturing plants—designed to produce on a regional level what is not economical at the national level and to free each of the members from the necessity of importing some large-scale, manufactured products from the industrial countries. A number of particular products were identified by the UN report as economically feasible and desirable for industrial development, and these formed the basis for both the list that the economic ministers were directed to consider and for the initial distribution.[60] These were urea plants for Indonesia and Malaysia, superphosphates for the Philippines, diesel engines for Singapore, and soda ash for Thailand, each allocated after extensive bartering among conflicting national aspirations. It was also established that the financing of the projects should be joint, with the host country contributing 60 percent of the equity and each of the other members 10 percent. The original projects each had some application to agriculture, in line with the emphasis in the Declaration of ASEAN Concord on basic commodities, "particularly food and energy."

The subsequent history of these ventures has been mixed. Japan provided a boost by offering $1 billion in unspecified types of soft financing after Prime Minister Fukuda's meeting with ASEAN in 1977; two conditions, feasibility and joint ASEAN sponsorship, were imposed, both of which have become somewhat problematic.[61] The Indonesian project, already started as a national project before allocation, is so far the closest to implementation, with the Malaysian project also approved, and the Thai effort close to the final stages; each of these, however, is subject to doubts about its economic viability.[62] Immediate discord broke out over the Singapore diesel plant, particularly as Indonesia already had similar plants planned or in operation, but eventually, virtually all of the other members objected, as they planned similar national projects.[63] As a result, Singapore will go ahead with the plant as a non-ASEAN project and will participate in the other regional industries only to the extent of 1 percent of equity, preserving the regional nature of the projects in form but not in fact.[64] In addition, the Philippines' original projects were dropped as uneconomical[65] and are slated to be replaced by a copper fabrication site.[66] Even the Basic Agreement for the industrial projects has been held up. Given the difficulties, it is hardly surprising that the second round of projects originally contemplated has been allowed to lie fallow. Conflicting national aspirations have not been overcome by regional harmony.

It is not merely the intransigence of national interest that has inhibited the ASEAN industrial projects. The complexity of planning is also considerable,[67] and world economic conditions change rapidly, affecting the feasibility of the projects. The Thai project, for example, was investigated by Japanese interests long before it was set as a cooperation project, and it required yet another 2.5 years of study by a Canadian firm before acceptance.[68] The Indonesian project was already a national project with a completed feasibility study before "ASEANization"; still, it is not yet in production, nor was the financing with Japan settled easily. The crawling pace and national conflicts have had a toll on ASEAN unity. Singapore has found it necessary to declare that it must make its own arrangements to maintain the required pace of economic progress to ensure its survival in the global economic arena, apart from ASEAN. [69] The centerpiece economic program is dividing, rather than uniting, ASEAN in the regional economic sphere.

The industrial complementation schemes, the final major area of cooperation, are the least developed. [70] As a supplement to the larger industrial projects of the ASEAN industry program, these projects seek to create transnational production within ASEAN, with some parts of a larger product produced in several ASEAN countries; in some cases, it is envisioned that specialization within a particular product line will be coordinated this way. Through this program, the various strengths of the manufacturing sectors in each country will be maximized, and "wasteful" competition will be minimized. The projects will be smaller in size and will build on existing national capabilities. In contrast to the high degree of government involvement in the industrial projects, the complementation program is left largely to the private sector for its planning, initiation, and implementation. Since the role of the private sector is discussed more fully in Chapter 6, only an overview of progress and of the major political issues is considered here.

To date, very little concrete cooperation has been achieved. Early agreements to coordinate and exchange information in several industries, particularly steel, glass, and petrochemicals, [71] have not been widely followed up with other sectoral agreements. Although a large number of products have been identified as potential complementation products, only one has been approved so far. [72] Automotive parts are the most advanced in the planning stages, and a series of allocations for each national industry has been suggested to avoid competition and to increase the regional content of automobile manufacturing. [73] With Japanese car makers dominant, coordination is necessary with their industry association, which has yet to have been achieved. [74] The first auto-products package is to go into effect June 1982, with a substantial tariff reduction, and the second is scheduled for 1984; this is the program that will test the complementation scheme. [75] The slow pace of the industrial projects seems to be replicated in the complementation schemes, with an additional hindrance: not only must governmental approval be secured, but transnational coordination of the private sectors is also required, adding another dimension to the problem.

One major problem has been in securing guidelines for complementation that are acceptable to the five governments and to each private sector. The task of formulating these guidelines has been passed back and forth between the ASEAN organization and the private-sector representative, the ASEAN Chambers of Commerce and Industry (ACCI), several times. [76] Each country seems to have different ideas on the allowable proportion of foreign investment, with all but Singa-

pore favoring some formula mandating majority ASEAN ownership. [77]
As a result, Singapore vetoed the complementation guidelines in
Jakarta in mid-1979, forcing an extensive review and delay of project
implementation; the Basic Agreement was reached only in June 1981. [78]

The second major problem is Singapore's fear of the erosion of
its international market position should it proceed with many complementation projects. Since each project would involve tariff and other
concessions, including some form of monopoly guarantee for the regional market, the private sector in Singapore is quite concerned that
the result would be to force it to purchase higher-cost inputs for manufactured exports, resulting in a less competitive, international marketing position. [79] This is also a domestic issue in Singapore, as the
government is seen as more willing to compromise than is the private
sector. Reversing its earlier enthusiasm, Singapore has replaced
Indonesia as the least willing to engage in regional industrial integration.

There is, however, an emerging area of ASEAN cooperation
that Singapore finds quite attractive and that may counter declining
enthusiasm for ASEAN economic programs. As an aspiring financial
center, Singapore has led cooperation in the banking sector. Initial
efforts in this area were limited to the establishment of an ASEAN
Swap Facility in 1977 (which apparently has never been used). More
ambitious is the establishment of the ASEAN Finance Corporation to
assist in the capitalization of development projects throughout the
region. [80] This fits with Singapore's vision of itself as a center for
the diffusion of finance and technology in ASEAN.

The major internal ASEAN economic programs, then, are all
plagued by slowness, internal divisiveness, and marginal economic
benefits. It is apparent that the major benefits of these programs are
not to be found in rapid economic integration of the members into
something resembling an economic community in the near future. Nor,
I would suggest, is this the intention of the members in pursuing these
programs. Rather, it seems evident that they are being exploited for
their effect in the wider international economic sphere. To the degree
that the ASEAN members appear to be building the basis of a future
economic association, their attractiveness to major international economic actors is enhanced. This image can be turned to good use at
the bargaining table. The PTA raises the possibility of enhanced regional trading for any company with a regional base and of costs for
those outside. The industrial projects signal decreased reliance on
major industrial countries for some products, encouraging the shift
of industry to the region. Complementation schemes guarantee a regional market for an increased range of products with monopoly possibilities. In each case, it is the image of economic robustness that
is being cultivated to a far greater extent than is the reality. At least

in the short term, the primary gain to the members of ASEAN from
the internal economic programs is in external economic relations.

External Economic Programs

    Coordination of international economic policies among the
ASEAN members developed slowly before 1976, but as has been previously pointed out, it was of some significance in the early 1970s.
As early as 1971, coordination of representatives at regional and international forums was identified as a "necessity" by the foreign ministers, "so that members of ASEAN would always present a united
stand to advance their common interest."[81] But on the whole, ASEAN
kept a low profile in affairs thought to be "political."
    All of this changed with the Bali Summit. Political cooperation
was reaffirmed and, in several ways, was made the central element
of cooperation emphasized by the heads of government.[82] The Declaration of ASEAN Concord entitled a major section "Joint Approach
to International Commodity Problems and Other World Economic
Problems," and the follow-up meeting of economic ministers a month
later detailed a program of diplomatic conferences to be carried out
with major countries and groups. Further, it was agreed to adopt
joint approaches to a wide variety of international bodies on economic
issues.[83] However, with so much promised at Bali in so many areas
of cooperation, external cooperation on economic issues was left more
or less unattended until the Second ASEAN Summit in Kuala Lumpur
and until the following meeting of economic ministers in August and
September of 1977.[84] By this time, the value of external cooperation
had acquired a new fillip: "In our external relations we share common
views. . . . It is easier psychologically to deal with ASEAN's external
partners than to sort out the intraregional arrangements between the
ASEAN partners" (Prime Minister Lee).[85] With the major ASEAN internal programs in stagnation, external cooperation offered a means
of visible and quick success.
    The forums have been the major instrument of formal coopera-
tion with external actors. Responsibilities for coordinating these in-
termittant conferences are divided among the members: Indonesia
for Japan and the EEC; Malaysia for Australia and west Asia; the
Philippines for the United States, Canada, and the Group of 77; Singapore for New Zealand; and Thailand for the United Nations Development Programme (UNDP) and ESCAP.[86] The substance of these
meetings is set jointly, but as the ASEAN machinery is neither extensive enough nor delegated enough authority to conduct them, primary
responsibility falls to a particular ASEAN member.[87] The stated objective is to establish regular means for economic collaboration in

order to build up long-term, complementary, economic relationships with the more developed countries, [88] but the intent is obviously to exercise collective political will for the benefit of the members. There are numerous areas in which some concrete gain has been achieved.

Group participation in international organizations and conferences has enhanced the image of ASEAN as a bloc. Common objectives have been pursued in conferences such as the United Nations Conference on Trade and Development (UNCTAD) after extensive preliminary meetings to resolve separate, particular interests, resulting in group support for each country's special problems. [89] In addition, the coordination and monitoring of various technical-assistance programs extended through UN agencies has been the goal of meetings with the UNDP, ESCAP, the Asian Development Bank (ADB), the Food and Agriculture Organization (FAO), and the United Nations Industrial Development Organization (UNIDO). [90] The wide range of economic development among ASEAN members allows the group to argue for programs benefiting all, programs that would be difficult to win from international agencies individually.

With economic partners, the most benefit has come from Australia, probably because of its relatively weak position in the global political and economic order. This is one of the oldest relationships for ASEAN, dating from early 1974, and it produced the first extension of bilateral aid for technical cooperation to the group. [91] The relationship has, however, not remained altogether harmonious. An early demonstration of ASEAN solidarity was an objection to Australian trade protectionism against Malaysia and the Philippines in late 1976, which was followed by an invitation to meet with the ASEAN heads of government after their 1977 summit to press the issue. Australian Prime Minister Frasier's inability to meet ASEAN demands cooled his initial enthusiasm at the prospect of inclusion in regional development plans, especially with the application of sanctions by Malaysia and the Philippines in the form of a slowdown of approval for imports of Australian goods. ASEAN was reportedly "growing weary" of Australia's desire for close ties but unwillingness to extend incentives. [92] Singapore's Prime Minister Lee made it quite explicit that the tenor of relations with Australia would depend on the resolution of economic issues, and in the context of stating ASEAN desires, he warned that Australia was becoming "less relevant" to ASEAN. [93] This blunt threat prompted Australia to extend special quotas to the ASEAN industries affected and to establish "early warning" links between the ASEAN ambassadors and the Australian cabinet to allow ASEAN to make representations on industrial policy changes before decisions were final. [94] Australia also undertook to sponsor trade and investment fairs in an attempt to respond to criticism that these areas of exchange were being inhibited by lack of government support. [95]

Before these disputes were placated, an agreement between Quantas and British Airways on direct discount airfares between London and Australia raised charges of damage to Singapore's airline and tourist trade. Clumsy efforts to offer concessions to the other ASEAN countries in order to prevent the emergence of a united front behind Singapore failed and, in fact, led to a special ASEAN economic ministers meeting on the subject. [96] Group sanctions were again threatened, and attacks were launched directly at Australia and indirectly at "developed-country protectionism" at the conveniently timed UNCTAD V meeting in Manila in May 1979. [97] A favorable compromise was accepted by ASEAN on behalf of Singapore before the end of the year. [98] ASEAN had again demonstrated that it was capable of obtaining results even when the interests threatened were those of a single member.

The higher profile of ASEAN and a feeling that Australia's role as speaker for the Asia-Pacific area is increasingly being usurped by ASEAN have reportedly led to some reexamination by Australia of its role in the region. The relative position of Australia in international forums, its role as a conduit between the developed countries and the less developed of the region, and its relative weight with the United States—all seen as traditional roles for Australia—are felt to be diminished by the emerging weight of ASEAN political muscle. [99] Perhaps Australian enthusiasm for the concept of a Pacific community is in part accounted for by its promise to provide a new basis of attachment in Asia and the Pacific, compensating for the erosion of more traditional connections. [100] Clearly, Australia has emerged as a relative loser in its disputes with ASEAN, and some realignment of power positions in the Pacific has resulted. On the other hand, Australia has proved the value of unity to ASEAN, both in specific economic issues and as a foil to demonstrate diplomatic aggressiveness without the repercussions that could result from challenging a major economic actor.

No other relationship has been marked by the same degree of acrimony, although that with Japan, "in spite of 'symbolic' cooperation and 'generous' aid extended by Japan to ASEAN, is by no means cordial."[101] Long-standing disputes over the degree of access to the Japanese market, exacerbated by a chronic balance-of-trade deficit on the part of ASEAN, have appeared regularly on the agendas of the ASEAN-Japan Forum. Only very limited concessions have been won, with the major trade benefit having been the introduction of a tariff scheme featuring a cumulative, rules-of-origin clause, and this was won only in 1978. [102] Japan's promise to "represent" ASEAN's interests in the Geneva round of multilateral trade negotiations (MTNs) failed to gain any significant advantages, and it eroded any attempt by Japan to project an image of ASEAN's protector against the other developed countries. [103]

The major outstanding issue is ASEAN's quest for a commodity-price-stabilization agreement with Japan, known as STABEX. A proposal patterned on the Lomé Agreement advanced by ASEAN in 1977 was reportedly on the verge of approval in mid-1978. [104] But this stalled when a minimal Commun Fund emerged from UNCTAD V, and negotiations were unproductive. Press reports placed the blame on ASEAN's lack of preparation for scheduled talks and on the Philippines' desire to await the outcome of UNCTAD, which it was hosting; but interviews presented a reversed picture of Philippine interest and Japanese reluctance to commit anything to STABEX before seeing how far UNCTAD would go. [105] Regional observers represent Japan as being more sympathetic to an UNCTAD approach as it fits more consistently with the global, rather than regional, posture that Japan would like to project. Surely, it is less expensive. [106]

The issue remains unresolved, and the whole tenor of relations between Japan and ASEAN is being subjected to a new strain with the development of closer ties between Japan and China, bumping ASEAN to fourth place in Japan's declared hierarchy of regional interests. [107] The relationship with Japan seems to be characterized by mutual recognition of importance, but with each side paying particular attention to a firm bargaining image in order to make minimal concessions. Even the 1981 Japanese plan for focusing aid to ASEAN was received with considerable reservation. [108] Although ASEAN has gained advantages from Japan, they have been far fewer than those sought.

In contrast, relations with the more distant EEC have been most amicable, if less productive. Despite growing institutionalization of the form of the relationship and despite political support from Germany within the community, very little aside from minor concessions has been won by ASEAN in trade issues. [109] But the EEC as the "senior region"[110] has taken an active interest in ASEAN, and in addition to sponsoring a major study of industrial complementation between the two areas[111] and giving seminars on the transfer of technology, [112] it is the only major partner that consistently deals with ASEAN as a unity instead of focusing on bilateral relations with the members. [113] Growing interest on both sides was indicated by ASEAN-EEC Industrial Cooperation Conferences in 1977 and 1978, by the first extension of development assistance from the EEC in 1978, and by the negotiation of a cooperation agreement. [114] Despite some skepticism on the part of ASEAN that the economic relationship is not being altered from a basically colonial pattern, [115] it is clearly being given priority and high hope for the future. [116] The concessions granted so far have been more of form than of substance, but this is equally appreciated by ASEAN for its diplomatic utility.

Other forums have progressed smoothly and without major substantive disputes. New Zealand has extended technical cooperation
and has agreed to sponsor a program of ASEAN trade promotion on a
continuing basis.[117] Canada has initiated a solid program of technical cooperation and some investment promotion.[118] A minor concession to ASEAN was made by the United States in continuing a tax de-
ferral for U.S. corporations operating abroad, which had been scheduled for cancellation, and contacts between the private sectors of the
United States and ASEAN have been facilitated.[119] ASEAN has won
some support for which the more developed members would not have
been eligible, and it has used established bilateral relations to gain
access for the views of the group.

Overall, it would appear that ASEAN has been able to achieve
some solid economic success and greater diplomatic leverage acting
as a "collective-bargaining force."[120] Certainly there are more
signs of success in external actions than there seem to be in internal
economic cooperation.[121] The benefits of guaranteeing that ASEAN
views will be heard in the developed countries and of bolstering the
bargaining position of ASEAN over that of the individual states have
been emphasized by several trade and development officials in the
region.[122] ASEAN's effectiveness in external relations is receiving
general recognition.[123]

The process of regional development in Southeast Asia, then,
has produced an organization that is increasingly effective in building
a base for more effective negotiation in the international economic
sphere. This is a result of an extensive period of low-level cooperation on a wide front of projects in the 1950s and 1960s, which contributed to the creation of ASEAN and provided a background of cooperative experience. In addition, a wide range of common problems in
domestic and international politics has contributed to a substantial
degree of commonality in the perception of problems and approaches.
ASEAN has slowly extended the range of cooperative ventures to include almost every conceivable area—cultural, social, economic,
political, and even security. By the mid-1970s, the earlier hesitant
and low-profile stance in the international system was abandoned for
precisely the opposite, bolstered by a new surge of regional projects.
While progress in internal economic areas has been slow and plagued
by disputes, it has had the effect of enhancing the image of ASEAN in
the international economic system and has drawn increasing attention
to the organization. External economic diplomacy has been closely
coordinated, producing results probably beyond the ability of any of
the members acting alone. As a group of developing countries, regionalism has been more focused on redressing the unbalanced relationships between the members and their developed partners than on
economic integration. Regionalism has emerged as a convenient diplomatic tool in Southeast Asia.

NOTES

1. Discussions of early regionalism are to be found in William Bucklin, "Regional Economic Cooperation in Southeast Asia: 1945-1969" (Ph.D. diss., Michigan State University, 1972), pp. 11-64; Peter Lyon, "ASEAN and the Future of Regionalism," in New Directions in the International Relations of Southeast Asia: The Great Powers and Southeast Asia, ed. Lau Teik Soon (Singapore: Singapore University Press, 1973), pp. 156-59; and Somsakdi Xuto, Regional Cooperation in Southeast Asia: Problems, Possibilities and Prospects (Bangkok: Institute of Asian Studies, Chulalongkorn University, 1973), pp. 20-43.

2. Estrella Solidum, "The Nature of Cooperation among the ASEAN States as Perceived through Elite Attitudes—A Factor for Regionalism" (Ph.D. diss., University of Kentucky, 1970), p. 34.

3. On ASA, see Bernard Gordon, The Dimensions of Conflict in Southeast Asia (Englewood Cliffs, N.J.: Prentice-Hall, 1966), pp. 141-77; and Vincent Pollard, "ASA and ASEAN, 1961-1967: Southeast Asian Regionalism," Asian Survey 10 (March 1970): 244-55. On Maphilindo and ASPAC, see Michael Leifer, Dilemmas of Statehood in Southeast Asia (Vancouver: University of British Columbia Press, 1972), pp. 135-44; on other organizations, see Michael Haas, comp., Basic Documents of Asian Regional Organizations (Dobbs Ferry, N.Y.: Oceana, 1974), vols. 1-4.

4. Solidum, "Elite Attitudes"; Somsakdi Xuto, Regional Cooperation; and Pollard, "ASA."

5. Lyon, "ASEAN," p. 157.

6. ASA met only four times. On Indonesia's position, see Gordon, The Dimensions, p. 167.

7. "Opening Address," Regionalism in Southeast Asia (Jakarta: Centre for Strategic and International Studies, 1975), p. 7.

8. Gordon, The Dimensions, has the best treatment of these, pp. 9-40, 68-119.

9. Shee Poon Kim, "A Decade of ASEAN, 1967-1977," Asian Survey 17 (August 1977): 765; and Michael Leifer, "The ASEAN States and the Progress of Regional Cooperation in Southeast Asia," in Politics, Society and Economy in the ASEAN States, ed. Bernard Dahm and Werner Draghn (Wiesbaden: Otto Harrassowitz, 1975), p. 3.

10. Lau Teik Soon, "ASEAN and the Future of Regionalism," in New Directions in the International Relations of Southeast Asia: The Great Powers and Southeast Asia, ed. Lau Teik Soon (Singapore: Singapore University Press, 1973), p. 167.

11. Frank Golay, "Economic Underpinnings of Southeast Asia," in Southeast Asia, An Emerging Center of World Influence? Economic and Resource Considerations, ed. Wayne Raymond and K. Mulliner

(Athens: Ohio University, Center for International Studies, 1977), pp. 4-6.

12. Malcolm Caldwell, "ASEANization," Journal of Contemporary Asia 4 (1974): 36-70.

13. Arnfinn Jorgensen-Dahl, "Southeast Asia and Theories of Regional Integration" (Ph.D. diss., Australian National University, 1975).

14. Russell Fifield, National and Regional Interests in ASEAN (Singapore: Institute of Southeast Asian Studies, 1979), pp. 25-44.

15. Bucklin, "Regional Economic Cooperation," p. 43. The following section is the best treatment of the subject.

16. Particularly, Hans Indorf, ASEAN: Problems and Prospects (Singapore: Institute of Southeast Asian Studies, 1975), pp. 45f.; and Ernest Corea, "ASEAN: The Road from Bali," in Development and Underdevelopment in Southeast Asia, ed. Gordon Means (Ottawa: Canadian Council for Southeast Asian Studies, 1976), p. 180.

17. Arnfinn Jorgensen-Dahl, "ASEAN 1967-1976: Development or Stagnation?" Pacific Community 7 (July 1976): 527-28; Indorf, Problems and Prospects, pp. 2-3; and Shee Poon Kim, "A Decade of ASEAN," pp. 763-64.

18. Shee Poon Kim, "A Decade of ASEAN," p. 765.

19. Corea, "The Road from Bali," p. 180.

20. Somsakdi Xuto, Regional Cooperation, pp. 15f.

21. Solidum, "Elite Attitudes," p. 243.

22. Alejandro Melchor, Jr., "Assessing ASEAN's Viability in a Changing World," Asian Survey 17 (April 1977): 422-23; and Russell Fifield, "ASEAN: Image and Reality," Asian Survey 19 (December 1979): 1207-8.

23. Jorgensen-Dahl, "Theories of Regional Integration," pp. 337-38; and idem, "Development or Stagnation?" p. 524.

24. "Address," in The ASEAN: Problems and Prospects in a Changing World, ed. Sarasin Viraphol, Amphan Namatra, and Masabide Shibusa (Bangkok: Institute of Asian Studies, Chulalongkorn University, 1976), pp. 4-5.

25. Shee Poon Kim, "A Decade of ASEAN," p. 755; and Melchor, "Viability in a Changing World," p. 423.

26. Arnfinn Jorgensen-Dahl, "Extra-Regional Influences on Regional Cooperation in S.E. Asia," Pacific Community 8 (April 1977): 427; Malaysia's first prime minister, Tunku Abdul Rahman, suggested ASEAN to meet the threat from China: Shee Poon Kim, "A Decade of ASEAN," p. 753n.

27. As reflected in the Joint Statements, Special Meeting of ASEAN Foreign Ministers, Bangkok, January 12, 1979, reproduced in ASEAN: Travel, Trade and Development 2 (1979): 18.

28. A recent statement of this concept is in Carlos P. Romulo, "A Perspective on ASEAN," Asia-Pacific Community 2 (Fall 1978):

1–6. See also Marvin Ott, The Neutralization of Southeast Asia (Athens: Ohio University, Center for International Studies, 1974); Sheldon Simon, Asian Neutralism and U. S. Foreign Policy (Washington, D. C. : American Enterprise Institute for Public Policy Research, 1975); Dick Wilson, The Neutralization of Southeast Asia (New York: Praeger, 1975); Michael Leifer, "The ASEAN States: No Common Outlook," International Affairs 49 (October 1973): 600–7; Tan Sri Muhammad Ghazali bin Shafie, "ASEAN's Response to Security Issues in Southeast Asia," Regionalism in Southeast Asia (Jakarta: Centre for Strategic and International Studies, 1975), pp. 17–37; and Interview with Malaysian Prime Minister Razak, Far Eastern Economic Review, July 18, 1975, p. 28.

29. Sheldon Simon, "The ASEAN States: Obstables to Security Cooperation," Orbis 22 (Summer 1978): 415–34; Justus van der Kroef, "ASEAN's Security and Development: Some Paradoxes and Symbols," Asian Affairs 9 (June 1978): 143–60; idem, "ASEAN's Security Needs and Policies," Pacific Affairs 47 (1974): 154–70; and T. B. Millar, "Prospects for Regional Security Cooperation in Southeast Asia," in Conflict and Stability in Southeast Asia, ed. Mark Zacher and R. S. Milne (New York: Anchor, 1974), pp. 451–67.

30. Michael Leifer, "Regionalism, the Global Balance and Southeast Asia," Regionalism in Southeast Asia (Jakarta: Centre for Strategic and International Studies, 1975), pp. 55–70.

31. Van der Kroef, "Paradoxes and Symbols," p. 147.

32. Tun Ismail, at the Fourth Ministerial Meeting, Manila, March 12, 1971, quoted in Jorgensen-Dahl, "Extra-Regional Influences," p. 423.

33. Indorf, Problems and Prospects, p. 12.

34. Reported in Straits Times (Malaysia), August 2, 1973; and Foreign Affairs Malaysia 6 (September 1973): 13–14.

35. Straits Times, November 10, 1973.

36. The UN Sugar Conference, for example, Straits Times (Malaysia), August 24, 1973; and General Assembly, Straits Times, September 5, 1973.

37. Far Eastern Economic Review, July 20, 1967, pp. 151–53; and Indorf, Problems and Prospects, pp. 23–24.

38. Straits Times (Malaysia), July 8, August 7, and November 19, 1973; and Foreign Affairs Malaysia 7 (March 1974): 44–45.

39. Asia Research Bulletin, May 1974.

40. Asia Research Bulletin, August 1975; and Far Eastern Economic Review, August 8, 1975, p. 18.

41. Asia Research Bulletin, December 1975, p. 152.

42. Reprinted in Asia Research Bulletin, March 1976, para. 5.

43. Indorf, Problems and Prospects, p. 12, table I.

44. Reproduced as Journal of Development Planning, vol. 7 (1974).

45. Dr. Vichitvong na Pambhejara, then employed as a senior economist by the Thai government; interviewed in Singapore, September 1979.

46. Association of Southeast Asian Nations, 10 Years ASEAN (Jakarta: ASEAN, 1978), p. 36; Wilson, Neutralization, p. 173; and New Straits Times, May 17, 1975.

47. For assessments of the Robinson Report (alternatively called the Kansu Report), see H. W. Arndt and Ross Garnaut, "ASEAN and the Industrialization of East Asia," Journal of Common Market Studies 17 (March 1979): 195-97; and S. Y. Lee and Ann Booth, "Towards an Effective Programme for ASEAN Cooperation from 1978 to 1983" (Paper presented at the Third Conference of the ASEAN Federation of Economic Associations, Kuala Lumpur, 1978).

48. Text in Asia Research Bulletin, March 1977, pp. 302-3.

49. Far Eastern Economic Review, November 21, 1975, p. 51.

50. Straits Times, January 25, 1976; New Nation, January 28, 1976; and Far Eastern Economic Review, March 26, 1976, pp. 27-28. Indonesia is consistently insecure in its ability to compete and, therefore, is hesitant to open itself up to the ASEAN partners.

51. New Nation, December 27, 1975, carried excerpts from a column from "a source close to Marcos" attacking the Indonesian leadership for dragging its feet on the PTA and hurting Philippine interests: "In the past Indonesia's neighbors have done most of the yielding to her."

52. Straits Times, January 29, 1976.

53. Far Eastern Economic Review, February 6, 1976, p. 18.

54. Ibid., February 18, 1977, p. 33.

55. Lim Chong Yah, "Singapore's Position in ASEAN Economic Cooperation," University of Singapore staff seminar paper, 1979, pp. 15-16.

56. These are set at quarterly meetings of the economic ministers.

57. Straits Times, April 23, 1979.

58. See, for example, Asia Research Bulletin, July 1977, p. 342; Arndt and Garnaut, "Industrialization of East Asia," p. 206; Lim, "Singapore's Position," pp. 17-18; ASEAN Business Quarterly 3 (1978): 16; and Gerald Tan, "Extra-ASEAN Trade Liberalization: An Empirical Analysis," Journal of Common Market Studies 20 (June 1982): 321-32.

59. Far Eastern Economic Review, March 12, 1976, pp. 48-49.

60. The 13 items from the UN report considered by the ASEAN ministers are listed in Amado Castro, "The Meaning of Economic Cooperation in ASEAN," ASEAN Trader (Manila: ASEAN Trade Fair, 1978), pp. 35-36; the Joint Press Communiqué of the Bali Summit, sec. 10 (iii), sets the agenda for the Second Meeting of the Economic

Ministers, which allocated the initial projects. The actual UN rec-ommendations are contained in "Economic Cooperation among Member Countries of the Association of South East Asian Nations: Report of a United Nations Team," Journal of Development Planning 7 (1974): 107-50.

61. Far Eastern Economic Review, August 19, 1977, pp. 27-29.

62. See the evaluative essays on each of the projects in Mohamed Ariff, Fong Chan Onn, and R. Thillainathan, eds., ASEAN Coopera-tion in Industrial Projects (Kuala Lumpur: Malaysian Economic As-sociation, 1977), pp. 111-50.

63. Lim Chong Yah, "ASEAN's Package Deal Industrial Proj-ects," Asia Pacific Community 2 (Fall 1978): 135-36; and H. W. Arndt, "ASEAN Industrial Projects," Asia Pacific Community 2 (Fall 1978): 124-25.

64. Far Eastern Economic Review, October 10, 1978, p. 61.

65. ASEAN Briefing 19 (February 1980); and Far Eastern Eco-nomic Review, January 27, 1978.

66. Far Eastern Economic Review, August 13, 1982, p. 66.

67. Ariff, Onn, and Thillainathan, ASEAN Cooperation, pts. 1 and 2, examine approaches to planning and allocation.

68. Far Eastern Economic Review, Asia 1979 Yearbook, p. 83.

69. As stated by Tan Boon Seng, Singapore's ASEAN director, in Far Eastern Economic Review, Asia 1979 Yearbook, p. 70.

70. It seems ironic that the UN team cited this area as the most promising and "particularly well-suited to ASEAN conditions," Jour-nal of Development Planning 7 (1974): 58.

71. Glass—Amado Castro, "Regional Cooperation in Southeast Asia: Implications for World Leadership," in Southeast Asia, An Emerging Center of World Leadership? ed. Wayne Raymond and K. Mulliner (Athens: Ohio University, Center for International Studies, 1977), p. 55; steel—Asia Research Bulletin, April 1977, p. 315; and petrochemicals—Abdul Rahman bin Yusof, "Effective Program for ASEAN Industrial Cooperation 1978-1983" (Paper presented at the Third Conference of the Confederation of ASEAN Economic Associa-tions, Kuala Lumpur, 1978), p. 6.

72. ASEAN Business Quarterly 4 (1978): 48.

73. Straits Times, February 27, 1979.

74. Far Eastern Economic Review, February 15, 1980, p. 48.

75. Far Eastern Economic Review, August 13, 1982, pp. 46-48.

76. Thomas Allen, The ASEAN Report, vol. 2 (Hong Kong: Dow-Jones, 1979), pp. 62-63; ASEAN-CCI Handbook (Bangkok: Joint Standing Committee on Commerce and Industry, 1978), p. 45; and Asian Wall Street Journal, September 5, 1979.

77. New Nation, April 27, 1978; ASEAN Chambers of Commerce and Industry, Report of the 1st Plenary Meeting of the ASEAN-CCI

Working Group on Industrial Complementation (Singapore: ASEAN Chambers of Commerce and Industry, June 16, 1976), pp. 23, 50, 58-66.

78. Author interview, Malaysian Industrial Development Authority, Kuala Lumpur, October 1979; and Far Eastern Economic Review, August 13, 1982, pp. 46-48.

79. Author interview with the secretary-general of the Singapore Federation of Chambers of Commerce and Industry, Singapore, September 1979.

80. See Michael Skully, ASEAN Regional Financial Cooperation: Developments in Banking and Finance (Singapore: Institute of Southeast Asian Studies, 1979); reports on new proposals are contained in Far Eastern Economic Review, February 1, 1980, pp. 34-37; February 15, 1980, pp. 60-61; January 30, 1981, p. 46; and August 13, 1982, pp. 113-16.

81. Point 6 of the Joint Communiqué of the Fourth Ministerial Meeting (March 1971), quoted in Edward Sinaga, "ASEAN: Economic, Political and Defense Problems, Progress and Prospects in Regional Cooperation with Reference to the Role of Major Powers in Southeast Asia" (Ph.D. diss., George Washington University, 1974), p. 23.

82. Chia Siow Yue, Singapore and ASEAN Economic Cooperation (Bangkok: UN Asian and Pacific Development Institute, 1978), sec. 6.1.

83. Joint Communiqué, Kuala Lumpur, March 9, 1976.

84. Association of Southeast Asian Nations, 10 Years ASEAN, p. 305.

85. Quoted in Charles Morrison and Astri Suhrke, Strategies of Survival: The Foreign Policy Dilemmas of Smaller Asian States (St. Lucia: University of Queensland Press, 1978), p. 283.

86. Association of Southeast Asian Nations, 10 Years ASEAN, pp. 228-29.

87. However, the ASEAN secretariat is establishing some contact with other regional groups outside of the dialogue format. Straits Times, May 2, 1979.

88. Association of Southeast Asian Nations, 10 Years ASEAN, p. 220.

89. UNCTAD precaucusing is reported in New Nation, May 3, 1979; see also R. J. G. Wells, "ASEAN Commodity Trade Policies: Objectives and Strategies" (Paper presented at the Third Conference of the Federation of ASEAN Economic Associations, Kuala Lumpur, November 24, 1978).

90. Association of Southeast Asian Nations, 10 Years ASEAN, pp. 228-29; and Sinnathamby Rajaratnam, "ASEAN External Relations," ASEAN Trader (Manila: ASEAN Trade Fair, 1978), p. 30.

91. $A5 million was committed to five projects at the first dialogue in Canberra, April 1974, another $A10 million following the 1977 meetings.

92. Straits Times, July 1 and July 16, 1977; and Arndt and Garnaut, "Industrialization of East Asia," pp. 200-1.

93. Interview, Far Eastern Economic Review, February 24, 1978, pp. 34-35.

94. Ibid., March 17, 1978, p. 42; and November 24, 1978, pp. 44-47.

95. Reports in New Straits Times, August 24, 1978; Straits Times, October 20 and November 6, 1978; and Far Eastern Economic Review, November 24, 1978, p. 47.

96. Straits Times, October 20, 1978; January 11, 12, and 20, 1979; and New Straits Times, January 5, 1979.

97. Far Eastern Economic Review, March 9, 1979, p. 51; and Straits Times, February 23, May 8, and May 9, 1979.

98. New Straits Times, September 10, 1979.

99. "Report from Canberra," New Straits Times, March 7, 1979.

100. Far Eastern Economic Review, December 21, 1979, pp. 47-59; February 1, 1980, pp. 24-25; and February 29, 1980, pp. 34-36.

101. Mohamed Ariff, "ASEAN's External Economic Relations—The Quest for a Common Approach" (Paper presented in Kuala Lumpur to the Malaysian Economic Association, 1979), p. 6.

102. Association of Southeast Asian Nations, 10 Years ASEAN, pp. 225-26; Far Eastern Economic Review, October 20, 1978, pp. 56-58. The clause in question treats products made in several stages in different ASEAN countries as eligible for Generalized System of Preferences benefits, a major benefit for Singapore.

103. Far Eastern Economic Review, July 18, 1978, p. 97.

104. Ibid., July 25, 1977, pp. 18-22; and June 23, 1978, p. 90.

105. Ibid., October 20, 1978, pp. 56-58; and author interviews, Ministry of Trade, Manila, October 1979.

106. Ariff, "External Economic Relations," p. 7.

107. As stated by Japan's Prime Minister Ohira, after the United States, the People's Republic of China, and the Republic of Korea, Straits Times, September 5, 1979.

108. Far Eastern Economic Review, October 31, 1980, pp. 50-51; November 21, 1980, pp. 42-43; January 9, 1981, pp. 22-27; and January 16, 1981, pp. 48-50.

109. Malcolm Subhan, "ASEAN-EEC Relations," in Southeast Asian Affairs 1977, ed. Kernial Sandhu (Singapore: Institute of Southeast Asian Studies, 1977), pp. 49-63; and Far Eastern Economic Review, April 21, 1978, pp. 38f.

110. Far Eastern Economic Review, July 25, 1975, p. 43.

111. To be undertaken by the Economist Intelligence Unit. Far Eastern Economic Review, December 1, 1978, p. 57.

112. The first in mid-1977: Far Eastern Economic Review, September 30, 1977, pp. 50-51; the second in October 1978.

113. Author interviews. Malaysian Industrial Development Authority, Kuala Lumpur, October 1979; and Ministry of Trade, Manila, October 1979.

114. ASEAN Business Quarterly, 1979, pp. 24-25; "Joint Declaration of the First Ministerial Meeting, ASEAN-EEC," November 21, 1978, ASEAN Travel, Trade and Development 2 (1979): 9-17; and Far Eastern Economic Review, March 21, 1980, pp. 96-97.

115. "ASEAN and the EEC," New Straits Times, February 6, 1979, editorial.

116. Far Eastern Economic Review, February 23, 1979, p. 37; and "ASEAN and the EEC: Working toward a Growth Pact," Asian Finance (Hong Kong) 5 (February 1979): 113-15.

117. Association of Southeast Asian Nations, 10 Years ASEAN, pp. 227-28; New Straits Times, February 27, 1979; and New Nation, July 6, 1978.

118. Association of Southeast Asian Nations, 10 Years ASEAN, pp. 223-24; Straits Times, February 6, 1977; New Nation, June 11, 1977; and Douglass Small, "The Developing Dialogue between Canada and ASEAN," International Perspectives, March-April 1978, pp. 28-31.

119. U.S., Department of State, Bulletin, September 28, 1978, pp. 19-25.

120. The phrase is common to Ariff, "External Economic Relations," p. 12, and to Arndt and Garnaut, "Industrialization of East Asia," p. 199.

121. Morrison and Suhrke, Strategies of Survival, p. 283.

122. Malaysian Industrial Development Authority, Kuala Lumpur, October 1979; Ministry of Trade, Manila, October 1979; and ASEAN director, Philippines, October 1979.

123. See Far Eastern Economic Review, Asia 1978 Yearbook, p. 74; and Michael Haas, "The ASEANization of Asian International Relations," Asia Pacific Community 6 (Fall 1979): 73-86.

4

TRADE DEPENDENCE AND POLICY

The position of Third World states in the international economic system has become a contentious political issue over the last decade, generating a barrage of impassioned accusations and desperate pleas, but only marginal change. The cry of "trade, not aid" still resounds through international forums as developing countries attempt to overcome external obstacles to their national economic growth and welfare. This is particularly important to that group of countries engaged in an attempt to expand and develop their economies through trade with the global economy, with the members of ASEAN serving as primary examples. The linkage between domestic pressures to improve economic welfare and international economic diplomacy is particularly close.

There have been consistent attempts to change the structure of the international trading system in favor of the developing countries over the last several years, centered on the United Nations Conference on Trade and Development (UNCTAD), with little progress achieved. Specific bargains such as the Lomé Pact have been struck, but these, of course, have limited coverage and, if anything, make the situation worse for other developing states. Trade dependence has not been reduced by the actions of the general international community, leaving the burden of efforts on individual states to formulate policy and to pursue strategies designed to improve their situations as best they can.

Trade dependence is not a new concern, and strategies to control its political effects have been advanced. Albert O. Hirschman masterfully analyzed the political consequences of trade relations and the results of concentration of national trade on few partners in 1945,[1] and Raul Prebisch advocated regional import substitution as the route to reduced Latin American dependence on the United States in the early 1960s.[2] For the ASEAN states, both Weinstein[3] and Wong[4] have pointed to the precariousness of overdependence on Japan, a concern that has often been voiced in various ways in the region. The implicit strategy is the restructuring of trade to reduce the overbearing impact of any one partner through diversification and freeing of regional trade, a course designed to minimize the inequality of economic position and political influence between small, developing states and large industrial ones.

Additional support for this strategy is offered by major approaches to international political economy. The dependency school advocates disengagement and self-reliance to reduce the degree of penetration and concurrent loss of autonomy,[5] a course resembling the early import-substitution, industrialization policies of the ASEAN states, rejected for its limitations on growth. The interdependence approach points to asymmetry in two facets of a relationship as the key to relative political influence.[6] "Sensitivity interdependence" in this context is largely a matter of relative size; the larger economic entity is less influenced by changes in the relationship than is the smaller and is thus less politically sensitive to the other's policy preferences. "Vulnerability interdependence" in trade can be interpreted as a result of concentration in partners; the larger the relative role of a given partner, the more significant the potential dislocations of changes and the greater that partner's political influence. Sensitivity, then, can be equalized by the formation of a larger trading bloc and by trading relatively less with the largest economic powers, while vulnerability can be minimized through diversification of major trading partners.

The ASEAN states are highly dependent in their structure of trade. They are largely commodity exporters to the industrial machines of the developed countries, which limits their potential export markets. In the mid-1970s, for example, the share of commodities to total exports for ASEAN was Indonesia, 97.8 percent; Malaysia, 69 percent; Philippines, 71 percent; Singapore, 53.7 percent; and Thailand, 73.3 percent.[7] They are linked to the international trading system closely and are thus quite sensitive to its general influence. Although not a completely accurate index, the proportion of their total trade to gross domestic product (GDP) indicates the magnitude of this sensitivity: Indonesia, 37.2 percent; Malaysia, 77.9 percent; Philippines, 35.7 percent; Singapore, 27.4 percent; and Thailand, 43.1 percent.[8] The asymmetrical nature of the sensitivity relationship with the major industrial nations is illustrated by the relative size of trade on each side as a proportion of total trade.[9] In 1978 the United States took 17.7 percent of ASEAN's trade, while ASEAN was only 4 percent of the U.S. trade market; in the same year, the European Economic Community (EEC) accounted for 14.3 percent of ASEAN's trade, and ASEAN for 1.1 percent of the EEC's; Japan's share was

24.9 percent of ASEAN trade, while ASEAN was 10.5 percent of Japan's. Trade partners for each country have tended to be overwhelmingly the major industrial nations, often with one of these clearly dominant, which heightens political vulnerability. Trade dependence for the ASEAN members is a matter of being narrowly economically developed, extremely sensitive to the international trading system in an asymmetrical fashion, and politically vulnerable to particular industrial nations. They are so dependent on the international system as to have little or no control over its effects.

The response of the ASEAN members has been conditioned by a new economic nationalism. The old nationalism, which emphasized decolonization and the transfer of economic activity from Chinese minorities to "national" ethnic groups,[10] has not entirely faded away and has been, to a degree, institutionalized.[11] But as Singapore Foreign Minister Rajaratnam predicted in 1969, nationalism has become more national-development oriented and internationally manifested;[12] one of the authors of a major work on economic nationalism in Southeast Asia now argues that the emphasis has shifted from control of resident aliens to issues such as dependence on Japan for trade.[13] The new economic nationalism melds domestic and international issues in the modern fashion.

One interesting aspect of this process is the reinterpretation of national security, a goal traditionally pursued through military means, as derived from domestic development. As one Southeast Asian scholar puts it, summarizing the views of regional leaders: "The concept of strengthening security in order to make possible development must . . . be discarded in favor of a more realistic and promising notion that development is security."[14] Faster economic development, providing the resources to defuse the primary security threat to the ASEAN governments—from domestic opposition by militant, armed groups protesting economic inequality—requires a greater degree of international cooperation.

This requirement is reflected in the Declaration of ASEAN Concord: "The stability of each member state and of the ASEAN region is an essential contribution to international peace and security. Each member state resolves to eliminate threats posed by subversion to its stability, thus strengthening national and ASEAN resilience." As "economic self-defense," ASEAN cooperation is seen as a means to guard economic stability and independence against "superpowers and economic giants,"[15] while one leader contends that "a consensus exists among the governments of the member states that ASEAN is the appropriate mechanism for evolving appropriate defensive strategies to minimize the disruptive effects of rapid changes in . . . the developed countries."[16] Domestic instability is being countered by regionalism.

One of these "defensive strategies" seems to be the diversification of economic relations away from two economic superpowers: Japan and the United States, particularly Japan. Public demonstrations against the increasingly visible presence of Japan in the region by nationalistic mobs in the early 1970s illustrate one basis for this strategy, but at the same time, governmental frustration with the lack of follow-up on the Fukuda Doctrine seems equally important.[17] The result has been a policy aimed at attracting attention from what the ASEAN nations term the middle powers of Europe, in order to balance Japanese dominance[18] and ASEAN's position in international relations generally. Interestingly, the basis of the argument has been picked up by the Soviet Union to justify a greater role for socialist nations in the region: "Under these conditions, activation of trade with such an alternative supplier of manufactured goods as the socialist states would, no doubt, weaken the economic diktat of the capitalist powers."[19] The new nationalism has resulted in a desire to balance the economic relations of the region more equally through diversification of partners and in the elevation of ASEAN as an instrument of economic defense. The general motivation for a strategy of economic defense is found in a combination of internal and external political threats.

This chapter describes in more detail the evolution of trade policies for each of the countries and the regional association leading up to diversification. In addition, trade statistics for the period from 1967 to 1979 are analyzed in order to assess the effectiveness of these policies. Finally, the reasons for different degrees of success in diversifying trade partners on the part of the five ASEAN members are discussed.

TRADE POLICIES FOR DIVERSIFICATION

The ASEAN Organization

A few remarks seem desirable regarding the nature of policy making in the ASEAN context. To regard the ASEAN organization itself as the initiator of policy would be misleading. It appears more often as a collection of states than a collectivity, which is reflected in the rule of unanimity in all decisions; policy initiatives come from the members, not the association itself. Public pronouncements often understate some members' positions while, at the same time, going farther than the least enthusiastic would like, concealing what may be significant differences in national policy under the cover of vague and diplomatic verbiage. Since there is a decided bias against recognizing any country as a leader in ASEAN, everyone becomes a follower; one anonymous official revealed that his delegation had been specifically instructed not to take the initiative on any issue in order to avoid alienating the other members (particularly Indonesia). In order to discern policy in ASEAN one must look to the actions of the association for areas of agreement and then to the national policy makers for the directions they are likely to pursue.

Despite the difficulties, there are some indications of the nature of the trade policy pursued collectively through ASEAN. The general content flows from the commitment made in the Declaration of ASEAN Concord to (1) jointly work to accelerate improved market access for ASEAN products, (2) adopt common approaches in dealing with regional groups and individual economic powers, and (3) formulate joint approaches to international commodity problems, to the reform of the international trade system, and to the establishment of a new international economic order. This cooperation is designed "to improve the trade structure of individual states and among countries of ASEAN conducive to further development," a broad but vague mandate.

Specific policy preferences are largely available only by inference from actions undertaken under ASEAN auspices. In the area of foreign trade cooperation, this includes the "dialogues" and "forums" conducted with the major economic partners and international organizations, trade fairs, industrial cooperation conferences, and united fronts regarding specific economic disputes. The common themes that seem to emerge from these activities flesh out the generalities of the declaration's intent.

The primary objective appears to be to increase the overall flow of trade from the ASEAN states to all market countries by cultivating and penetrating the major markets of Japan, the United States, and Europe and by gaining entry into other, nontraditional markets. The dialogues have focused on the reduction of specific barriers to trade, on increasing quotas and Generalized System of Preferences (GSP) coverages, and on extracting promises of increased imports.[20] The same dominant concern is reflected in ASEAN participation in UNCTAD, discussions of the new international economic order, and negotiations surrounding changes in the General Agreement on Tariffs and Trade (GATT).[21] In addition to sponsoring its own trade fair in Manila in 1978, ASEAN has solicited support from dialogue partners to do the same, with the result that there have been numerous fairs in the European Economic Community (EEC), Australia, New Zealand, and Japan. Since each ASEAN member is striving to increase exports as the leading developmental sector, a focus on increasing the volume of trade is central to their common concerns and reaches an easy consensus.

The second major objective appears to be market diversification. As has been mentioned, the energy expended in cultivating relations with the EEC is justified on the grounds that, relative to Japan and the United States, Europe is underrepresented economically in the ASEAN area and should be encouraged to balance the other two. At the same time, Australia, New Zealand, and Canada have drawn ASEAN attention despite their marginal importance in the present structure of trade; this appears to be a reflection of the expectation that they will each be more important to ASEAN in the future as it diversifies trade relations to the smaller industrial nations, an expectation that includes non-EEC Europe.[22] Considerable effort has been devoted to attempts to broaden the base of trade partners.

National policy also draws on the strength of ASEAN in more particular ways. Each ASEAN country has a slightly different set of established trade partners, and these connections are looked to by the other members as creating an "extension effect" of ASEAN membership, which will assist individual efforts to diversify.[23] Membership in ASEAN is thought to increase the perceived importance of each national market to new partners. This contribution may become more significant in the future as requests for a more formalized economic relationship with ASEAN come from a number of areas outside the traditional arena, including at present South Asia, the South Pacific Forum, and the Soviet Union. As one Philippine official commented: "Developing countries like India and Sri Lanka come to us now for economic cooperation because of ASEAN, not because of the Philippines."[24] Thus, at present ASEAN contributes both some direct efforts to diversification and some indirect effects by providing a larger political platform and a psychological boost to national policy.

Finally, some reference should be made to the effect on diversification that may result from the freeing of intraregional trade through the Preferential Trade Agreements. This has traditionally been a major focus of regional movements, from the EEC to the various Latin American customs unions. In the ASEAN case, there is no evidence that this will be of significant import in the near future. Although regional trade is already high for a group of developing states, efforts to reduce tariff barriers have so far been mostly symbolic and have not had a visible effect on the pattern of regional trade. The entrepôt trade of Singapore continues to be important, although less so, and the only other ASEAN member that puts much stock in the growth of regional trade is the Philippines, presently the least involved. The others are convinced that the outside world will continue to supply their major markets, at least in the near future.

Common ventures through the ASEAN organization have made some changes in trade policy possible. Efforts have been directed toward increasing the volume and range of trading partners and toward eliminating specific obstacles to access in major market areas. Expansion with diversification is the evident policy consensus. However, ASEAN itself is clearly supplementary to national trade policy, and for the development of trade policy in the ASEAN area to be clearly set out, it is necessary to examine each country in turn.

Singapore

Singapore has by far the longest-standing commitment to diversification. Diversity of trade partners has been a part of Singapore's policy almost from independence in order to minimize the adverse effects of undue dependence on any single major partner. This is in part a result of the political imbroglio surrounding its establishment as an independent state, which included the continuation of the Indonesian trade embargo against Singapore, started in 1964 as part of Indonesian opposition to the creation of a Malaysia that included the North Borneo territories. In addition, with the ejection of Singapore from Malaysia in 1965, a tariff wall was erected to the Malaysian market, which had been Singapore's most important one. Surrounded by protected, if not hostile, states, Singapore was forced to look to the outside world. The result was a realization that the path to survival led to diversification to the global market.[25] This concern has remained a high-level, urgent one continuously since 1965, as it was expected that the desired results would only be achieved in the long term.[26] The policy was never worked out closely, but the rhetoric set daily working patterns nonetheless.[27]

Trade policy has been reinforced by a political policy of balancing the presence of each major power with that of the others to as great an extent as possible. The government believes that competing interests will cancel each other out, with the result that no single group will be strong enough to pressure the government effectively. This has obvious economic benefits, as well as providing political defense; future strategic safety is to a degree guaranteed by the presence of diverse economic interests.[28] As a small state, the only way that Singapore saw to minimize the adverse effects of any single large state's presence was to induce diversity and to invite them all in.

However central a policy of diversification may have been in Singapore's first decade, the major efforts to achieve it seem to have been focused in the last several years. As late as 1974, the Department of Trade was reported to have justified the recruitment of more trade commissioners to be posted overseas by maintaining that "very little has been done to take advantage of foreign markets."[29] And in a 1975 interview, Prime Minister Lee, while recognizing that Europe could serve a purpose to balance the United States and Japan, was reluctant to do more than "facilitate administratively" closer ties with Europe, as he maintained that all ASEAN countries did, in face of the possibility of losses of GSP privileges and violations of GATT provisions.[30] No mention was made of specific means available to implement a policy of diversification.

By 1976 a positive strategy of trade development emerged. A domestic export drive was launched, focused on new market areas in South America, the South Pacific, West Asia, West Africa, and South Asia, as well as a more thorough approach to less explored regional markets in the major trade areas of the United States and Europe.[31] By 1978 the government could respond to a parliamentary question on what it was doing to diversify trade markets by pointing to 11 trade missions since 1976, to the establishment of three major overseas trade offices with others under consideration, and to reports from teams sent to investigate trade potential in Africa, the Pacific, and Latin America.[32] In addition, the government trade company, Intraco, has been tapped to break new ground for Singapore's trade in new market areas and in the command economies of China, Vietnam, and Eastern Europe through its own trade missions and joint missions with the Singapore Manufacturers Association (SMA).[33] The SMA on its own sponsored a first trade mission, with government encouragement, to Latin America in 1979, and it negotiated both trade contracts and several joint ventures.[34] Thus, in more recent years, the earlier policy has been put into a higher gear to foster diversification through trade missions, public enterprise, and private associations.

The old rationale of dependence reduction has also acquired a new twist with the fast pace of Singapore's growth as a trading power. A concern that the slow pace of growth in the industrial countries will inhibit Singapore's own growth seems to be adding economic logic to the policy:

> We must accept and adjust to the slower pace at which the developed countries are growing. Unless and until these countries make real efforts to restructure their economies, protectionism will remain a problem in world trade. So we must knock on the doors of new markets in the developing countries around us—in Asia Pacific countries, the Mideast and China. [Minister of Trade and Industry Goh Chok Tong][35]

Thus, Singapore has as a matter of policy not only attempted to balance the major economic powers, but is also engaged in reducing the relative importance of overall linkages to the major industrial nations. Diversification, as both a political and an economic doctrine, seems to be a major, active part of Singapore's trade policy.

The Philippines

The Philippines developed its policy of diversification later than Singapore, but it has been a most enthusiastic ASEAN member in this regard. Rather than being a reaction to local political and economic threats as in the case of Singapore, relations with the United States as the single dominant partner for the Philippines was the stimulus to diversity. Colonial ties, rather than fears of future dependence, provided the motive. Although U. S. -Philippine economic relations have a long and contentious history,[36] developments in the late 1960s and early 1970s stimulated domestic debate over their immediate future, prompting President Ferdinand Marcos to explore alternatives to the U. S. -oriented policy that would be acceptable in the context of rising Philippine nationalism. In his 1966 State of the Nation address, he predicted the loss of the U. S. export market with the expiration of the Laurel-Langley Treaties in 1974, and he urged the shift to new markets in Europe and Asia. With his reelection in 1969, evaluation of the consequences of dependence on the United States for economic relations started, and alternatives were seriously explored, although some of the measures eventually taken reversed previous, more nationalist policies.[37]

The more immediate push to formulate a policy of economic defense came, however, with the opening of relations between the United States and the People's Republic of China, which ended the era of U. S. -imposed isolation from socialist regimes followed by the Philippines. With the declaration of martial law in the Philippines in late 1972, Marcos moved to shift the whole framework of the Philippines' economic relations, turning toward a "development-oriented" foreign policy. The major features were increased regional cooperation, the opening of relations with socialist countries, and increased "self-reliance" without excessive dependence on any one country or group of countries.[38]

The foreign affairs ministry subsequently became a primary focus of "development diplomacy," with a variety of tasks. Relations with socialist countries were expanded in 1973 and 1974, with emphasis on the expansion of trade ties, export promotion, market diversification, and new sources of economic assistance.[39] The transformation of relations with the United States toward the end of "special relations" and the beginning of "pragmatic relations" was undertaken.[40] An economic treaty with Japan—stalled since 1960 for political reasons—was negotiated in 1973 and renegotiated in 1977, as Japan emerged as a new source of potential dependence, to provide more formal relations in economic matters, but primarily to supply a firmer base for an alternative economic partner to balance the United States.[41] Economic nationalism became the centerpiece of

foreign policy as the Philippines sought a wider political and economic
base for development, a redefinition of relationships with the United
States and Japan, and diversification to provide an alternative to overdependence on particular partners. The political role of the foreign
ministry was subjugated to economic interests.

By 1976 a wider, domestic institutional basis had been established to support diversification. The Institute of Export Development
of the Board of Investment, which had been supporting export diversification by promoting Australia, the EEC, and the Mideast since
1973,[42] was supplemented by the creation of the Philippine Export
Council (Presidential Decree 941 of May 29, 1976). This body was
designated to develop a strategy to promote, expand, and diversify
exports to existing and prospective markets by defining specific product and market targets and to coordinate both government and private-
sector efforts in the implementation and monitoring of the new "National Export Strategy."[43] For the first time, export goals were to
be formally integrated into the planning process of the government,
with the particular goal of diversifying trade away from the United
States, and now Japan; the latter had become the Philippines' largest
trade partner in 1975, creating anxiety over a new dependence relationship. In order to coordinate implementation, a network of Export
Council permanent committees for particular product groups was set
up starting in 1977; the committees, in conjunction with the Philippine
International Trading Corporation and joint export groups previously
established in some sectors (cement, bamboo products, handicrafts),
are to work to meet trade guidelines established by the Export Council, especially in diversifying to new markets.[44] The private sector
is to be rationalized and guided by government in order to meet developmental and political goals, giving detailed form to the general
policy.

The broad policy is explicitly incorporated in the current mas-
ter development plan. Trade diversification and rationalization are
held up as primary aspects of the strategy for development, "to minimize undue dependence on particular countries" both as sources of
supply and as export partners.[45] Long-term goals for the geographical distribution of Philippine foreign trade are set out:[46] by 1987 the
United States and Japan are expected to account for only 50 percent
of the Philippines' trade; ASEAN, 10 percent; the Mideast, 13 percent; and Europe, 16 percent—considerably more diversified than at
present. Institutional responsibilities for a wide variety of government agencies are closely set out to involve a broad range of the public sector in this effort; the government trading arm, the Philippine
International Trading Corporation, for example, is given primary responsibility for tapping socialist markets, perhaps to insulate the
private sector from the effects of the political policy of actively pur-

suing these markets. Performance in attainment of the goal of diversification is monitored, and it is publicized in the annual development report.[47] An indication of the extremely long-term nature of the goal setting is contained in a speech by Vincente Paterno, then minister of industry, when he elaborated on the desired pattern of trade for the year 2000; targets include 45 to 55 percent of trade with the industrial nations as a group, 20 to 25 percent with the rest of ASEAN, and the rest with non-ASEAN Third World nations, a pattern that would substantially reduce the leverage of any single industrial nation, or of the group as a whole, in favor of politically less influential economic partners.[48]

By all indications, the government is serious in its intention to shift progressively more of Philippine economic intercourse away from the United States and Japan, in particular. To a limited degree, preferences are now accorded for government-agency imports to countries other than the United States and Japan by the Board of Investment, despite generally higher prices for alternative sources of supply; this only affects the public sector because the private sector will generally not pay the higher prices, and resources to subsidize private purchases are not available.[49] Private-sector purchasers are encouraged to find nontraditional suppliers, but existing contacts and more aggressive marketing by Japanese and U.S. firms make the effort one that will have an effect only over the very long term. The government is able at this time only to lead by example.

In addition to organizing and directing efforts on the domestic side, the government places some emphasis on the role of international political initiatives in contributing to its development efforts. ASEAN is seen as a vital part of the development plan and receives firm support, both as a future market in itself and as a booster for official efforts to diversify into markets traditionally close to other ASEAN partners, particularly those in Europe.[50] The UNCTAD-sponsored cooperative scheme among developing countries strikes a sympathetic response as a means to Philippine "self-reliance." Economic Cooperation among Developing Countries (ECDC) aims at reinforcing the political and economic self-reliance of developing countries through increased mutual trade and cooperation in the areas of finance, production, infrastructure and service development, technology, and science.[51] Study groups in the Philippine Ministry of Trade are now working on the import profile of developing countries, with the aim of expanding exports in that direction and with the firm conviction that this is the most promising direction for the Philippines to attain its own development goals with the least potential political dependence.[52] To a considerable degree, the foreign policy of the Philippines has directed itself toward goals of economic self-defense.

Malaysia

Malaysia has expressed a desire to diversify external trade
partners, but neither with consistent effect nor with the enthusiasm
of Singapore and the Philippines, and with considerably more restraint in form. Economic nationalism has found its primary expression in other, more pressing areas, such as foreign investment, than
in restructuring trade directions, although the latter is again emerging as an area of concern.

Soon after independence, Malaysia sought to alter the pattern
of its trade away from heavy dependence on the United Kingdom,
which had resulted from colonial ties. In addition, confrontation with
Indonesia stimulated a foreign policy of "external outreach,"[53] which
included development and trade issues and which prompted Malaysia
to seek to widen trade ties. For example, economic relations were
opened with the Soviet Union in 1967, long before other Southeast
Asian countries were willing to deal with socialist regimes. By the
end of the decade, these efforts had resulted in some diversification
away from the United Kingdom; 25 percent of imports were of U. K.
origin in 1958, and only 10. 6 percent were in 1969.[54] With the erosion of U. K. influence, interest shifted to other areas, and trade
diversification was accorded lower priority.

International issues and forums became the new focus. By the
late 1960s, extensive rethinking of Malaysian foreign policy re-
oriented it toward the Third World position in economic issues.
Malaysia became one of the original supporters of UNCTAD and, to
some extent, a speaker for the then "radical" critique of the industrial countries. Finance Minister Tan Siew Sin addressed the International Monetary Fund (IMF) in this vein in 1970:

> Whatever the sacrifices needed, we must reduce our im-
> ports of manufactured goods from the highly industrialized
> countries, and we must do this as quickly as possible. We
> must also form trading blocs which would be in a position
> to compete on more equal terms with the developed world. [55]

This rhetoric, however, found expression in few concrete forms; one
of the few actions that can be identified as contributing to a change in
trade patterns was the establishment of a permanent trade mission
in Nairobi, which was to increase trade with developing Africa as
part of the "united fight" to gain a fair share of world trade for developing countries.[56] Institutional attention to the problem was not focused until late 1972, when it was found necessary to establish the
Committee of Officials on Foreign Investment and Trade to formulate
policy among the various departments involved with investment, trade,

and tourism;[57] at the same time, the Ministry of Trade first set up an internal division to be responsible for the expansion and diversification of trade.[58] Strategic problems of trade were largely overshadowed by other nationalist concerns.

Despite some continued support for altering the pattern of trade, the thrust of Malaysian nationalism was focused on the issue of foreign investment and on the distribution of ownership in Malaysia generally (see Chapter 5). Japanese dominance in external economic relations had replaced that of Britain of an earlier generation and had stimulated popular sentiment against Japanese business practices, which resulted in a call by government leaders[59] for "breaking new ground" with alternative partners and for guarding against Japanese "domination" in 1976. Local observers even accorded anti-Japanese feeling the status of being the only element directing Malaysian external economic policy.[60] Even if this may exaggerate the actual case, the increasingly visible role of Japanese interests appears to have resurrected an active policy concern about the structure of trade partners by the middle of the 1970s, to echo that of the early 1960s. The Third Malaysia Plan, admitting that exports to West Asia, Eastern Europe, Latin America, and mainland China were negligible as a result of inattention, promised a renewal of efforts to establish closer and more active trade and economic relations with these countries,[61] a significant step toward diversification. Nationalism appears to have spilled into the area of trade again at the end of the 1970s.

Continued emphasis on expanding trade links for both new sources of supply and for new outlets for exports is unlikely to change in the near future. It is voiced as a policy basis, with Malaysia reported to be "eager to diversify" its trade market by the deputy minister of trade and industry,[62] and it fits closely with policy regarding foreign investment (see Chapter 5). Some reliance is placed on ASEAN as an instrument in achieving this goal.[63] However, the policy is not to the exclusion of other interests. Actual practice moderates the effect of diversification with more narrowly economic considerations—as, for example, the "price-sensitive" import policy and the recent "Look East" policy, which have resulted in an increasing share of imports from Japan, the nominal target of economic nationalism.[64]

As part of this pragmatism, Malaysia follows rather cautious lines in the enunciation of policy in this area. There appears to be a sensitivity to the necessity of preserving the present close relationships with the major industrial nations and a concern to not disrupt them through seeming hostility.[65] For Malaysia, Indonesia's cautious and pragmatic attitude appears to set an example for the tone and pace of policy; there is a feeling that pushing too far and too fast might alienate Indonesia from ASEAN.[66] However, despite public moderation, Malaysia is searching for a more balanced relationship with all economic power centers, and diversification is one of the major conceptual bases of policy.

Indonesia

General support for the restructuring of trade partners has grown slowly in Indonesia, but hampered by pragmatic considerations, the policy has been marked by less effective commitment than either Singapore or the Philippines. The focus of Indonesian economic policy has been confined almost entirely to the domestic scene, especially in the years following Sukarno's fall, which were marked by the necessity of rebuilding the shattered national economy. Internal economic problems led to a belief that foreign markets would be needed only after the large, underexploited domestic market had been developed.[67] With the largest potential internal economy in Southeast Asia, Indonesian planners gave little attention to external factors other than aid.

Even though the primary focus was internal, some consideration was accorded to external trade, although at low levels. Some governmental measures to expand trade and export production were undertaken as early as 1970. Regulatory agencies were set up to license trade, to set quotas, and to regulate markets, followed in 1971 by the establishment of the National Institute for Export Development. The main targets for export growth at this time were in "Southeast Asia's new markets"—Japan, Australia, South Korea, Hong Kong, and Taiwan—as these were identified as expanding faster than the United States or Europe in import growth and, therefore, as more promising partners.[68] During the early 1970s, Indonesian exports did expand considerably, but the major emphasis in policy was in rationalizing the domestic structures for export, rather than considering the pattern of external trade or the political consequences of that pattern.

By the mid-1970s, concern was beginning to rise on several fronts that trade policy was having an undesirable political effect. A feeling of anxiety over the growing preponderance of Japan as an economic partner produced the dilemma of whether to reduce that role to restrain overdependence or to go ahead and exploit the opportunity; it would be "preferable" to maintain a relative balance among external markets, but "foolish" not to expand trade with Japan.[69] Popular sentiment on the subject was expressed by mass riots in Jakarta during the Japanese prime minister's visit in January 1974. Following these riots, President Suharto moved to expand relations with the socialist nations and to give priority to U.S. and, even more, to European economic presences to dilute the strongly negative image of the Japanese.[70]

Japan's role was not the only source of apprehension. During Adam Malik's tour of Eastern Europe in July of 1974, he expressed concern on a broader basis. "Worried" that aid and investment all from the West through the Intergovernmental Group on Indonesia (IGGI), chaired by the Netherlands, would create an undue dependence on the West that could constrain Indonesia's "active and independent" foreign policy, he concluded that Indonesia needed trade from new, diversified sources, including Eastern Europe.[71] This appears to have been a straw in the wind intended for the consumption of those very Western partners, as a very "selective" opening with the socialist states is the most that the Indonesian military is willing to countenance for security reasons.[72] Nevertheless, it was a symbolic opening that was required, as growing concentration of economic power, such as in the EEC, the Council for Mutual Economic Assistance (COMECON), and Japan, raised the specter in Indonesian minds that trade development on a global scale would bypass the developing countries and foreclose future options.[73] Indonesian readings of the pattern of global trade development created some concern for their future welfare.

This concern, reinforced by developments in international organizations, produced an active search for alternatives. The failure of the United Nations to produce concrete, unified approaches to development of trade in the interest of the developing countries that would allow them to deal effectively with the economic superpowers provided an impetus for Indonesia to seek the development of solutions on a regional scale.[74] Ali Moertopo, maintaining that an "economic triangle" set conditions for developing countries, advocated a greater regional infrastructure to moderate competition among developing countries and to serve their national interest, but he seemed uncertain as to exactly which regional framework would be best. On the one hand, he suggested an "Asia-Pacific Triangle," composed of ASEAN, Japan, and Australia, and on the other, greater ASEAN cooperation to the exclusion of outside powers, proposing specifically that "in the framework of international trade ASEAN has to formulate a policy of diversification."[75] The next year, 1974, he was elaborating another approach, focused on the complementary development of resources in the region as a route to an improved trade position with the developed countries.[76] Although none of these proposals was necessarily mutually exclusive, throwing several rapidly into the diplomatic wind would indicate that Indonesia was apparently searching for a solution to the political consequences of excessive trade dependence, but was unable to settle on, and follow, any one specific strategy. Instead, very diffuse solutions, such as "regional resilience," which was taken as a capacity to absorb without excluding potential hostile pressures and to neutralize them in the process, were advanced as the philosophical basis of policy.[77]

Only in the last years of the 1970s has an approach that is complementary to that pursued by other ASEAN states emerged. A mid-
level Indonesian trade official surveyed Indonesia's options in the
"post-détente" era and advocated a more coherent policy mix. He
observed that the existing environment of policy was based on a search
for a balanced relationship with all economic power centers in order
to avoid excessive dependence on any one, which was the basis of a
"re-equilibrating effort" in the mid-1970s to correct the global balance. Analyzing Indonesia's options, he advocated a more cohesive
ASEAN trade policy, which would result in a better "pre-negotiating
position" with the major economic powers at the regional level, combined with a comprehensive strategy of diversification on geographic
and product lines at the domestic level, as the best route to directly
reduce Indonesian vulnerability to the political effects of economic
relations.[78] This seems to portray the development of Indonesian
policy accurately for the final years of the decade. In 1976 another
export drive was launched, with two of the major goals being the penetration of new markets to balance the old ones and renewed emphasis
on the use of marketing institutions organized to strengthen the position of individual exporters in their dealings with foreign partners.[79]
Repelita III, the national plan for 1979-84, emphasizes an export policy geared to diversification by product and market and supported by
export promotion in the Mideast, socialist countries, ASEAN, and
Europe "to reduce the country's dependence on Japan and the U.S."[80]
In addition, efforts undertaken prior to Repelita III designed to diversify Indonesia's markets are to be continued: for example, a mission
sponsored jointly by the Indonesian National Agency for Export Development and UNCTAD to Australia and New Zealand in 1978, designed
to provide alternate markets for the timber industry.[81] It would appear that Indonesia has settled on a strategy of diversification, but
whether this choice is final is uncertain.

The problem for Indonesia in any strategy that sets out change
in the pattern of external economic relations is in political difficulties
that might arise. The weakness of the domestic economy has fostered
a preference to wait until a stronger economy emerges, which would
allow the luxury of political measures that might well have negative
short-term economic effects. If Indonesia were to use any form of
sanctions to direct a policy of diversification, or even to make it obvious that certain partners were less desirable than others, the result might well be negative, in reducing the flow of assistance from
the targets, which would be Japan and the United States. This has
resulted in a cautious, pragmatic approach to foreign economic policy. In addition, practical difficulties in obtaining trade credits from
new partners or, alternatively, in increasing the governmental role
in financing exports pose a problem for actively changing the pattern

of trade. These practical difficulties and pragmatic considerations were instrumental in delaying implementation of the policy of diversification that was preferred since 1969. [82] If the recent record of economic growth has allowed some departure from this restraint, only continued economic growth is likely to allow a policy of diversification to be institutionalized. Renewed concern would likely stimulate a return to a policy of noninterference in external economic matters.

Thailand

Thailand is perhaps the limiting case among ASEAN members in the area of trade policy. Preoccupied with concerns of security and governmental stability, there has been little political control over the flow of trade or over economic affairs generally, with the partial exception of recent relaxations of restrictions on trade with China. [83] Only very recently have economic affairs been accorded priority, and even now the focus is on domestic, rather than on international, policy.

Trade in particular has been marginal to policy concerns. Up through 1972 there were not even efforts to promote Thai exports by the government; in that year the Export Promotion Committee was set up, but it languished with disuse until the civilian government revived it, with the prime minister in the chair, in 1975. [84] It lapsed into its former obscurity with the return of the military to government. Similarly, trade negotiations were of very limited utility, as clear guidance or plans for the foreign sector were rarely forthcoming from the government, leaving the negotiators in a position of forced passivity. [85] Only in the latter part of 1978 did governmental efforts to stimulate trade increase to the point where they matched the magnitude of private efforts. [86] The structure of trade was left almost entirely to the invisible hand of the private sector.

The lack of governmental response was not, however, a result of a lack of stimuli. From as early as late 1972, anti-Japanese demonstrations became a principal activity of the growing nationalist movement, and the government aligned itself with the resentment of the Japanese economic position in Thailand, at least publicly. [87] Some limited response to this sentiment is reflected in the Foreign Investment Committee's 1974 report expressing concern over Japanese dominance in investment and trade and expressing a "preference" for diversification. [88] On the same line, the president of the Thai Board of Trade, Ob Vasuratna (later minister of trade), joined in the call for guarding against renewed Japanese domination in trade and commercial relations throughout Southeast Asia. [89] One observer of Thai foreign policy reported that the increasing criticism of Japanese "exploitation" had, by 1976, produced a policy of diversifying economic relations for "self-reliance."[90] However, another observer recognized the presence of Thai anxiety over the predominant position of Japan, but maintained that, aside from talk about market diversification, there was no directive policy as of late 1979.[91] The apparent conclusion is that concern over the pattern of economic relations existed in the private sector and was expressed through private organizations, but failed to produce government policy.

Recent evidence indicates that the government is slowly responding to public pressure and taking more control of economic policy, at least insofar as that involves reducing the impact of Japanese predominance. In a move to reduce exports from Japan to Thailand, a long list of "luxury goods," mostly originating from Japan, was banned in early 1978 (the ban was later lifted under pressure from the World Bank); this exhibition of resolve prompted the formation of the Thailand-Japan Joint Study Committee on Economic Cooperation to resolve a wide range of bilateral disputes.[92] The Thai government also approached the Group of 77 in mid-1978 to explore the potential market in the developing countries, particularly for manufactured products; West Asia, Africa, and Latin America were of particular interest as new trade partners to reduce the necessity of reliance on Japan.[93] A new trade push was under way by late 1978, with the Commerce Ministry, under the leadership of Ob Vasuratna, making an effort to identify new markets, planning to finance overseas export missions, and attempting to coordinate the efforts of other ministries for a coherent external economic plan.[94] Finally, the government was supporting the establishment of Thai-owned trading firms as a means of reducing Thailand's dependence on Japanese trading houses, which currently control up to half of Thailand's total trade.[95] Anti-Japanese sentiment has apparently stimulated the government to attempt to exercise more political control over trade policy, in an effort to diversify away from Japan and toward the Third World.

The government seems to be breaking away from indirection in economic policy in other areas as well. The Fourth National Economic and Social Plan, for 1977-81, contemplates more cooperation with the other ASEAN members in external and internal economic activities, which is a departure from frequent inaction in ASEAN economic activities of earlier years.[96] The earlier (and continuing) security-oriented interest in ASEAN has been complemented by greater economic interest.[97] A more centralized economic policy apparatus is one of the major aims of Prime Minister Prem's government, although the clique most involved with joint ventures with Japanese interests was high in the first cabinet, making it uncertain that a policy of diversification away from Japan will be continued.[98]

Thailand has been slower than the other ASEAN members to formulate a policy to respond to the political consequences of external trade patterns. In large measure, the government has left trade policy to private interests, only acting to supplement their efforts in the last few years, while it focused on security problems. Thailand, then, is an example of private-sector leadership in economic nationalism, with the government following far behind. To the extent that a policy of diversification has emerged as a basis of current policy, it is likely more a reflection of commercial interests, and perhaps practices, than a result of strategic thinking. Whether the government will continue on this track is uncertain.

Each ASEAN member, then, supports a policy of trade diversification, but the degrees and strategies of implementation and the emphasis in national policies vary widely. Only Singapore and the Philippines have a clear, long-standing commitment to diversification as a strategic policy. Malaysia and Indonesia have preferred to subordinate their existing efforts to diversify to pragmatic considerations of the acceptability of their diplomatic stances to their major economic partners for the major portion of the recent past, emerging with apparent commitment to diversification only in the last few years. Thailand is only now beginning to exercise political control over trade policy, and it appears to be leaning toward diversification. Each, however, agrees on trade expansion. ASEAN activities reflect this hierarchy of agreement. On the surface, expansion of trade is a publicized goal, while the direction of that expansion would appear to reflect an interest in diversification without an explicit statement to that effect. Only in the last few years, with the emergence of a national consensus on diversification, has ASEAN also publicly announced this goal.

Overall, the policies aimed at diversification in ASEAN aim to change the structure of trade partners slowly. It is expected that trade will continue to grow and that, in this context of growth, more of the additional increments will be with newer partners, leading gradually to a more balanced pattern. The governments of ASEAN are generally more active in sponsoring trade missions and directing the flow of trade, especially where the private sectors have not exploited opportunities. But this is also a conservative economic nationalism: none of the ASEAN members desires to discriminate overtly against the presently important industrial countries and to incur a damaging disruption of economic relations. The growing status of ASEAN is expected to provide higher visibility and, with its Third World and neutral credentials, to enhance the leverage of the members. The ultimate goal is to become truly "interdependent" members of the global community—a degree of mutuality that can hardly be said to exist at present. Trade diversification now appears to be the mutually accepted path to decreasing the political weight of preponderant economic partners.

TRADE PATTERNS: TOWARD DIVERSIFICATION?

If the policies of the ASEAN members are directed toward diversification of trade partners, the question of what effect this may have had on the pattern of recorded trade arises. Has trade followed policy? Or is the international trading system too constraining? Specifically, in line with the theoretical framework previously outlined, three questions are addressed. First, has there been movement toward balancing the relative positions of the major trading partners, so that none accrues an advantage owing to vulnerability? Second, has the overall position of the three dominant industrial areas together receded, reducing the degree of sensitivity? Third, has the overall pattern of trade been diversified, so reducing potential vulnerability to any particular area?

In order to provide some answers to these questions, I have gathered trade data from the International Monetary Fund's Directions of Trade: Yearbook for the period 1967-79. The data are aggregated for each year and for each ASEAN member into percentage totals for 15 units, defined by a combination of geographic and political criteria. These units are the United States, the European Economic Community, Japan (large industrial); Canada, other Western Europe, Australasia, newly industrializing countries (NICs) (small industrial); Latin America, West Asia, Africa, South Asia (Third World); the Soviet Union, Eastern Europe, China, Indochina (socialist); ASEAN. Hirschman's index of trade concentration has been calculated for each year (index of dispersion) to provide a measure of overall diversification. [99] Results for odd-numbered years only are presented in Tables 4.3-4.7.

The ASEAN region as a whole has become more vulnerable and less sensitive (see Table 4.1). Although no single major partner's role has increased, that of Japan has declined much less than have those of the United States or the EEC. Japan's role as the region's major trade partner has been maintained and has expanded relative to the rest, making the region as a whole potentially more vulnerable to Japanese pressure. At the same time, the reduction in trade proportions with the United States and the EEC has resulted in a declining degree of connection with the large industrial areas. This reduction in sensitivity has been small since 1971, and previous years are not exactly comparable owing to underreporting of trade between Singapore/Malaysia and Singapore/Indonesia, [100] which overstates the proportions of the remaining areas. A modest degree of diversification has been achieved, largely toward the socialist states [101] and other Third World areas, as evidenced by the consistent decline in the index of dispersion.

The political importance of trading relationships is largely a matter of the relative positions of the partners, and in some respects,

TABLE 4.1

ASEAN: Direction of Trade
(in percent)

	1967	1969	1971	1973	1975	1977	1979
Large industrial	68.7	71.1	58.4	58.6	57.6	56.4	55.5
United States	20.3	20.8	15.9	16.4	17.6	17.7	16.9
European Economic Community	22.2	21.1	17.4	16.1	14.6	14.5	13.9
Japan	26.2	29.2	25.1	26.1	25.4	24.2	24.7
Small industrial	15.3	16.2	11.8	12.1	12.2	12.4	11.3
Canada	0.9	1.2	1.1	0.7	0.8	0.8	0.8
Other Western Europe	2.6	3.0	2.0	2.2	2.1	2.0	2.2
Australasia	4.7	5.0	4.0	3.8	4.0	3.5	4.0
Newly industrializing countries	7.1	7.0	4.7	5.4	5.3	6.1	4.4
Third World	8.3	6.5	9.0	8.4	14.0	14.5	12.9
Latin America	1.1	1.2	1.0	1.0	2.1	1.9	1.5
West Asia	3.2	2.7	4.2	4.0	8.5	8.9	8.4
Africa	0.4	0.7	1.4	1.5	1.2	1.3	1.2
South Asia	3.6	1.9	2.4	1.9	2.2	2.4	1.8
Socialist	1.1	0.7	4.5	4.5	3.4	3.1	3.1
Soviet Union/Eastern Europe	0.2	0.1	1.4	1.4	1.2	1.1	1.3
China	0.0	0.0	1.8	2.2	1.9	1.8	1.6
Indochina	0.9	0.6	1.3	0.9	0.3	0.1	0.2
ASEAN	6.3	5.3	15.3	14.2	12.7	13.5	14.9
Index of dispersion	47.7	43.1	38.7	38.6	38.3	38.0	37.9

Note: Percentages do not add to 100 owing to unspecified trade included in totals.

Source: International Monetary Fund, Directions of Trade: Yearbook (Washington, D.C.: IMF, 1967-79).

TABLE 4.2

ASEAN: Asymmetry of Trade with Large Industrial Nations

	1967	1972	1978
Trade as percentage of ASEAN trade			
United States	20.3	16.6	17.7
European Economic Community	22.2	16.6	14.3
Japan	26.2	25.6	24.9
ASEAN trade as percentage of trade			
United States	2.8	2.7	4.0
European Economic Community	1.2	0.8	1.1
Japan	8.4	8.8	10.5

Source: International Monetary Fund, Directions of Trade: Yearbook (Washington, D.C.: IMF, 1967-79).

this is changing in favor of the ASEAN states. As Table 4.2 shows, ASEAN has become relatively more important to Japan and the United States as a part of their global markets, while the United States and Japan have become less important to ASEAN. This is not to say that they are by any means equal, only more so, with the balance still clearly weighted on the side of the industrial nations. An equally important point for the political balance is simply the existence of ASEAN as a political bloc on economic matters. As a group, ASEAN is far more important to any trading partner than as individual nations: the separate shares of Japanese trade in 1978, for example, range from a low of 1.3 percent for Thailand to a high of 4.1 percent for Indonesia, while ASEAN together takes 10.5 percent of Japan's trade. Thus, the continuing vulnerability of ASEAN toward Japan is moderated by some shifts in relative importance and by the more evident cohesion of the regional association.

The trade figures for the region as a whole, then, reveal only modest progress toward diversification, which would result in little change in political inequality. The aggregate figures, however, conceal significant differences among the ASEAN members in this regard.

Singapore has achieved a widely diversified balance of trade (see Table 4.3). The narrowly dominant partner, the EEC, was nearly equaled by Japan in 1967, and trade with the United States has increased so that the three large industrial areas are now closely balanced, leaving Singapore in no position of particular vulnerability toward any one. Similarly, trade with the large industrial nations has

TABLE 4.3

Singapore: Direction of Trade
(in percent)

	1967	1969	1971	1973	1975	1977	1979
Large industrial	49.9	59.0	42.2	45.2	41.8	40.0	40.1
United States	8.5	13.2	12.4	15.9	15.0	13.9	14.1
European Economic Community	21.2	21.7	15.0	15.3	13.2	12.1	12.1
Japan	20.2	24.1	14.8	14.0	13.6	14.0	14.0
Small industrial	24.8	23.3	14.0	14.7	15.8	16.4	14.5
Third World	15.0	10.9	13.4	13.4	21.3	22.9	20.4
Socialist	3.4	1.6	8.3	6.8	4.1	3.1	3.3
ASEAN	6.9	5.0	22.0	20.0	17.1	17.4	19.4
Index of dispersion*	36.1	38.6	35.2	35.2	34.9	34.7	34.7

*Calculated on the basis of trade with the 15 units.

Note: Percentages do not add to 100 owing to unspecified trade included in totals.

Source: International Monetary Fund, Directions of Trade: Yearbook (Washington, D.C.: IMF, 1967-79).

fallen off in favor of increases with other Third World states, resulting in less sensitivity to the major industrial nations than formerly was the case. With the single exception of the socialist states, Singapore's trade is very close to an even balance among the various units of the global system, leaving further diversification open to political decisions. Particularly since 1973, diversification is quite evident.

The Philippines has also moved toward a greater degree of diversification, as can be seen in Table 4.4. An initially high degree of concentration on the United States has declined substantially, as has a balancing concentration on Japan, which had been increasing up to 1973. Although the EEC still lags behind as a balancer, there is now a reduced degree of vulnerability toward the United States or Japan. As a result of the shifts away from the United States and Japan, the Philippines' degree of concentration on the major industrial nations has declined, reducing the level of sensitivity to these sources. The increasing role of Third World trade partners is partially due to increases in petroleum prices, which introduces another source of potential vulnerability, but other trading areas are also becoming more

TABLE 4.4

Philippines: Direction of Trade
(in percent)

	1967	1969	1971	1973	1975	1977	1979
Large industrial	81.9	79.2	78.8	78.8	70.1	65.9	66.6
United States	37.9	33.6	32.0	32.5	24.8	26.9	26.0
European Economic							
Community	13.6	14.3	14.9	12.5	14.1	14.7	16.5
Japan	30.4	31.3	31.9	33.8	31.2	24.3	24.1
Small industrial	8.5	10.6	11.5	11.4	10.5	11.7	11.8
Third World	5.2	5.0	5.2	6.5	13.8	12.3	11.5
Socialist	0.3	0.1	0.2	1.3	1.5	4.6	2.8
ASEAN	4.2	4.6	4.2	2.1	4.0	5.3	5.1
Index of dispersion	51.0	48.8	48.4	49.3	44.4	41.5	41.3

Note: Percentages do not add to 100 owing to unspecified trade included in totals.

Source: International Monetary Fund, Directions of Trade: Yearbook (Washington, D.C.: IMF, 1967-79).

important. The index of dispersion shows the largest shift toward diversification of any ASEAN member, so progress is substantial despite a continuing high level of potential political vulnerability and sensitivity to the United States and Japan.

Malaysia has changed the locus of potential vulnerability in a context of a mild degree of diversification (see Table 4.5). Earlier concentration on the EEC has declined, only to be replaced by Japan, but to a lesser degree. Since 1973 the degree of concentration on the large industrial nations has increased, a reversal of the trend of previous years. Similarly, overall diversification, which was evident up to 1973, has been almost totally reversed since. Malaysia had achieved a reduction in sensitivity through diversification in the early 1970s, but the present trend is toward increased concentration; diversification has not continued.

Indonesian trade has become very much concentrated on a single partner, Japan (see Table 4.6). This is apparently at the expense of reduced trade with all of Europe and most of East Asia. Although Indonesia is a major exporter of petroleum to Japan, the strategic value of this commodity is unlikely to balance the tenfold difference in their relative importance to each other; Indonesia is quite vulnerable to

Japan. A slight reduction in overall concentration on the large industrial powers has apparently been accomplished through some increased trade with other Third World states, but the reduction in sensitivity is only marginal. Indonesia has not diversified, but has done the opposite, replacing the Philippines as the least diversified in its international trade of the ASEAN members.

Thailand has reduced both forms of concentration of trade, although it remains moderately concentrated on Japan (see Table 4.7). The former level of concentration on Japan has been reduced by a significant amount, moderating the political leverage of Thailand's primary trade partner. At the same time, concentration on the large industrial nations has also declined, largely in favor of other Third World nations, reducing the level of Thailand's sensitivity to the most powerful trading nations. Although Thailand has not achieved a close balance among its largest trading partners, it has diversified more than any other ASEAN country except the Philippines.

TABLE 4.5

Malaysia: Direction of Trade
(in percent)

	1967	1969	1971	1973	1975	1977	1979
Large industrial	64.2	68.6	50.1	50.0	52.5	56.2	57.9
United States	13.9	18.0	9.9	9.5	13.5	15.7	16.3
European Economic Community	27.9	24.9	21.3	21.0	21.9	18.8	17.8
Japan	22.4	25.7	18.9	19.5	17.1	21.7	23.8
Small industrial	17.3	19.9	13.6	13.9	13.5	12.6	11.1
Third World	13.2	7.2	9.8	6.1	8.9	9.5	7.8
Socialist	0.3	0.1	5.4	7.0	5.1	4.5	4.6
ASEAN	4.9	4.2	20.9	19.9	19.9	17.1	17.4
Index of dispersion	40.7	41.8	38.1	37.6	38.1	38.2	39.1

Note: Percentages do not add to 100 owing to unspecified trade included in totals.

Source: International Monetary Fund, Directions of Trade: Yearbook (Washington, D.C.: IMF, 1967-79).

TABLE 4.6

Indonesia: Direction of Trade
(in percent)

	1967	1969	1971	1973	1975	1977	1979
Large industrial	72.5	78.4	72.6	72.2	71.1	70.6	69.1
United States	18.2	22.3	15.7	16.5	21.4	22.2	18.5
European Economic							
Community	29.7	22.7	17.5	13.5	10.9	13.0	9.9
Japan	24.6	33.4	39.4	42.2	38.8	35.4	40.7
Small industrial	19.7	14.8	3.7	5.6	8.1	8.3	7.1
Third World	2.1	1.3	2.8	4.2	7.8	7.6	5.8
Socialist	0.2	0.2	2.6	1.5	3.2	1.4	1.4
ASEAN	5.6	4.5	13.0	10.4	9.7	12.0	13.4
Index of dispersion	44.8	47.2	48.1	49.0	47.3	46.0	48.0

Note: Percentages do not add to 100 owing to unspecified trade included in totals.

Source: International Monetary Fund, Directions of Trade: Yearbook (Washington, D. C.: IMF, 1967-79).

TABLE 4.7

Thailand: Direction of Trade
(in percent)

	1967	1969	1971	1973	1975	1977	1979
Large industrial	66.6	68.5	66.1	62.3	60.7	55.9	56.0
United States	15.6	15.1	13.8	11.9	13.3	11.3	14.2
European Economic							
Community	20.6	22.2	19.8	18.7	16.9	17.7	17.9
Japan	30.4	31.2	32.5	31.7	30.5	26.9	23.9
Small industrial	12.3	13.8	13.2	15.5	12.3	12.4	11.0
Third World	8.3	7.4	9.5	9.0	16.3	17.7	15.4
Socialist	2.3	1.7	2.5	2.7	2.0	3.2	3.8
ASEAN	10.3	8.3	7.9	10.2	8.6	10.2	11.7
Index of dispersion	42.3	43.1	42.2	41.6	40.7	38.4	37.3

Note: Percentages do not add to 100 owing to unspecified trade included in totals.

Source: International Monetary Fund, Directions of Trade: Yearbook (Washington, D. C.: IMF, 1967-79).

EFFECTIVENESS OF POLICIES

Generally, the analysis of trade data confirms that the overall goals apparently pursued by the ASEAN members have been achieved to a moderate degree. Concentration on the largest trade partners has moderated, the degree of connection to the system of major industrial powers has been reduced, and a generally wider dispersion of trade is taking place. But, since there were substantive differences in national policies regarding diversification of trade, it should be useful to compare actual performance with these policies before discussing general limitations on the attainment of diversification in trade.

Philippine enthusiasm for a policy of diversification has been matched by striking results. Of the ASEAN members, the Philippines has achieved the most change in each of the three areas: reduction of concentration on the single largest partner, shifting trade away from the large industrial nations, and generally spreading trade more widely. Diversification is particularly apparent following 1973, which accords with the enunciation of specific policies in late 1972 and with concrete policy steps in the years thereafter. The particular sources of political conern, the United States and Japan, have both declined in importance, although the latter more than the former. The goal set for these states by 1987 (50 percent together) has already been attained, although some of the other quotas, particularly those for ASEAN and other Third World states, are quite far off. Although President Marcos is probably quite deserving of much of the criticism leveled by nationalists, in this regard his regime is not lacking in progress. Still, the Philippines is, after only Indonesia, the most dependent in its pattern of trade in ASEAN. Further diversification is required before Marcos's stated goal of self-reliance becomes more than rhetoric.

Thailand has, after the Philippines, achieved the most diversification of trade. This is particularly apparent since 1973 and is largely a result of shifts of trade with Japan to Third World areas. Since a coherent government policy has not been apparent, it is an intriguing speculation that this is a result of nationalist criticism of Japan; whether the results are due to private-sector responses to this pressure or to Japan retrenching in the face of opposition is not self-evident. Whatever the precise linkage, Thailand moved from being one of the more dependent ASEAN members to being one of the less dependent, through diversification.

Singapore's concern to diversify its trade predates the period examined here, although it was given renewed emphasis in the mid-1970s. Singapore was, in 1967—and continued to be in 1979, as it continued to tap new markets—the most diversified of the ASEAN countries. However, the trade data exhibit phases of diversification before the policies were enunciated: generally between 1973 and 1975, when the topic came to the surface in 1974, and with the Third World at the same time, when the trade drive was announced in 1976. Several informants described this as the typical pattern of behavior in the timing of Singapore's policy announcements, explaining that a policy was only made public after it was well under way. Whatever the nature of timing, it is evident that Singapore's concern to continue diversification is having results. The major trade partners are closely balanced, and industrial nations are being generally deemphasized, through effective diversification.

Malaysian expressions of concern about trade concentration and commitment to diversification have so far not been accompanied by real change. Trade diversification was an active topic during the whole decade of the 1970s, while Japan was becoming more important as the major trade partner and concentration on the largest industrial countries was increasing. Policy appears to have had only a nominal effect on trade patterns. To be fair, Malaysia is, by all measures used here, already well diversified relative to the other ASEAN countries (only Singapore is more so), and the trade data do indicate somewhat wider diversification over the entire period; however, how much the latter is an artifact of underreported trade with Singapore prior to 1970 is impossible to determine. At best, Malaysia is only slightly more diversified in 1979 than it was in 1967.

Indonesian policy has been relatively ineffective. Throughout the 1970s, diversification has been mentioned as a desirable goal of trade policy, but little progress is evident. Japan has remained by far the major trade partner, although slightly less predominant; concentration on the large industrial nations has remained high, although with a downward trend; overall diversification has fluctuated, but has remained consistently low. From the beginning of the period examined to the end, Indonesia is the only country to show changes contrary to diversification: concentration on the single largest partner is higher in 1979 than in 1967, and overall diversification is less in 1979. Indonesia is not diversifying, but becoming more dependent.

LIMITS TO DIVERSIFICATION

Each ASEAN country, with the exception of Indonesia, either has achieved some degree of diversification or is relatively diverse already, indicating that the goal is not unattainable despite the existence of presumed restraints in the international system. The extensive airing of the problems of the Third World in trade development in international forums points to the industrial countries as the source of inhibitions on the growth of Third World trade, especially in manufactured products. [102] Dependence is portrayed as a matter of the center keeping the periphery down.

While at the general level this may be the case, for the ASEAN states it is at most a partial answer. The major determinant of trade partners is structural, and it derives from the chosen pattern of economic growth. Singapore aside, the ASEAN countries are each engaged in building an industrial sector from little or no base. This dictates that imports will be largely capital goods: for Indonesia, 52.5 percent; for Malaysia, 51.5 percent; for the Philippines, 41.2 percent; for Singapore, 39.5 percent; and for Thailand, 48 percent. [103] Sources for these goods are limited largely to the major industrial nations. Ranked according to cost in the region, lowest to highest, this means that these imports will come from Japan, the United States, or Europe. Diversification of imports away from Japanese goods is expensive, and only the Philippines has, to a limited degree, encouraged the purchase of higher-cost goods for political reasons. The concentration of imports is sensitive to global factors, as a product of the interaction of industrialization policy and oligopoly in capital goods.

There are a number of factors that contribute to export concentration, and for Indonesia, Malaysia, and the Philippines, this is higher than import concentration. It is most often attributed to a narrow range of export commodities, [104] and certainly Indonesia's heavy reliance on petroleum fits this scenario. However, the rest of the ASEAN countries are both diversifying the primary commodities they export and increasing the proportion of manufactured products in their exports, which should contribute to geographical diversification. [105] That exports still go mainly to buyers from the large industrial countries is less a matter of necessity than of habit, as the global market for materials is increasingly an open one: "Shortages of supply have replaced shortages of demand . . . and the power position of suppliers and consumers has thus changed dramatically." [106] This is also apparently the conclusion of ASEAN trade officials, as promotion of exports to a wider variety of countries receives a much higher priority than diversifying imports. A structural problem does exist for the ASEAN members in their attempts to diversify exports, but the constraints are easing. Developed country restrictions are not exclusively responsible either. There has reportedly been increasing concern in Japan, for example, that its overdependence on ASEAN could have negative results, with the result that attempts have been made to diversify Japanese trade to other areas. [107]

The analysis of this chapter belies the conclusion that trade dependence is wholly a result of the effective structuring of the periphery by the center. There are real structural constraints on the pattern of trade partners that give some nations, mostly industrial, more opportunity to take advantage of trade dependence than others. [108] But patterns of trade do appear to be responsive to governmental policies. The degree to which trade is concentrated is partly a matter of how much control is exercised by governments in directing economic affairs, rather than allowing them to be directed by external actors. Trade patterns even appear to be responsive to social antagonisms in the absence of governmental control. The result of policies designed to reduce the economic influence of particular partners is an actual change in the indicators of trade dependence in the desired direction. With the exception of Indonesia, the ASEAN members appear to be reducing the degree of their trade dependence through diversification.

NOTES

1. Albert O. Hirschman, National Power and the Structure of Foreign Trade (Berkeley and Los Angeles: University of California Press, 1945).

2. Raul Presbisch, Toward a New Trade Policy for Development (New York: United Nations, 1964).

3. Franklin Weinstein, "Multinational Corporations and the Third World: The Case of Japan and Southeast Asia," International Organization 30 (Summer 1976): 373-404.

4. John Wong, ASEAN Economies in Perspective: A Comparative Study of Indonesia, Malaysia, the Philippines, Singapore, and Thailand (Philadelphia: Institute for the Study of Human Issues, 1979), pp. 12-24.

5. See Carlos F. Diaz-Alejandro, "Delinking North and South: Unshackled or Unhinged?" in Rich and Poor Nations in the World Economy, ed. Albert Fishlow et al. (New York: McGraw-Hill, 1978).

6. Robert O. Keohane and Joseph S. Nye, Power and Interdependence: World Politics in Transition (Boston: Little, Brown, 1977).

7. Indonesia, 1976; Malaysia, 1975; Philippines, 1976; Singapore, 1975; Thailand, 1973. All figures from United Nations, Statistical Yearbook, 1977 (New York: United Nations, 1978).

8. Computed from International Monetary Fund, Directions of Trade: Annual (Washington, D.C.: IMF, 1977); and idem, International Financial Statistics Yearbook: 1979 (Washington, D.C.: IMF, 1979).

9. Computed from International Monetary Fund, Directions of Trade: Annual (Washington, D.C.: IMF, 1978).

10. Frank Golay, ed., Underdevelopment and Economic Nationalism in Southeast Asia (Ithaca, N.Y.: Cornell University Press, 1969).

11. For example, in the Malaysian ethnic bargain. See R. S. Milne, Government and Politics in Malaysia (Boston: Houghton Mifflin, 1967), pp. 39–41.

12. Sinnathamby Rajaratnam, "Beyond Nationalism, More Nationalism," Solidarity (Manila) 4 (January 1969): 42–47.

13. Frank Golay, "National Economic Priorities and International Coalitions," in Diversity and Development in Southeast Asia, ed. G. Pauker, F. Golay, and C. Enloe (New York: McGraw-Hill, 1977), pp. 100–1.

14. Somsakdi Xuto, Regional Cooperation in Southeast Asia: Problems, Possibilities, and Prospects (Bangkok: Institute for Asian Studies, Chulalongkorn University, 1973), p. 20.

15. Amado Castro, "The Meaning of Economic Cooperation in ASEAN," ASEAN Trader (Manila: ASEAN Trade Fair, 1978), p. 35.

16. Vincente Paterno, "Address," Regionalism in Southeast Asia (Jakarta: Centre for Strategic and International Studies, 1975), p. 97.

17. Far Eastern Economic Review, December 22, 1978, p. 37.

18. Ibid., February 23, 1979, pp. 37–39.

19. Ibid., September 7, 1979, p. 52.

20. The dialogues are summarized in Association of Southeast Asian Nations, 10 Years ASEAN (Jakarta: ASEAN Secretariat, 1978), pp. 220–29.

21. Mohamed Ariff, "The New International Economic Order: ASEAN at the Crossroads" (Paper presented at the Third Conference of the Federation of ASEAN Economic Associations, Kuala Lumpur, 1978), pp. 4–7.

22. Author interview, Ministry of Trade, Manila, October 1979.

23. Ibid.

24. Ibid.

25. Chia Siow Yue, "Singapore's Trade Strategy and Industrial Development, with Special Reference to the ASEAN Common Approach to Foreign Economic Policy" (Paper presented to the Tenth Pacific Trade and Development Conference, Canberra, 1979), p. 5; and idem, Singapore and ASEAN Economic Cooperation (Bangkok: UN Asian and Pacific Development Institute, 1978), sec. 2.62.

26. Author interview, Chia Siow Yue, September 1979. Chia frequently advises the Singapore government.

27. Author interviews, Singapore, September 1979.

28. Lim Joo-Jock, ed., Foreign Investment in Singapore: Some Broader Economic and Socio-political Ramifications (Singapore: Institute of Southeast Asian Studies, 1977), p. 221.

29. Trade Director Ridzwan Dzafir, quoted in New Nation, April 6, 1974.

30. Straits Times, October 30, 1975.

31. Ibid., September 4, 1979.

32. Ibid., February 18, 1978.

33. Ibid., March 8, 1979; and September 4, 1979.

34. Business Times (Singapore), September 21, 1979.

35. Interview, Far Eastern Economic Review, August 10, 1979, p. 41.

36. For a Philippine nationalist perspective, see Renato Constantino and Letizia Constantino, The Philippines: The Continuing Past (Quezon City: Foundation for Nationalist Studies, 1978); and Benito Legarda, Jr., and Roberto Garcia, "Economic Collaboration: The Trading Relationship," in The United States and the Philippines, ed. Frank Golay (Englewood Cliffs, N.J.: Prentice-Hall, 1966), pp. 139-43.

37. Ralph Pettman, Small Power Politics and International Relations in South East Asia (Sydney: Holt, Rinehart & Winston, 1976), pp. 114-25. Court decisions restricting ownership by foreign nationals and their employment practices were reversed; the Laurel-Langley Agreements were extended for nearly a year; and opposition nationalists were severely repressed. See Robert Stauffer, "The Political Economy of Refeudalization," in Marcos and Martial Law in the Philippines, ed. David Rosenberg (Ithaca, N.Y.: Cornell University Press, 1979), pp. 209-11; Robert Stauffer, "The Political Economy of the Coup: Transnational Linkages and Philippine Political Response," Journal of Peace Research 11 (1974): 161-77, argues that the coup was timed to prevent nationalists from disrupting relations with the metropolitan nations.

38. Carlos Romulo, "Filipino Foreign Policy," Ambassador 3 (February 1973): 26-32; also see reports of Marcos's announcements of this policy in Straits Times (Malaysia), May 3, 1973.

39. Reports in New Nation, October 4, 1973; and Straits Times, January 8, 1975.

40. Republic of the Philippines, Philippine Army Civil Relations and Information Service, Guiding Principles of the New Society II (Manila: National Printing, 1978), pp. 49-57.

41. Charles Morrison and Astri Suhrke, Strategies of Survival: The Foreign Policy Dilemmas of Smaller Asian States (St. Lucia: University of Queensland Press, 1978), p. 257.

42. See its journal, Export Bulletin, initiated in August 1973, particularly vol. 2, no. 6 (August 1974); and vol. 3, no. 1 (January 1975).

43. Republic of the Philippines, Philippine Development 4 (July 1978): 19-25.

44. Republic of the Philippines, Board of Investment, Institute of Export Development, Export Bulletin, vol. 4, no. 4 (April 1976); and vol. 5, no. 1 (January 1977). For an example from the plywood

industry, see Far Eastern Economic Review, December 7, 1979, p. 93. Markets in Japan and Europe have been cultivated to offset dependence on the United States for the product's markets.

45. Republic of the Philippines, Five-Year Philippine Development Plan, 1978-1982 (Manila: Government Printers, 1977), p. 9.

46. Ibid., figures from table 5, p. 156. See Table 4.3, below, for comparison.

47. Republic of the Philippines, National Economic and Development Authority, Philippine Development Report, 1978 (Manila: National Economic and Development Authority, 1979), pp. 50-52, compares target and actual figures for 1977 and 1978.

48. Export Bulletin (Manila), vol. 5, no. 1 (January 1977).

49. Interview, Philippines Ministry of Trade, Manila, October 1979.

50. Interview, policy coordinating staff, National Economic Development Authority, Manila, October 1979.

51. The ECDC was launched in Mexico City in 1976, after the Manila meeting of the Group of 77 earlier that year; UNCTAD is now working on concrete proposals. A summary and the support by the Philippines is contained in Republic of the Philippines, Philippine Development, pp. 30-34.

52. Interview, Ministery of Trade, Manila, October 1979.

53. Jayaratnam Saravanamuttu, "A Study of the Content, Sources, and Development of Malaysian Foreign Policy, 1957-1975" (Ph.D. diss., University of British Columbia, 1976), p. 126.

54. International Monetary Fund, Directions of Trade: Annual (Washington, D.C.: IMF, various years).

55. Saravanamuttu, "Malaysian Foreign Policy," pp. 169-70.

56. Straits Times (Malaysia), December 18, 1973.

57. Malaysia, Third Malaysia Plan: 1976-1980 (Kuala Lumpur: Government Printers, 1976), p. 314.

58. Mohamed Ariff, "Development of Malaysia's Trade Policy," in ASEAN Cooperation in Trade and Trade Policy, ed. Seiji Naya and Vinyu Vichit-Vadakan (Bangkok: UN Asian and Pacific Development Institute, 1977), p. 186.

59. Particularly Datuk Musa Hitam, "Frowning at the Zaikai," ASEAN Review (Kuala Lumpur), May 29, 1976, pp. 26f.

60. Author interviews, Kuala Lumpur, October 1979.

61. Malaysia, Third Malaysia Plan, p. 313.

62. Encik Abdul Manan bin Othman, interviewed in New Straits Times, February 15, 1978.

63. Ariff, "Development of Malaysia's Trade Policy," p. 199.

64. Far Eastern Economic Review, August 3, 1979, p. 36.

65. This concern was prominent in author interviews with Malaysian Industrial Development Authority officials, Kuala Lumpur, October 1979.

66. Mohamed Ariff, Malaysia and ASEAN Economic Cooperation (Bangkok: UN Asian and Pacific Development Institute, 1978), secs. 1.25, 1.27.

67. Suhadi Manghusuwondo, "Economic Interdependence: The Indonesian View," in New Directions in the International Relations of Southeast Asia: Economic Relations, ed. Lee Soo Ann (Singapore: Singapore University Press, 1973), p. 124.

68. Sumitro Djojohadikusumo, "Indonesia's Trade Policies," Embassy of the Republic of Indonesia, Singapore, Information Bulletin 16/PEN/ING/71 (1971).

69. Suhadi Manghusuwondo, "Economic Interdependence," p. 130.

70. Charles Morrison, "Southeast Asia in a Changing International Environment: A Comparative Foreign Policy Analysis of Four ASEAN-Member Countries" (Ph.D. diss., Johns Hopkins University, 1976), pp. 277-87.

71. Reported in New Nation, July 15, 1974.

72. Author interviews with Indonesian diplomats, May 1980.

73. Suhadi Manghusuwondo, "Economic Interdependence," p. 125.

74. Sumitro Djojohadikusumo, "Foreign Economic Relations: Some Trade Aspects," Indonesia Quarterly 1 (January 1973): 18-26.

75. Both positions are contained in Ali Moertopo, Indonesia in Regional and International Cooperation: Principles of Implementation and Construction (Jakarta: Centre for Strategic and International Studies, 1973), pp. 18-21.

76. Reported in Straits Times (Malaysia), September 21, 1974.

77. Justus van der Kroef, "Indonesia's National Security: Problems and Strategy," Southeast Asian Spectrum 3 (July 1975): 37-49.

78. H. S. Kartadjoemena, The Politics of External Economic Relations: Indonesia's Options in the Post-Detente Era (Singapore: Institute of Southeast Asian Studies, 1977), especially pp. 18, 60, 112. The author was on leave from the Indonesian Ministry of Trade while writing this and returned afterward.

79. Sumardi Reksoputranto, "Development of Trade Policies of Indonesia in the Context of ASEAN Cooperation," in ASEAN Cooperation in Trade and Trade Policy, ed. Seiji Naya and Vinyu Vichit-Vadakan (Bangkok: UN Asian and Pacific Development Institute, 1977), pp. 149-54.

80. Indonesian Development News, vol. 2, no. 10 (June 1979).

81. Ibid., vol. 2, no. 2 (October 1978).

82. This paragraph is based on an interview with Indonesian diplomats, May 1980; the dilemma is described as one between development (with dependence) and self-reliance. See Franklin Weinstein, "Indonesia," in Asia and the International System, ed. W. Wilcox, L. Rose, and G. Boyd (Cambridge, Mass.: Winthrop, 1972), pp. 116-45.

83. Narongchai Akrasanee, "Development of Trade and Trade Policies in Thailand and Prospects for Trade Cooperation with ASEAN," in ASEAN Cooperation in Trade and Trade Policy, ed. Seiji Naya and Vinyu Vichit-Vadakan (Bangkok: UN Asian and Pacific Development Institute, 1977), p. 304.

84. Ibid., p. 324.

85. Ibid., p. 328.

86. Bangkok Bank, Monthly Review, August 1978, p. 353.

87. Morrison, "Changing International Environment," p. 118.

88. Seiji Naya and Narongchai Akrasanee, "Thailand's International Economic Relations with Japan and the U.S.: A Study of Trade and Investment Interactions," in Cooperation and Development in the Asia/Pacific Region: Relations between Large and Small Countries, ed. Leslie Castle and Frank Holmes (Tokyo: Japan Economic Research Center, 1976), p. 121.

89. ASEAN Review, May 29, 1976, p. 26.

90. Sarasin Viraphol, Directions in Thai Foreign Policy (Singapore: Institute of Southeast Asian Studies, 1976), p. 36.

91. Author interviews, Bangkok, October 1979.

92. Far Eastern Economic Review, March 10, 1978, pp. 42-43.

93. Ibid., June 9, 1978, p. 32.

94. ASEAN Briefing, vol. 13 (August 1979).

95. Far Eastern Economic Review, November 9, 1979, pp. 77-81.

96. Narongchai Akrasanee, "Development of Trade," p. 332.

97. Sarasin Viraphol, Thai Foreign Policy, p. 46.

98. Far Eastern Economic Review, March 21, 1980, pp. 17-20; and April 11, 1980, p. 44. Chart Thai members Pramat-Adireksan and Chatichai Choonhaven in particular, although the latter has left the government.

99. Hirschman, National Power, app. A. The index varies from a value of 100 (all trade with one partner) to a lower limit of around 20 for the method used here; see also James Caporaso, "Methodological Issues in the Measurement of Inequality, Dependence and Exploitation," in Testing Theories of Economic Imperialism, ed. S. J. Rosen and J. R. Kurth (Toronto: Lexington, 1974).

100. For a discussion of the difficulties inherent in the trade data for the region at the beginning of the period examined here, see Seiji Naya and Theodore Morgan, "The Accuracy of International Trade Data: The Case of Southeast Asian Countries," SEADAG Paper 41, July 1968.

101. For a more detailed discussion of this subject, see John Wong, "Southeast Asia's Growing Trade Relations with Socialist Economies," Asian Survey 17 (April 1977): 330-44.

102. For a summary of the arguments on Third World trade, see David Blake and Robert Walters, The Politics of Global Economic Relations (Englewood Cliffs, N.J.: Prentice-Hall, 1976), pp. 26-41.

103. United Nations, Economic and Social Commission for Asia and the Pacific, Statistical Yearbook for Asia and the Pacific, 1977 (Bangkok: ESCAP, 1977), pp. 199, 294, 389, 415, 455; all figures for 1977, except Malaysia—which is for 1974.

104. Hirschman, National Power, p. 106, links this tendency to commodity concentration.

105. John Wong, ASEAN Economies in Perspective, p. 16 and table 2.5, p. 141. For growth of manufacturing exports, see Table 5.1, below.

106. C. Fred Bergsten, "The Threat Is Real," Foreign Policy 14 (Spring 1974): 85.

107. Far Eastern Economic Review, April 30, 1976, pp. 43-48.

108. One recent study of export concentration concluded that the major variable was national age, or the colonial syndrome. Elijah M. James, "The Political Economy of Export Concentration," Journal of Economic Issues 15 (December 1980): 967-75.

5

INVESTMENT DEPENDENCE
AND POLICY

The countries of ASEAN all rely to a great degree on foreign sources of investment to provide the capital deemed necessary to their development plans. According to an early 1979 estimate the total foreign investment in ASEAN amounted to $9 billion.[1] Foreign-owned companies currently control well over 45 percent of the total manufacturing investment in the ASEAN area, according to another estimate.[2] On a country-by-country basis, foreign capital as a share of total investment is highest in Singapore, lowest in Thailand, and quite significant for all: Singapore, 69.4 percent; Philippines, 59.7 percent; Indonesia, 56.9 percent; Malaysia, 54.8 percent; Thailand, 29.1 percent.[3] The magnitude of investment and the degree of penetration of the region by external economic interests only roughly indicate the seriousness of the issue and its sensitive nature.

Because one current goal of most developing countries, with ASEAN certainly no exception, is to increase the degree of their industrialization, it is interesting to note that the ASEAN countries have made significant progress in this effort. As Table 5.1 indicates, the share of manufacturing in total gross domestic product (GDP) has increased, manufacturing has contributed to overall growth of GDP to a significant degree, and the structure of exports has shifted toward a higher proportion of manufactured goods. Indonesia has been the least successful and Singapore the most successful in this effort, but with the exception of Indonesia, each of the ASEAN countries appears to be moving toward the goal of industrialization. Foreign investment has certainly been influential in contributing to this growth.

At the same time, growth based on foreign investment is not universally applauded as contributing to autonomous national development.[4] The multinational corporations (MNCs), as the agents of

TABLE 5.1

ASEAN Industrialization
(in percent)

	Share of Manufacturing in Gross Domestic Product		Share of Manufacturing in Gross Domestic Product Growth	Structure of Exports Primary/Manufacturing	
	1965	1975	1970–75	1960	1975
Indonesia	8.4	10.5	13.9	100/0	99/1
Malaysia	10.4	14.3	19.3	94/6	82/18
Philippines	17.5	20.9	27.3	93/7	83/17
Singapore	15.3	21.5	23.2	74/26	57/43
Thailand	15.5	20.1	28.5	98/2	77/23

Sources: Share of manufacturing: U.N. Economic and Social Survey of Asia and the Pacific, 1976 (Bangkok: UN Asian and Pacific Development Institute, 1977), p. 15; and structure of exports: ASEAN Business Quarterly 2 (1978): 16.

direct foreign investment, stand at the center of an ongoing debate over their consequence, for both host and home countries. The political effects of their impact on balances of payments, patterns of exports and imports, future availability of exploitable resources, the development of skilled work forces, research and development of new technologies, patterns of consumer preferences, local entrepreneurial activities, state revenues (and control over them), currency exchange rates, and the availability of local capital are much discussed but largely indeterminate. Developing countries tend to be both highly critical of the activities of multinational corporations that might threaten state control and desirous of more foreign investment. Domestic nationalism has made the control of foreign investment a matter of high priority. For the ASEAN countries, this issue is particularly germane, as their commitment to some sort of "open economy" is balanced by equal concern to avoid potentially negative domestic and international consequences from large pools of foreign investment.

There is little dispute that foreign investment is subject to a climate of closer control, but little agreement on the reasons for this among ASEAN members. On the one hand, several political analysts point to renewed Japanese imperialism accomplished by economic rather than military means[5] or confirm that many of the criticisms leveled against the multinationals are accurate for the region as a result of "conflicts inherent in the relationship between MNCs and underdeveloped countries," particularly when a single country comes to occupy a dominating role in investment.[6] Increased control is, then, a result of essentially political concern. On the other hand, business analysts tend to point to the relative diversity of sources of investment in the region as a factor relieving just these tensions, producing a relatively soft and more tolerant attitude toward foreign investment.[7] Policies leading to more stringent control are seen not so much as a reaction to fear of foreign domination as the result of learning and greater knowledge on the part of governments of what they want to achieve. The treatment of control of foreign investment that follows mediates this gap; it denies neither a basis of conflict nor a degree of cooperation as parts of an economic relationship.

Two major areas of political concern relating to the issue of foreign investment are examined here. In the context of domestic political relations, the relative roles of foreign owners and domestic owners influence the distribution of newly created wealth, providing an incentive to governments to regulate the terms of entry of foreign capital to maximize local benefit; governments regulate the terms of transnational exchange. In the context of external relations, the relative roles of nationals investing from different countries influence the potential leverage of their home governments over the host country, providing an incentive for governments to diversify sources of

investment to maximize local autonomy; governments try to regulate
the patterns of transnational exchange. These two types of control interact to influence the flow of investment and, presumably, the power
of the developing country over the MNC. Barnet and Muller see the
power relationship between developing countries and multinational corporations shifting as a result of the diffusion of knowledge about their
control. There is "the increasing awareness that the industrial world
is no longer a bloc," that competition among the United States, Japan,
and Europe can be exploited, as developing countries learn to diversify
their sources of investment to maximize their leverage.[8] As Singapore's former foreign minister, S. Rajaratnam, put it: "Interdependence is now accepted, if somewhat cautiously, as not only a fact of
life but also as something which could be exploited for national advantage."[9]

    This chapter explores the topic of control of foreign investment
in the ASEAN region. The focus throughout is on diversification as a
strategy of reducing dependence on particular states; domestic regulation is also discussed, as it seems to be a major factor influencing the
growth rate of foreign investment and, therefore, affecting the success
of a policy of diversification through growth. I briefly describe the
policies pursued by each country, separately and jointly through the
ASEAN organization. Then available statistics are analyzed to evaluate
the effectiveness of these policies. Finally, the limitations on a
strategy of diversification of foreign investment are discussed.

CONTROL OF FOREIGN INVESTMENT:
POLICIES AND STRATEGIES

    Three aspects of control that merit particular attention struc-
ture the following discussion. First, each of the countries has developed plans that attempt to allocate ownership between domestic
and foreign interests in various ways. None of the ASEAN countries
allows unrestricted foreign ownership; this is the most basic level
of control, reflecting national development plans and nationalistic
desires for increasing local ownership. Second, each ASEAN member plans for some total amount of foreign-investment flow and pur-
sues potential investors accordingly. Generally, there is some
question as to whether the desired flow can be attained, creating a
perception of capital shortage; this results in an avid concern over
the "investment climate" as an indicator of comparative advantage.[10]
Third, some concern to balance the economic presence of investor
countries through diversification is present in each country to varying degrees; this has resulted in policies designed to attract new
partners to balance the old.

The major locus of policy to achieve control over foreign investment is in the five national governments, but the ASEAN organization is also used to some degree to pursue national objectives, and in various other ways, it is relevant to investment policy in the region. Both the national policies and the regional organization require examination in order to clarify the nature of policy to regulate transnational exchanges and dependence in investment. Control involves a mix of policies designed to both attract and restrict foreign investment, producing several types of internal and international conflict.

Indonesia

The Indonesian government is quite adamant in its desire to control foreign investment. Initial penetration by the Dutch, with almost 74 percent of all entrepreneur investment from that single source in the interwar period,[11] produced an acute sensitivity to foreign investment as an aspect of political domination. The result was widespread nationalization immediately after independence. The Suharto regime acted to reverse the active hostility of the Sukarno government with early legislation on foreign investment, compensation for much of the former Dutch property, and return of the rest.[12] Even though foreign investment was again welcomed, particularly in partnerships with military officials and their Chinese partners, economic nationalism continues to influence attitudes, qualifying the invitation. This reservation is embodied in the basic foreign investment law, which specifically raises the concern of dependence on foreign countries.[13]

Specific limitations are put on the form, duration, and type of investment allowed. With few exceptions, commercial activities were to be transferred to majority Indonesian ownership by December 31, 1977 (they were), and manufacturing activities by December 31, 1997; all foreign investments are limited to a 30-year contract. Joint ventures with Indonesian nationals were initially encouraged and were required after 1974.[14] Other limitations are not clearly spelled out, but they include limitations on certain industrial areas designated "overcrowded" from time to time, in addition to the published lists of open and closed sectors. Preferences are given to labor-intensive, foreign-exchange-earning projects, as well as to the transfer of technology. Oil, banking, mining, and in 1977, forestry are sectors that can only be pursued in joint venture with the government, and the contracts are being tightened to favor the government in stages.[15] These policies are directed at increasing Indonesian ownership and control. The governing philosophy is that foreign investment is supplementary, temporary, and to be "domesticated," reflecting continued economic nationalism, albeit a more pragmatic version.[16] The chairman of the Indonesian Board of Investment expressed it thus in 1977: "Our policy is to make efforts so that at an appropriate time there will be no foreign investment whatsoever existing in the country."[17]

Despite this long-term goal, the overall industrialization program relies on a continuous flow of foreign investment, to be directed to specific types of activities. The Repelita series shifts the priority areas more and more toward industrial projects that require large increments of foreign investment: Repelita I (1969-74) focused on infrastructure development and agricultural industries, Repelita II (1975-78) on the processing of raw materials, Repelita III (1979-84) adds export and agricultural projects to further processing, and Repelita IV will focus on producer goods.[18] The current plan, Repelita III, calls for foreign investment to equal 42 percent of all private investment (government investment will be about half of the plan total).[19] This is remarkably low, since the historical level of foreign investment is far higher: as previously noted, the level in 1972 was 56.9 percent, and reported foreign investment at the end of 1979 was only slightly lower, at 55.9 percent.[20] The foreign component of investment is still a substantial, although declining, proportion of the total required by Indonesian development planning. Domestic ownership has not increased substantially in the past decade, but it is apparently scheduled to do so in the early 1980s.

The Repelita plan for a reduced flow of foreign investment may simply reflect a degree of realism, rather than government desires. The investment climate in Indonesia has not been positive since 1975, resulting in reduced flows of direct investment.[21] Recession in the industrialized countries probably accounted for the initial lag, but this has been reinforced by investor wariness owing to the Pertamina crisis, by signs of domestic instability, and by rising economic nationalism signaled by increased governmental restrictions on investment contracts.[22] Most of the approvals granted in the last few years have been for expansions in existing projects, rather than for new inflows, despite increased government efforts to attract investment by restructuring incentives and by sending out investment-promotion teams.[23] Control over the flow of investment has been reduced by attempts to control the structure of domestic ownership; this basic conflict has forced a revision of long-term plans in the direction of increased promotion and reduced total investment.

In addition to problems involving the level of investment, the political implications of concentrated sources of investment are subjects of concern. To a substantial degree, this is a reaction to the high visibility of Japanese investors, but also to the nature of Japanese ventures and joint-partner practices, which have contributed to the image of exploitation.[24] Anti-Japanese feelings persist, al-

though expressed in less violent forms than the riots of 1974, requiring the attention of Japanese diplomatic personnel.[25] Popular
sentiment has to a degree been manipulated to the government's advantage, as, for example, in the establishment of a bilateral committee between Japan and Indonesia to assuage the latter's feelings.[26]
Indonesia is, as a consequence, attempting to give priority to other
sources of investment to dilute the more conspicuous Japanese
presence.[27]

The desire to diversify foreign investment sources is not, however, simply a reaction to the Japanese role. There is also a long-
term concern dating from the late 1960s over the viability of Indonesia's "active and independent" foreign-policy stance.[28] In 1970 the
Indonesian ambassador to the United States pointed to the strategic
implications:

> It so happens that for the moment private foreign invest-
> ment comes from Western sources. However, we are
> in the process of negotiating with the Soviet Union on a
> final settlement of our debts. We hope that this will
> clear the way for participation by the Soviet Union and
> other Communist countries in our economic develop-
> ment. We do not conceive of our economic develop-
> ment in the narrow terms of an exclusively Western
> orientation. It is in our national interest to involve
> as many countries as possible in the economic develop-
> ment of Indonesia. In this light, neutrality is removed
> from the impact of economic pressures because these
> tend to cancel each other out.[29]

Adam Malik carried this theme out in his 1974 tour of Eastern Europe, expressing a "worry" that dependence on the West alone could
compromise Indonesia's neutrality and soliciting investment to balance
the Western presence.[30] Development of a non-Western counter has,
however, been curtailed by a cautious attitude on the part of the Indonesian military.[31]

The focus of diversification efforts has shifted to balancing
largely Western partners against each other. The overall "re-equilibrating effort" has taken the form of a more avid pursuit of the
"middle powers" of the European Economic Community (EEC) in the
last few years,[32] particularly of France, which has been "lectured"
on the low level of investment in Indonesia relative to its industrial
status.[33] There has also been a degree of openness to investment
from other developing countries of East Asia (including ASEAN),
which would appear to bolster the neutral image of Indonesia and to
dilute the Japanese presence, but since projects from these sources

tend to be smaller and less advanced in their technology, they are
not likely to increase greatly in the future; the Indonesian government
would like to reserve this sort of investment for pribumi (native) entrepreneurs.[34] The major thrust of diversification remains toward
Europe.

Owing to the need to increase the flow of investment, a policy of
diversification has become secondary. As stated by Widjojo Nitisastro, chairman of the National Development Planning Agency, in
reference to financial dependence on Japan: "There are other sources
and other markets and we continue to diversify. But we would like
to see this diversification develop, together with overall growth, so
that proportionately there will be growth overall."[35] Indonesia has
shifted toward a policy of diversification, but the level of commitment appears to be rather low.

Malaysia

Nationalism in Malaysia has lead to a similar concern over the
degree of foreign economic presence and to a desire to control foreign investment. Early reactions were directed at the role of the former colonial power. British investments were something over 70 percent of total foreign investment in the interwar period,[36] and the
United Kingdom continued to dominate as the largest single investor
during the 1960s, declining to 21.4 percent by 1968.[37] As the colonial
situation was gradually relieved, economic nationalism did not disappear, but continued to direct hostility toward foreign investment,
as illustrated by these comments of more recent vintage:

. . . An independent state must exercise full sover-
eignity over its natural resources rather than . . .
be at the behest of multinational corporations.[38]

. . . Foreign firms are not responsive to the needs of
the people. The time has come for Malaysians to free
the nation from foreign domination of its economy.[39]

Nevertheless, Malaysian development policy has required the continued use of foreign investment.

Malaysia's economic development planning has evolved in the
direction of more manufacturing, particularly for export, which has
kept the demand for foreign investment high. The First Malaysia
Plan (1966-70) emphasized import-substitution industries and resource processing for export; however, as the domestic market
limited further growth in this type of project,[40] manufacturing for

export gradually absorbed more of foreign-capital allocations, reducing the role of import-substitution projects from almost 29 percent of approvals in the Second Malaysia Plan (1971-75) to only 12 percent in the Third Malaysia Plan.[41] The New Industrial Strategy emphasizes exports and labor-intensive industrialization, while maintaining a commitment to agricultural development;[42] however, the major requirement for expansion is export growth in manufactured goods.[43] In order to implement these policies, Malaysia requires a continuous flow of foreign investment.

Attracting further foreign investment is a fundamental part of government policy. As the Second Malaysia Plan commented: "Thus an essential ingredient of policy to reach the investment targets is the maintenance of a favourable economic and political climate in Malaysia."[44] This has consisted of a wide range of incentive systems offered to investors, starting in 1958 with the Pioneer Industries Act, now supplemented by a series of locational and labor-use incentive schemes. In addition, industrial estates and free-trade zones have been extensively developed, with considerable success.[45] Infrastructure and psychological boosts are necessary to maintain a planned growth rate of foreign investment in excess of 10 percent per annum.[46]

At the same time as investment is sought, governmental controls have imposed increasing limits on the role of foreign investors. Currently, in order to qualify for Pioneer status, an investment project has to meet approval by being some combination of a priority product, labor-intensive, export-oriented, designed to use local raw materials, integrated with existing firms, or agriculturally based. No formal criteria are published, and there are unpublished lists of areas considered "overcrowded" where no new investment is normally accepted. Ownership is also restricted according to the type of project: any firm targeted at the domestic market or exploiting primary resources must be 70 percent Malaysian; all projects are encouraged to start as joint ventures or to go public; only firms exporting a high percentage of their product are allowed full foreign ownership. The extent of incentives granted is dependent on the planned upstream or downstream processing of a project. With the exception of export-platform projects, the type of status, approval itself, and incentives granted are the result of bargaining between the government and the potential investor.[47] The Malaysian Industrial Development Authority (MIDA)[48] has consistently sought to increase the proportion of local participation in manufacturing activities through this set of controls. These efforts seem to be having an effect: in 1977, for example, 50.2 percent of all projects approved were wholly Malaysian owned, 47.8 percent were joint ventures with a foreign partner (74 percent of these majority Malaysian), and only 2 percent were wholly foreign.[49] MIDA makes it clear that a major goal of government

control is to reduce the role of foreign investment as a proportion of
each project to the benefit of Malaysian nationals.

Increasing participation of Malaysians is dictated by another
consideration aside from nationalism, unique to Malaysia. Serious
racial riots in 1969 resulted in a radical shift in economic planning,
to focus on the distribution of business ownership among the several
racial groups. The New Economic Policy (NEP)[50] was promulgated
in 1971, designed to achieve an economic balance among Chinese,
Indian, foreign, and Malay ownership in the context of overall growth;
this applied explicitly to foreign investment. The structure of ownership of corporate assets is to change drastically: Malay ownership
from 1 percent in 1969 to 30 percent in 1990, Chinese from 22.8 percent to 40 percent, foreign from 62.1 percent to 30 percent.[51] The
reduced foreign share is a substantial realignment from the 60 percent of limited companies, 75 percent of agriculture and fisheries,
72 percent of mining, 63 percent of commerce, and 59 percent of
manufacturing owned by foreigners in 1970.[52] Since this is to occur
along with substantial growth, it does not imply an absolute curtail-
ment of foreign investment, but a substantially reduced relative role
nevertheless.

Some progress has in fact been made toward the achievement
of these goals. In projects approved between 1971 and 1977, Malay
ownership was 32.3 percent, Chinese ownership 36.1 percent, and
foreign ownership 31.6 percent, very close to targeted figures.[53]
Government holding companies account for most of the Malay ownership;[54] in fact, large government organizations have become a central feature of economic development, participating on behalf of various groups in myriad forms.[55] In the period from 1970 to 1975, total
foreign ownership fell from 63.3 percent to 54.9 percent, but indications were that the goal of 43.6 percent for 1980 was overambitious.[56]
The combination of previous domestic controls and the NEP is increasing the share of ownership of domestic groups, particularly
Malays, at the expense of foreigners, both in the aggregate and in
individual projects, resulting in enhanced control over the effects of
foreign investment.

Domestic ownership is increasing, but nationalism is also
making it more difficult to attract more foreign investment. Domestic regulation and new clashes with foreign investors in 1974 and 1975
unsettled the investment climate. The government shifted from
traditional concession agreements to a production-and-management
sharing system with the oil companies in 1974 through the Petroleum
Development Act, which raised charges of "nationalization" and, at
the same time, established the Foreign Investment Committee to ensure progressive achievement of NEP goals.[57] The prime minister
announced guidelines to discourage mergers, takeovers, and other

such activities that could erode the Malay position and nullify the NEP.[58] Passage of the Industrial Coordination Act, 1975, further eroded investor confidence, domestic and foreign. Designed to ensure "orderly development" of manufacturing, the act required all larger manufacturing concerns (more than 25 employees or capital of $50,000) to seek a license from the government within one year. The license could be withdrawn if the concern changed its production, failed to comply with the targets of the NEP, or otherwise became not "consistent with national economic and social objectives." This act extended government control substantially beyond that previously exercised through the granting of preferred tax status, to virtually all large manufacturing firms. Malaysian Chinese were unsettled at the prospect of implementation that could operate on the basis of racial bias, while foreign investors were concerned that the act would lead to eventual de facto nationalization.[59]

The apparent change in the government policy of nonintervention seriously eroded investor attitudes toward Malaysia,[60] particularly given the uncertainty resulting from events in Indochina. The result was that little new investment was made from early 1975 to the end of 1977, with most investment growth being from the expansion of existing projects.[61] Investors required assurances that the government desired more funding and that they were not going to change equity requirements further.[62] Some minor changes were made in the framework of legislation to restore investor confidence and to stimulate the flow of capital.[63] The government had apparently overstepped the boundary between acceptable control and cutting off the necessary flow of investment.

As the control strategy at the domestic level seems to have reached the point of diminishing returns, diversification of investment sources is apparently taking its place as a means of reducing the political impact of foreign investment. The present primo minister, Datuk Seri Mahathir bin Mohammad, has since early 1978 systematically circled the globe in search of investment, concentrating on Europe and the smaller industrial nations, with Canada and Singapore included; MIDA has sponsored investment seminars in virtually every developed country.[64] The purpose of these trips is reported to be to seek greater diversification of the sources of foreign investment, with the government "in earnest about diversifying the investment pool."[65] Diversification is thought to avoid the limitation in investment flow inherent in a focus on domestic controls as well as to provide insulation against undue political influence from any single economic center. But the emphasis is on returning the flow of funds to a higher level. As an official of MIDA put it: "The government wants as much (investment) as possible from as many places as possible."[66] The ethnic imperatives of the government's economic policy require continued growth of foreign investment and make a significant dismantling of provisions for joint partnership and domestic ownership highly undesirable. If this has the undesirable effect of curtailing the flow of capital, another means of sustaining growth must be found. The restructuring goals conflict with promoting foreign investment only with stagnation, not with growth.[67] It would appear that the current choice is diversification.

The Philippines

Policies in the Philippines have vacillated between close control of foreign investment and a virtual open door, as a result of the dilemma imposed by nationalism on the one hand and the need for accelerated economic development to alleviate domestic economic inequality on the other. The United States, as the major investor from the colonial period, with 52 percent of all direct investment,[68] was the target of the "Filipino First" policy of the 1950s. Inspired by the thinking of Sen. Claro Recto, the Garcia administration attempted to reverse the "parity" rights of U.S. nationals embodied in the Laurel-Langley Agreements of 1956. Repudiated by President Macapagal, Filipino First was replaced by more relaxed controls in the 1960s, tightened by the courts in the early 1970s, then partially implemented under martial law by President Marcos after 1972, with "parity" ending in 1974.[69] The current policy of control is, as stated by President Marcos, a response to "apprehension about foreign domination of our national economies, remembering as we do the unpleasant memories of unrestricted entry of foreign capital during the colonial era and noting the aggressive instincts of foreign investments when allowed to do or go as they please."[70] However, the actual degree of control is questionable, as the Marcos administration has sought to preserve an important role for foreign investment in the Philippines.[71]

The structure of controls aims to order the growth of the economy as well as to increase Philippine ownership. The decontrolled growth of the 1960s produced a chaotic result[72] as well as a net outflow of investment.[73] Capacities are set for the production of all major products, with new investment allowed only in industries not yet meeting their set capacities, mostly in intermediate industries.[74] Increasingly, the effort is to channel new investment into areas producing for export of manufactures or commodities, ending the long import-substitution focus of industrialization.[75] Foreign investment is to find its place as a supplement to domestic investment in achieving the "organic development" of the Philippines.[76] A complicated set of guidelines for initial ownership prohibits any foreign ownership in a few industries, mandates majority Philippine control in "basic industries" such as mining, forestry, and finance, and encourages joint ventures in all areas; up to 30 percent foreign ownership is allowed without approval, and only in Pioneer areas is 100 percent foreign ownership allowed. All majority foreign control is to be phased out by conversion to 60 percent Philippine ownership within 40 years.[77] In order to prevent disguised control, the maximum debt to equity ratio is set at 75/25, a policy opposed by all foreign investors but most cumbersome for the Japanese firms that tend to use smaller initial equity investments and to fund the enterprise through loans.[78] This is designed to prevent a recurrence of the experience of the 1960s, when many Philippine joint-venture partners were forced to drop out, leaving foreigners in complete control.[79] The complex set of controls attempts to utilize foreign investment in a manner that will develop the economy and benefit domestic economic actors.

Despite the complexity of controls and the apparent bias toward increasing Philippine ownership, the role assigned to foreign investment remains large and appears to be increasing. Planned private-investment requirements for 1972 through 1977 allocated an increasing proportion to foreign resources: 25.5 percent in 1972, 30.5 percent in 1975, 35.3 percent in 1977. In the industrial program for the same period, only 25 percent of the funds were expected to come from foreign sources.[80] In fact, these expectations have been exceeded by quite a margin. In projects granted approval, foreign dominance is clearly increasing, from 24.4 percent in 1968 to 53.3 percent in 1972, reaching 56.7 percent in 1976. The yearly increments of approved investment were above 60 percent from foreign sources for 1972 through 1975, far above the original estimates.[81] With targets for the future inflow of foreign investment calling for yearly flows up to $134 million by 1987,[82] the position of foreign investors relative to Philippine investors is not likely to erode. It would appear that the verbiage of the Marcos regime restricting the role of foreign investment has not been matched by policies that would actually increase the relative control of Philippine investment. Ownership continues to be dominated by foreign investors.

Reliance for control of political effects appears to be placed on diversification, particularly away from the United States. For the most part, this has taken the form of soliciting Japanese capital. While the relationship with the Japanese is not free from conflict,[83] it produced a considerable flow of capital and closer economic relations in the late 1970s,[84] although now there is some attempt to balance the Japanese presence as well. The focus of diversification has shifted toward encouraging investment from the EEC through investment centers and conferences, but the overall effect has not been productive, leading most recently to partial deregulation.[85] As a supplement, there is an emerging emphasis on finding smaller multinationals as joint venture partners, which is intended to allow participation from smaller industrial countries, increasing the potential leverage of Philippine partners. [86] Since the announcement of a "self-reliance" policy for the Philippines by President Marcos in early 1973, it has been emphasized that foreign investment is welcome from any source, in line with the general broadening of Philippine economic relations, and the Board of Investments has consistently reported new investment from nontraditional partners, largely the smaller industrial nations, as contributing to progress in diversification. [87] According to the development plan, this is expected to continue in the future: "While a substantial portion of these (planned) investments is expected to originate from traditional investors, a gradual diversification is foreseen in the light of existing foreign policy."[88] However, as was pointed out in an interview with an official from the National Economic Development Authority, the task is a difficult one when the implementation must exclude sanctions and must rely on positive incentives in order to avoid damage to the Philippines' investment climate with the United States and Japan, the sources of most investment. [89] Diversification is seen as a politically expedient means of allowing investment from foreign sources to increase without suffering undue dependence on any single source.

Singapore

Singapore occupies a unique position in ASEAN, derived from both its small size and the emphasis that has been placed on industrialization. With no large domestic market to protect, foreign investment is seen as a basic resource, and the issue of control revolves around means to draw more rather than around how to domesticate alien influence. In contrast with the other ASEAN states, Singapore has maintained a largely positive attitude toward foreign investment; although the opposition Barisan Sosialis voices some criticism, it apparently fails to strike a responsive note. [90]

Singapore's industrial planning reflects consistent change in order to maintain an internationally competitive position, which requires a consistent inflow of foreign capital. The forced separation from Malaysia stimulated a shift from import substitution to export promotion in labor-intensive projects for the last years of the 1960s; beginning in 1970, higher technology and skills were emphasized, particularly after 1975, and by the end of the decade, a strategy of "high wage, high value-added" was in place for the 1980s. [91] The last policy, billed as Singapore's second industrial revolution, reflects full employment as well as a desire to curtail the growth of visiting workers from neighboring ASEAN countries.[92] Singapore's industrial strategy has been built on foreign capital.

The importance of foreign investment is reflected both in output and in ownership of the Singapore economy. In 1977 foreign projects accounted for more than 73 percent of total manufacturing output and for more than 84 percent of export sales.[93] Ownership of the most important group of industrial firms, those enjoying Pioneer status, has become overwhelmingly foreign: local capital constituted 47 percent of total investment in 1963, but only 16 percent by the end of 1972.[94] Singaporean investors, with the government prominent among them, play an important minority-ownership role in perhaps as many as half of the foreign-controlled firms,[95] but the situation remains that most of the larger manufacturing enterprises are beyond the scope of national capitalists. It is quite apparent that the role allocated to foreign investment is the crucial one for significant industrialization, with local capital playing a supporting role in services and commerce.[96] This division of labor (or capital) makes Singapore extremely dependent on the flow of foreign investment.

In order to attract this investment, the Singapore government has developed an extensive infrastructure of facilities, agencies, and incentives. The Economic Development Board (EDB) implements government policy in industrial development and is closely tied in with the execution of foreign policy; one of its senior officers has recently been seconded to take the position of ambassador to the EEC, indicating the degree of overlap between foreign and commercial policy.[97] The EDB is responsible for most aspects of investment in Singapore,[98] including soliciting investment through 13 worldwide offices, granting incentives, and monitoring performance of existing firms. Differential incentives are granted through negotiation between the EDB and the proposing investor, with the EDB emphasis on promoting large export projects with high levels of technology and planned diversification of product lines; labor-intensive projects are not absolutely discouraged but have rarely been given incentives since 1975, and they are frequently admonished that their viability will become less tenable with Singapore's high-wage policy.[99] Since the result of government policy is to favor large foreign investment over the smaller local entrepreneur,[100] several programs have been developed to encourage smaller projects of a desirable technological nature. These include a program offering permanent residence to investors bringing in a substantial sum of capital, which has attracted investment from Hong Kong,[101] and the Capital Assistance scheme, which has provided government loans and equity on a small scale since 1976.[102] The latter program in particular was developed to counter flagging levels of foreign-investment flow during 1975-76, in order to attract new types of capital and to keep the total flow of investment up.[103]

Since there are few restrictions on foreign capital—almost no areas
are closed to it—and no real requirement for local participation, the
emphasis of policy has been consistently on attracting the desired
flow to fuel Singapore's industrialization.

One measure of the success of Singapore's policies on foreign
investment is Singapore's emergence as a center for the distribution
of investment to other countries of the region. Traditionally a large
investor in Malaysia, Singapore is now supplying funds to Indonesia,
Thailand, the Philippines, Sri Lanka, and Bangladesh.[104] Some of
this is overflow from Singapore-based multinationals, but with the
new high-wage policy, there may be more Singaporean investment
based on smaller-scale, labor-intensive manufacturing driven out to
neighboring lower-wage areas; the EDB is suggesting to some investors interested in labor-intensive projects that they consider other
ASEAN countries rather than Singapore as an original location.[105]
The Singapore Manufacturers Association is also starting to send out
its own investment missions to various parts of Asia and the Pacific,
looking for future investment sites.[106] Along with the Philippines,[107]
Singapore is becoming a significant source of investment in the ASEAN
region, particularly as the type of investment required in Singapore
differs from that required in the other ASEAN countries.

Although extensive policies to increase local participation are
lacking, Singapore relies on diversification of sources for political
control over the effects of foreign economic presence. With the major
focus of investment promotion on Japan, the United States, and the
EEC, a rough balance among these globally predominant economic
actors is attempted by the simple expedient of setting quotas for the
overseas missions of the EDB.[108] Although there are now numerous
projects from the smaller industrial nations,[109] less effort is devoted
to them; only Australia has been singled out for its future potential.[110]
This is perhaps a result of the policy of preferring high-technology
projects. Recent policy has shifted "to intensify the EDB's activities"
in Japan,[111] as Japanese investments are relatively smaller than those
from U.S. and EEC sources in total capital, although there are more
projects from Japan. As was pointed out in 1973, the early strategy
of diversifying sources of foreign investment "protected Singapore
from undue influence by foreign investors, as the government insured
that foreign investments came from a multiplicity of countries so that
no single one could exert undue economic influence over the Republic."[112] Political considerations are as important as economic or
geographic ones; the goal is to produce competition among investors
in order to cancel out individual influences.[113] Singapore follows an
economic balance-of-power doctrine to control foreign investment,
which complements the same policy followed on the diplomatic front.

Thailand

Thai interest in controlling foreign investment has only recently become important. Perhaps because of the lack of formal colonial status, a high degree of investment dependence on Britain before the war (70 percent to 80 percent)[114] appears not to have caused a reaction similar to that in other ASEAN countries. Rather, the initial focus of control was to prevent exclusive, Chinese, resident control of industry through the creation of government monopolies, which remain quite extensive. [115] Only in the 1970s did concern over foreign investment surface.

Industrial development policy has lagged behind that of other regional states, resulting in some uncertainty over the desired role for foreign investment. Import substitution has been the main goal of industrialization since the mid-1950s and was the continuing focus of the first two national plans (1961-66, 1967-71); this attracted significant foreign investment during the late 1960s.[116] By 1970 interest was beginning to shift toward promoting exports, and criticism was leveled at the Board of Investments that past policy had not taken into account the need for export growth;[117] Japanese projects, for example, were exporting less than 2 percent of their production. [118] The third plan (1972-76) accordingly shifted emphasis to labor-intensive export projects, but with little apparent effect; this is still being touted as the direction of change in policy for the 1980s. [119] As planning shifts toward larger export projects, the need for foreign investment will increase over that required previously for smaller investments for the domestic market.

Policy instability and domestic controls have reduced the relative role of foreign investment in Thailand. Throughout the 1960s, foreign investment constituted exactly one-third of registered capital; in the 1970s, this gradually declined to approximately 27 percent. [120] Major restrictions on foreign investment were introduced with the 1972 Alien Business Law, which closed many areas to future majority-foreign ownership and required some to divest to the extent required to achieve majority Thai ownership. [121] Joint ventures are preferred, and nearly all approved investments take this form. [122] Despite a very uneven reputation on the actual enforcement of these controls and their ultimate effect on limiting foreign control of particular enterprises, [123] the result does appear to be an increase in the relative position of Thai to foreign owners.

Languishing levels of foreign investment have been a consistent problem. This is due in part to the extensive control and bureaucratic delay involved in seeking approval, but also to political instability that has disrupted the degree of policy consistency desired by foreign business in making investment decisions. Despite higher levels of protection offered to promoted projects than in other countries of the region, and despite extensive tampering with the investment laws to increase their attractiveness, foreign interest is less than desired. A recent revision even includes a guarantee against strikes and places the prime minister at the head of the Board of Investments. [124] In 1979 the Alien Business Act was relaxed to allow increased expansion of investment in existing projects without approval, and industrial-promotion zones were revamped in a continuing attempt to reverse the decline in foreign business interest. [125] Nevertheless, foreign investment continues to be static. [126]

Another major concern is emerging in the form of political consequences of the pattern of investment. The dominant role of Japan has become an issue, complicating attempts to balance domestic control over forms and areas of investment against a capital shortage. A rising fear of Japanese domination during the 1970s has resulted in the promotion of economic nationalism as a defense, even by business interests and the Foreign Investment Committee. [127] As early as 1972, government policy was reported to discourage complete control of any industry by a single foreign nation, but this policy was largely ineffective. [128] It is impossible to tell to what degree anti-Japanese policy statements are a result of economic nationalism and, therefore, are permanent, or whether they are merely a reflection of factional strife; interests tied to Japanese joint ventures have replaced those closer to U.S. investments in the Prem government, [129] so the future will test the degree of national concern. Since the unification of Vietnam, the diversification of economic relations has been given more priority in an effort to become more self-reliant and to keep "equidistance" among the major powers, [130] so it may be that the concern over the Japanese presence is at the strategic level. Efforts to increase the flow of capital from the EEC are justified, in these terms, as contributing to a more healthy diversification. [131] Diversification as a means of reducing dependence on Japan, and to a lesser extent on the United States, appears to have become at least an undertone of Thai foreign economic policy.

Policies Pursued through ASEAN

The ASEAN organization itself has in recent years emerged as an important tool of economic policy for the members, and where common interests exist, it is used to attain mutually agreed objectives. In this, as in other areas of policy, the ASEAN organization supplements national policy, as stated by Foreign Minister of Singapore S. Rajaratnam in 1971: "ASEAN is used more for national than for regional interests by its member countries and it is an instrument for national consolidation."[132] In the area of foreign investment, the common interests appear to be in expanding the flow and range of sources of funding.

The most important type of ASEAN initiative has been in joint "dialogues" (the ASEAN term for a diplomatic conference) between the five members and the major external partners. Each of the dialogues has included a substantive focus on investment issues, with the exception of that with New Zealand.[133] In each case, some type of program focused on the investment area has resulted. These meetings have allowed ASEAN to move ahead in coordinating common programs involving investment with the industrial countries,[134] likely more attractive to the members than could have been expected had ASEAN not prenegotiated the issues and presented a common front to the industrial countries.

The relationship with Australia is the most obvious example of collective influence. From the earliest meetings in 1974, Australia was put on the defensive, with restrictions on investment flow to ASEAN a prominent issue. In an attempt to overcome the acrimonious tenor of relations, Australia sponsored the ASEAN-Australia Industrial Cooperation Conference in 1978, designed to bring together likely Australian investors and potential ASEAN partners. Despite the gesture, the conference was marred by threats from the ASEAN delegates that Australia would be excluded from the developing ASEAN economic bloc if further moves to loosen trade and increase the flow of investment were not forthcoming. This flexing of collective muscle produced five planned joint ventures.[135] Despite the lack of grace in the courting, Australia is becoming a more important investor in ASEAN.

Another, less important, industrial country, Canada, has drawn the attention of ASEAN. A series of meetings in 1977 were low-key and focused mainly on bilateral assistance, but two programs initiated subsequently by the Canadian government pertain to increasing the flow of investment from Canada to the ASEAN area. As industrial development is to be the major thrust of Canadian programs in Southeast Asia, the programs sponsored by the Canadian International Development Agency (CIDA) provide funds for prefeasibility studies of ASEAN industrial-complementation projects to be done by Canadian firms, with the hope that the early contact will result in larger contracts and Canadian ventures at a later date. In addition, an industrial-cooperation program sponsors meetings between Canadian and ASEAN manufacturers in fields in which there is some possibility of joint ventures; for example, these have included furniture and auto parts manufacturers. As the pilot of a larger CIDA program, the purpose is to raise the level of information about the capabilities of Canadian investors, which has been a major factor hindering interest in ASEAN for investments from Canada. The currently low level of interest in Canada as a potential partner for diversifying investment relations results from the ASEAN perception that Canada is merely an extension of the U.S. industrial system. This appears to be changing, and Canada is likely to become more important to ASEAN in the future as a source of investment. [136]

The search for ASEAN investment partners perhaps reached the limits of imagination with the ASEAN-West Asia Investment Conference. Designed rather obviously to include ASEAN in the recycling of "petrodollars," the 1977 conference drew little interest from the potential partners and largely demonstrated the present lack of relations between the two regions as well as the limited potential. The goal, however, was made quite explicit: the only practical way for developing countries to further the necessary interdependence of nations without losing their independence is to diversify. [137]

The theme of diversification is carried out in the three previously noted regional approaches, but by far the most significant action to achieving this goal is with the EEC. The EEC is the single region with the capacity to balance the investment influence of Japan and the United States, and this potential forms a large part of ASEAN motivation to foster closer relations. Again, it was Rajaratnam who expressed the preferences for ASEAN; at the ASEAN-EEC Industrial Cooperation Conference in Brussels, April 1977: "We'd feel more comfortable with diversification of investment sources" as ASEAN is currently too dependent on the United States and Japan. [138] This conference and its larger, more productive follow-up in Jakarta the next year both attempted to match specific projects in ASEAN countries with European investors in an ambitious way, [139] in line with the EEC commitment to step up efforts to expand European investment in the ASEAN region. [140] The promising part of this relationship is the interest on both sides in expanding economic relations. The Commission of the EEC and Germany are particularly concerned to assure access to ASEAN raw materials and to reverse the relative decline of European business interests in the region. [141] ASEAN's interest is captured aptly in the title of an article announcing diversification to the economic "middle powers." "Once we pinned our faith on Japan—now it's the EEC." [142] ASEAN has been the vehicle of choice in the development of broader region-to-region relations.

Despite a desire to reduce the predominance of Japan as an investment partner, it is not the case that further financial relations with Japan have been deemphasized. Japan has consistently been most concerned to foster close economic relations with ASEAN, and it even sought a permanent role as a development partner in 1968, which ASEAN vetoed. [143] Japan is extending a large part of the financing for the large industrial projects, [144] and it has agreed to en-

courage more, and higher technology, investment in the region. [145]
Early Japanese irritation at ASEAN initiatives to cultivate the EEC
as a counterweight stimulated the consideration of means to tighten
ties with ASEAN, [146] and now the governmental ties have been reinforced by the ASEAN-Japan Economic Council, which joins the private-sector organizations of the six countries in an effort to promote
cooperation in investment and technology transfer. [147] At the same
time as the relationship with Japan seems to have failed ASEAN expectations, most of the members have increased their efforts to promote investment from Japan, leading to the conclusion that the shift
toward Europe is as much aimed at increasing bargaining leverage
with Japan as it is at actually changing the pattern of investment.

Meetings with the United States have had almost no results outside the field of investment. The first, in 1977, produced only a
minor tax concession of interest to ASEAN, [148] while the second meeting, in 1978, resulted in a mission to the region to reassess the investment climate and, ultimately, in the convening of an ASEAN-U. S.
Business Council. [149] The latter private-sector conference, similar
to those with the EEC and Australia, produced a number of joint-venture proposals and an organization to promote investment from the
United States. [150] The relationship with the United States has been
muted, according to one informant, because the United States is ap-
prehensive about the possibility of transferring the stigma of the
Southeast Asia Treaty Organization to ASEAN. [151] Future economic
relations will apparently remain the preserve of private business.

A regional policy of potential significance for investment is currently being debated. Proposals for the establishment of common
incentives and policies on foreign investment are working their way
through the regional mechanism. First appearing on the agenda of
the Second Heads of Government Meeting in Kuala Lumpur in 1977,
but dropped from the final communiqué, [152] the proposal was passed
to the economic ministers and considered in both 1977 and 1978 without
resolution. [153] The idea is supported by Malaysia as an element
strengthening national bargaining power and reflecting a stronger
ASEAN position in attracting investment from the industrial countries;[154] several private-sector organizations have also added their
approval. [155] The issue is now being considered by ASEAN economic
planners in the form of pilot guidelines for investment in industrial-
complementation projects as a preliminary step to a general set of
common policies. [156] According to one observer, [157] the economic
ministers favor the proposal while the foreign ministers are uncon-
vinced, but the governments are unwilling to expand the cost of the
ASEAN secretariat to cover this new area. Now that private-sector
plans for the ASEAN Investment Corporation to fund regional projects
have been carried through, [158] this may add impetus to the harmonization of policy on investments.

The focus of policy regarding the control of foreign investment, then, has shifted from domestic regulation toward a diversification strategy. Increasing the benefits for domestic interests through closer control of foreign investment in various sectors of the economy and through mandated joint partnership arrangements has characterized each ASEAN country, with the exception of Singapore. However, this manifestation of economic nationalism has had serious effects on the flow of investment as the footloose industries looked elsewhere for less restrictive platforms. Especially with the shift to export industrialization, the ASEAN countries have sought higher flows of investment to satisfy national aspirations for economic growth. Diversification of investment sources has emerged as a policy strategy that allows the pool of foreign investment to grow while minimizing the potential political effects. It is this policy that has emerged as the focus of control in the ASEAN area, with the ASEAN organization being used to contribute to its furtherance.

However, a primary criticism of developing countries is that they are unable to implement their policies, particularly in relation to the industrialized states, as a result of being "soft states" or dependencies. Thus, an examination of policy is only preliminary to determining a shift in reality. If diversification is being pursued effectively, it should be reflected in actual patterns of foreign investment over time, and it is to this that I now turn.

INVESTMENT PATTERNS:
TOWARD DIVERSIFICATION?

The analysis of the pattern-of-investment sources informs conclusions as to whether policies have been effective in sponsoring diversification as a defensive political strategy. As in the case of trade, three particular questions are addressed. First, has there been progress in balancing the relative positions of the major investment partners, so that none accrues an advantage due to excessive concentration? For this condition to be met effectively, no more than one-third of total foreign investment should come from a single source, and at least one other investor should be in a position to balance the major one. Second, has the overall position of the three major investing areas receded, reducing the degree of sensitivity to the major industrial nations? Third, has the pattern of investment become more diversified in general, as indicated by Hirschman's index of concentration?

There are difficulties in attempting to analyze foreign investment data for the ASEAN countries. Aside from the problem of obtaining data that are consistent over time, the several governments collect slightly different forms of data. Indonesia, Thailand, and the Philippines indicate investment intended at the date of approval of the investment proposal, which may not actually be transferred later in the same amount. Malaysia indicates registered equity, but has kept these records since the initiation of company registration in 1975; earlier data are not strictly comparable. Singapore presents gross fixed assets, but does not publish a complete breakdown by source country; some figures have to be interpolated through comparison of different published data sets. Thus, while the data for each state are internally consistent, some reflect intentions rather than realized capital, imposing a limitation on crossnational comparison. Since the primary purpose is to examine changes in the relative roles of foreign investors in each country's investment pool, the data are sufficient; crossnational comparisons, however, can be only approximate.

The data used here derive from the government agencies responsible for investment: the Board of Investments for Thailand, Indonesia, and the Philippines;[159] the Malaysian Industrial Development Authority; the Economic Development Board of Singapore. Tables 5.2 through 5.6 present the data for each ASEAN country by percentage distribution of investment sources for as long a time span as availability of data permits. The regions and the calculation of the index of dispersion are identical to those used in discussing trade (see Chapter 4).

Investment in Indonesia has remained relatively concentrated on a few sources. The reversal of Sukarno's policy of expropriation by the Suharto regime led to the return of foreign investors after 1967. Starting from a base of almost zero (British investments were returned and all U.S. investments had not been nationalized), the initial investment was even more concentrated on U.S. sources than had been true for the prewar Dutch dependence. Thus, relatively small investments from new partners result in large changes in proportional standing among the lesser partners, especially up through 1970. The predominant position of the United States was steadily eroded with the inflow of Japanese investment in the mid-1970s. Aside from the dominant role of Japan, the only other investors of significance are those from the United States and new textile investments from Hong Kong and Taiwan (NICS in Table 5.2). Indonesia is heavily concentrated on Japan specifically and on the large industrial countries generally, and it shows little general diversification. This is equally evident when the comparison is made starting from 1970, when a sufficient pool of investment had accumulated to moderate large proportional changes due to relatively small increments of new investment. Indonesia has not diversified, except to exchange a preponderant U.S. role for a dominant Japanese one.

Malaysia's pattern of foreign investment underwent large changes prior to 1975, when regular statistics became available. For

TABLE 5.2

Indonesia: Cumulative Foreign Investment, Percentage Distribution

	1967	1968	1969	1970	1971	1972	1973	1974	1975	1976
Large industrial	91.7	60.6	57.8	58.80	55.10	58.1	58.80	62.20	69.10	67.30
United States	82.5	43.1	39.9	37.10	30.70	35.5	30.00	22.30	18.10	17.40
European Economic Community	7.2	12.5	6.0	8.50	7.90	6.8	6.90	12.40	10.10	10.10
Japan	2.0	5.0	12.0	13.20	16.40	15.8	21.80	27.60	40.90	39.80
Small industrial	0.8	33.2	14.0	14.70	21.40	20.7	22.80	23.20	19.00	21.10
Canada	—	18.3	6.7	5.40	4.40	3.4	2.80	2.00	1.60	1.50
Other Western Europe	—	1.3	0.7	1.80	1.40	1.2	1.20	1.80	1.50	1.40
Australasia	0.6	0.3	0.4	0.80	6.30	5.1	5.40	4.50	3.70	3.50
Newly industrialized countries	0.2	13.3	6.2	6.70	9.30	10.9	13.30	14.90	12.20	14.60
Third World	5.0	2.1	1.0	0.90	1.30	1.9	2.10	1.80	1.60	1.60
Latin America	5.0	2.1	1.0	0.90	1.30	1.3	1.20	0.90	0.70	0.70
Africa	—	—	—	—	—	—	0.02	0.01	0.01	0.01
South Asia	—	—	—	0.04	0.03	0.6	0.80	0.90	0.90	0.90
Socialist	—	—	—	—	—	—	—	—	0.10	0.06
ASEAN	2.5	4.0	27.3	25.50	22.30	19.4	16.40	12.80	10.20	9.90
Philippines	2.5	2.2	22.6	18.60	14.90	12.0	10.20	7.60	6.00	5.80
Singapore	—	1.6	3.0	4.50	4.00	4.3	3.60	3.30	2.60	2.60
Malaysia	—	0.2	1.4	2.10	2.40	2.3	1.90	1.40	1.20	1.10
Thailand	—	—	0.3	0.30	1.00	0.7	0.60	0.50	0.40	0.30
Total	100.0	100.0	100.0	100.00	100.00	100.0	100.00	100.00	100.00	100.00
Geographical dispersion index	83.0	50.6	48.8	45.50	40.80	43.4	42.00	41.70	48.10	47.60
Annual growth rate	—	136.8	175.1	22.80	26.20	27.5	22.10	37.30	26.50	4.80

Source: Board of Investments, Jakarta, Indonesia. Excludes petroleum, banking, and insurance.

TABLE 5.3

Malaysia: Cumulative Foreign Investment, Percentage Distribution

	1975	1976	1977	1968[a]
Large industrial	48. 70	53.2	53.20	58.5
United States	11.40	12.3	10.40	15.0
European Economic Community	17.70	19.1	22.70	42.2
Japan	19.60	21.8	20.10	1.3
Small industrial	19.60	17.4	16.90	—
Canada	1.00	1.2	0.50	—
Other Western Europe	2.30	2.3	1.60	—
Australasia	2.40	2.4	2.60	—
Newly industrializing countries	13.90	11.6	12.10	10.0[b]
Third World	3.70	3.7	3.80	—
Latin America	1.70	1.6	1.70	—
South Asia	2.00	2.2	2.20	—
ASEAN	28.00	25.7	26.20	—
Indonesia	0.10	0.1	0.05	—
Philippines	0.07	0.2	0.10	—
Singapore	27.60	25.0	25.90	22.1
Thailand	0.20	0.2	0.10	—
Total	100.00	100.0	100.00	90.6
Geographical dispersion index	42.40	42.2	43.20	50.9
Annual growth rate	—	23.6	32.00	—

[a]For comparison only.
[b]Estimate.

Sources: Malaysian Industrial Development Authority, Kuala Lumpur (1975, 1976, 1977); and Census of Manufacturing Industries (Kuala Lumpur: Government Printers, 1968).

purposes of rough comparison, the distribution as indicated by the
1968 Census of Manufacturing Industries is included in Table 5.3.[160]
Although the statistics are not precisely comparable, two points are
apparent. First, the position of British investment (almost all of that
under EEC) was still large in 1968, but the former colonial tie was
almost gone by 1975. Second, Japanese investments have largely occurred in the 1970s, without becoming more than a counterweight to
remaining British investment. Other sources of investment appear
relatively stable, with Singapore becoming the largest source of investment once the British share declined. Since 1975 investment in
Malaysia has become slightly more concentrated on the large industrial nations, but with three roughly equal major investors, no pattern of dependence is apparent—a large change from 1968.

Foreign investment in the Philippines has become more evenly
spread among several sources, as shown in Table 5.4. Steady erosion of the U.S. role through newly important investments from Hong
Kong (NIC) and Japan have provided three roughly equal investment
partners, erasing the vestiges of U.S. colonialism.[161] The result
is a significant degree of diversification of particular partners, but
still a high degree of concentration on the major industrial countries
for investment. The Philippines has changed from being quite dependent on a single, foreign investment source to not being exces-
sively vulnerable to anyone, but it is still quite sensitive to large industrial partners.

Singapore has reduced the relative role of its single largest investment source, the EEC, but it draws almost all of its investment
from the large industrial countries (see Table 5.5). The EEC still
plays the largest role, but it has been balanced by the United States,
while Asian countries together provide an equivalent proportion of
investment. The inflow of U.S. investment during the 1970s resulted
in an extremely high level of sensitivity to the large industrial nations
for foreign investment. General diversification of sources has been
steady but moderate in effect. Despite the trend toward greater diversification, the level of concentration is relatively high, contra-
dicting the image put forward by Singapore of a high degree of geographical diversification; figures published by the EDB foster the
misleading idea of close balance by dividing the whole into nearly
equal portions for North America, the EEC, and Asia. Nevertheless,
an earlier dependence on the EEC has been changed through diversification to other large industrial countries.

As shown in Table 5.6, Thailand is consistently dependent on
Japan for its investment. The relative position of that single source
changed little during the 1970s, although 1975 saw a peak in concentration, which declined somewhat thereafter. This small reduction
in specific partner concentration appears to have been the result of

TABLE 5.4

Philippines: Cumulative Foreign Investment, Percentage Distribution

	1968	1969	1970	1971	1972	1973	1974	1975	1976	1977
Large industrial	60.70	64.8	61.10	36.80	47.70	57.50	66.80	64.60	64.30	59.70
United States	59.00	60.4	55.40	32.40	40.20	41.30	30.10	29.70	30.90	29.80
European Economic Community	0.01	2.6	3.80	1.90	3.50	9.50	10.80	10.00	9.80	8.70
Japan	1.70	1.8	1.90	2.50	4.00	6.70	25.90	24.90	23.60	21.30
Small industrial	1.20	5.9	6.50	46.80	37.70	29.30	23.80	26.90	28.10	32.40
Canada	—	—	0.01	0.05	1.60	1.10	2.70	2.40	2.10	1.80
Other Western Europe	—	0.5	0.40	0.20	1.00	0.80	2.20	2.30	5.10	4.50
Australasia	—	—	—	—	0.02	0.10	2.20	3.50	4.30	3.80
Newly industrializing countries	1.20	5.4	6.10	46.60	35.10	27.20	16.70	18.70	16.70	22.40
Third World	—	—	0.30	0.20	0.20	0.60	0.80	0.90	0.80	0.70
Latin America	—	—	—	—	—	0.40	0.50	0.60	0.50	0.40
South Asia	—	—	0.30	0.20	0.20	0.20	0.30	0.30	0.30	0.30
West Asia	—	—	—	—	—	—	0.01	0.01	0.01	0.01
ASEAN	—	—	—	—	—	0.01	0.30	0.30	0.30	0.30
Indonesia	—	—	—	—	—	—	—	—	<.01	<.01
Singapore	—	—	—	—	—	0.01	0.20	0.20	0.20	0.20
Thailand	—	—	—	—	—	—	0.05	0.10	0.10	0.10
Not specified	38.10	29.3	32.10	16.30	14.40	12.50	8.30	7.30	6.50	6.90
Total	100.00	100.0	100.00	100.00	100.00	100.00	100.00	100.00	100.00	100.00
Geographical dispersion index	61.40	62.1	57.70	57.30	54.10	51.10	44.80	44.60	44.10	44.40
Annual growth rate	—	119.0	44.90	169.20	37.00	47.10	85.10	14.90	17.40	16.30

Source: Board of Investments, Manila, Republic of the Philippines.

TABLE 5.5

Singapore: Cumulative Foreign Investment, Percentage Distribution

	1967	1968	1969	1970	1971	1972	1973	1974	1975	1976	1977	1978
Large industrial	68.0	59.9	65.7	82.1	77.8	80.6	80.5	79.6	79.4	80.1	80.2	82.2
United States	8.9	11.7	21.8	34.5	31.8	36.8	37.3	35.4	33.1	33.0	33.0	30.5
European Economic												
Community	48.8	40.7	37.8	40.8	39.1	37.8	34.3	32.6	32.8	33.1	31.9	36.4
Japan	10.2	7.5	6.0	6.8	6.9	6.0	8.9	11.6	13.4	14.0	15.3	15.3
Small industrial	n.a.	n.a.	n.a.	n.a.	22.2	19.4	19.5	20.4	20.7	19.9	19.8	17.8
Canada	n.a.	n.a.	n.a.	n.a.	0.3	0.3	0.3	0.3	0.3	0.3	0.3	0.2
Other Western Europe	n.a.	n.a.	n.a.	n.a.	1.6	1.6	1.6	1.2	1.8	1.8	2.0	1.9
Other Asia*	n.a.	n.a.	n.a.	n.a.	20.3	17.5	17.6	18.8	18.6	17.8	17.5	15.7
Not specified	32.0	40.1	34.3	17.9	0.0	0.0	0.0	0.0	0.0	0.0	0.0	0.0
Total	100.0	100.0	100.0	100.0	100.0	100.0	100.0	100.0	100.0	100.0	100.0	100.0
Geographical dispersion												
index	59.9	58.8	55.8	56.8	54.8	55.9	54.4	53.0	52.0	52.0	51.5	52.3
Annual growth rate	—	49.8	32.2	65.8	58.3	44.9	16.5	14.9	10.7	10.6	10.9	26.5

n.a. = not available

*Includes Australasia, South Asia, newly industrializing countries, and ASEAN.

Source: Economic Development Board, Singapore.

TABLE 5.6

Thailand: Cumulative Foreign Investment, Percentage Distribution

	1970	1971	1974*	1975	1976*	1977	1978*
Large industrial	62.4	62.9	64.3	62.6	63.2	62.6	63.0
United States	18.1	17.0	16.2	13.8	15.4	15.6	15.4
European Economic Community	11.1	10.6	10.8	10.4	10.3	12.3	12.8
Japan	33.2	35.3	37.3	38.4	37.5	34.7	34.8
Small industrial	17.5	19.1	19.2	20.4	20.4	22.5	22.3
Other Western Europe	1.7	1.6	1.4	2.6	2.5	2.7	2.6
Australasia	0.6	0.6	0.6	0.5	0.5	0.7	0.7
Newly industrializing countries	15.3	16.9	16.0	17.3	17.3	19.2	19.0
Third World	1.8	2.4	2.1	4.1	4.0	5.2	5.2
Latin America	0.3	0.9	0.7	0.8	0.8	1.4	1.4
South Asia	1.2	1.2	1.0	1.3	1.2	1.5	1.5
West Asia	0.3	0.3	0.5	2.0	2.0	2.3	2.3
ASEAN	5.7	5.8	5.4	4.3	4.0	4.6	4.5
Indonesia	0.2	0.2	—	—	—	—	—
Malaysia	3.7	3.9	3.6	2.6	2.6	2.8	2.8
Singapore	1.1	1.1	1.3	1.2	1.0	1.3	1.3
Philippines	0.7	0.6	0.5	0.5	0.5	0.5	0.5
Not specified	12.5	9.8	9.0	8.6	8.5	5.0	5.0
Total	100.0	100.0	100.0	100.0	100.0	100.0	100.0
Geographical dispersion index	42.5	44.2	45.2	45.8	45.5	44.7	44.7
Annual growth rate	—	2.6	10.1	18.7	4.2	-9.1	4.5

*1974 as of January 31; 1976 as of June 30; 1978 as of March 31; all others as of December 31.

Source: Board of Investments, Bangkok, Thailand.

an increased flow of investment from the NICs, now Thailand's second most important source of foreign investment. The level of concentration on the large industrial nations has been consistently high. Overall concentration has increased by a small amount. Thailand has not diversified its investment sources, and it remains potentially vulnerable to Japan as the largest single source.

EFFECTIVENESS OF POLICIES ON INVESTMENT

In general, there has been some progress toward diversification of foreign investment sources. Specific partner vulnerabilities have been reduced for several countries, and only Thailand has failed to reduce the concentration of foreign investment sources from the earliest date to the latest for which there were data available. At the same time, most of the countries drew more of their investment from the large industrial countries over time. Comparing the foreign investment data with the policies should clarify these changes.

Indonesian policies have had only a marginal effect. The ambivalent attitude toward Japan has not curtailed increasing dependence on this source of investment. There has been a small growth in sources intended to balance Japan, the EEC, and the NICs, but not enough to fulfill the objective. To be fair, Indonesian concern has continued beyond the last date for which data were available, and further changes may have occurred. Nevertheless, all forms of concentration of sources of investment were less in 1976 than in 1967. But despite a fear of compromising its foreign policy autonomy through such concentration, Indonesia remains heavily dependent on the large Western industrial nations for investment and is potentially quite vulnerable to Japan.

Malaysian policies have been quite effective in reducing the role of the former colonial power and in achieving the most diversified pattern of foreign investment in ASEAN. Recent concern over the rising role of Japan has stimulated a renewed drive to diversify, which is too recent to evaluate, but this is hardly a problem compared with the other ASEAN states. Malaysia is neither heavily concentrated on the largest industrial countries nor particularly dependent on any one of them for its sources of foreign investment.

Philippine policies of diversification have met with considerable success. The predominant position of the United States was substantially eroded, both before and after martial law, and the secondary target, Japan, has also lost relative ground as a source of foreign investment. Policies to attract investment from the EEC have showed some results, although small in effect on the overall balance. Japan and the NICs have become credible counterweights to the United States

as sources of investment. The Philippines should no longer be seen
as overly dependent on the United States in investment relations, a
large change from the situation in the late 1960s.

Singapore has also been relatively effective in fostering diversification. The predominant role of the EEC has been progressively
eroded and balanced by the United States, while policies intended to
draw in Japan as an investment partner have shown less success so
far, but they are the major current focus. A substantial role for the
smaller Asian countries has been maintained, one of the goals of policies in the 1970s. The EEC remains Singapore's largest source of
investment, yet not a dominant one. At the same time, the effects of
policy should not be overestimated; Singapore remains the least diversified ASEAN country and the most concentrated on the large industrial countries.

Thai concern over the role of Japan has had only marginal effects. Increasing concentration up through 1975 was reversed by a
small amount thereafter, which corresponds to the peak of domestic
agitation against Japan. A small growth in investments coming from
the EEC is also apparent but not enough to balance the role of Japan.
Some general diversification has taken place since 1975 as well, but
not enough to compensate for increasing concentration prior to that
date. Since there is no apparent government policy, these changes
cannot be related to effectiveness. Thailand is almost as dependent
on Japan as is Indonesia, and like Indonesia, has not effectively dealt
with what is recognized as a problem.

LIMITATIONS ON DIVERSIFICATION

Some of the ASEAN countries have made progress toward diversifying their sources of foreign investment. Those with specific
government policies to achieve this goal—Singapore, Malaysia, and
the Philippines—have produced results; Indonesia's vacillation between
political concern and pragmatic acceptance and Thailand's political
concern but lack of policy have been associated with little or no progress toward diversification. Government policies, then, would appear to be a major variable in achieving a wider range of sources of
foreign investment.

However, the major form of diversification has been related to
the relative roles of the few largest sources. In 1967 each of the
ASEAN countries was dependent on a single foreign source, often the
former colonial power. This has changed through balancing the former
dominant partner with one other in Singapore, Malaysia, and the
Philippines, while Indonesia exchanged a large U.S. role for a slightly
smaller Japanese one. Although each of the ASEAN countries but

Thailand shows some diversification to a wider global community, each has also either maintained or increased relative concentration on the large industrial countries: close to two-thirds or more for all but Malaysia and the Philippines. An important limitation on diversification is that there are only a few large capital-exporting countries, especially for relatively advanced-technology projects.

Another limitation stems from domestic regulation of foreign investment. Each ASEAN country, except Singapore, has attempted to increase the ownership of its nationals, although with varied success; Malaysia and Thailand have done so, while Indonesia and the Philippines appear not to have. All five have regulated the terms of foreign participation with increasing vigor to meet their domestic economic goals. Planned divestment of foreign control[162] and closer government regulation unsettle potential foreign investors, who are closely concerned about the stability of the "investment climate" in host countries. Published ratings of the ASEAN countries by investment analysts[163] rank them roughly in the reverse order of the extent of regulation: Singapore is highest, Malaysia lower, followed by the Philippines, Thailand, and Indonesia. These ratings are issued to guide prospective investors, and they do not necessarily determine the actual flow of capital. Still, domestic regulation has a negative effect on the ability of these countries to attract the kind and volume of capital considered desirable, and less choice results in less bargaining advantage over terms. This tension between the desire to regulate more closely and the desire to maintain an attractive image in the investment market was quite evident in the mid-1970s, when global recession dampened the flow of capital, causing several of the ASEAN states to moderate their regulations and to increase overseas promotional activities.

It is in order to circumvent these limitations that diversification has become more attractive as a strategy. Not only does diversification serve the political goal of reducing the potential influence of economic partners, but in the case of investment, it also allows an increased flow of foreign investment by tapping a larger market. In a global system characterized in investment relations by oligopoly and hostility to regulation, diversification can be achieved through government policy.

NOTES

    1. ASEAN Briefing 10 (May 1979).
    2. V. Kanapathy, "Investments in ASEAN: Perspectives and Prospects," United Malayan Banking Corporation, Economic Review 15 (1979): 19.

3. Indonesia, 1972; Malaysia, 1976; Philippines, 1975; Singapore, 1975; and Thailand, 1975. Indonesia and Singapore manufacturing investment: John Wong, ASEAN Economies in Perspective (Philadelphia: Institute for the Study of Human Issues, 1979), p. 178; Bangkok, Thailand and Manila, Philippines: Boards of Investments; Malaysia: Malaysia, Federal Industrial Development Authority, Annual Report, 1977 (Kuala Lumpur: Government Printers, 1978), p. 224 (Pioneer companies). It should be pointed out that comparisons of this nature are indicative only, as the basis of national statistics varies too widely to allow close comparison.

4. The literature on multinational corporations is quite large, but concise summaries are contained in David Blake and Robert Walters, The Politics of Global Economic Relations (Englewood Cliffs, N.J.: Prentice-Hall, 1976), pp. 76-126; and Elizabeth Smythe, "Foreign Investment, Foreign Policy and Interstate Relations: Towards a Propositional Inventory" (Paper delivered to the International Studies Association, Los Angeles, March 1980). Standard works include Raymond Vernon, Sovereignty at Bay (New York: Basic Books, 1971); Jack Behrman, National Interests and the Multinational Enterprise (Englewood Cliffs, N.J.: Prentice-Hall, 1970); Richard Barnet and Ronald Müller, Global Reach (New York: Simon & Schuster, 1974); and Robert Gilpin, U.S. Power and the Multinational Corporation (New York: Basic Books, 1975).

5. Jon Halliday and Gavin McCormack, Japanese Imperialism Today (New York: Monthly Review Press, 1973), pp. 31–49; and Raul S. Manglapus, Japan in Southeast Asia: Collision Course (New York: Carnegie Endowment for International Peace, 1976), pp. 5–23.

6. Franklin Weinstein, "Multinational Corporations and the Third World: The Case of Japan and Southeast Asia," International Organization 30 (Summer 1976): 373-404, quote at 378.

7. Buu Hoan, "Asia Needs a New Approach to the Multinationals," in ASEAN and a Positive Strategy for Foreign Investment, ed. Lloyd Vasey (Honolulu: University Press of Hawaii, 1978); Donald Sherk, "Foreign Investment in Southeast Asia: A Reconsideration," in Conflict and Stability in Southeast Asia, ed. M. W. Zacher and R. S. Milne (Garden City, N.Y.: Anchor Books, 1974); Wong, ASEAN Economies; Thomas Allen, "Policies of ASEAN Countries toward Direct Foreign Investment," in Asian Business and Environment in Transition, ed. A. Karpoor (Princeton, N.J.: Darwin Press, 1976).

8. Barnet and Müller, Global Reach, pp. 195, 203.

9. Quoted in the Mirror, May 27, 1974, in an address to the Singapore International Chamber of Commerce.

10. This "ratings game" is formalized in international business reports comparing national investment climates. See Thomas Allen,

ASEAN Report, vol. 1 (Hong Kong: Dow-Jones, 1979), pp. 142-43; and Business International Asia/Pacific, reported in Christian Science Monitor, September 20, 1979.

11. Helmut Callis, Foreign Capital in Southeast Asia (New York: Institute of Pacific Relations, 1942), p. 34. British holdings were about 14 percent and U. S. 7 percent in 1937.

12. Mohammad Sadli, "Foreign Investment in Developing Countries: Indonesia," in Direct Foreign Investment in Asia and the Pacific, ed. Peter Drysdale (Toronto: University of Toronto Press, 1972), pp. 202-3.

13. "Nevertheless this principle of relying on our own capacity should not lead to reluctance to make use of foreign capital, technology and skill, so long as these are truly devoted to serving the economic interests of the people without causing dependence on foreign countries." Law 1 of 1967, Preamble; and Richard Robinson, "Toward a Class Analysis of the Indonesian Military Bureaucratic State," Indonesia 25 (April 1978): 17-39.

14. The Indonesian interests are to become majority partners within 10 years, from an actual ownership of 20 percent: Indonesian Investment Focus (August 1979).

15. Indonesia Development News 2 (October 1978); and the "third generation" mining contracts have unsettled prospective investors: Far Eastern Economic Review, February 1, 1980, pp. 51-52.

16. Sadli, "Foreign Investment in Developing Countries," p. 215.

17. Barli Halim, quoted in Straits Times, February 16, 1977.

18. Wong, ASEAN Economies, pp. 59-60.

19. Asia Research Bulletin, March 31, 1979, p. 544; Indonesia Development News 2 (June 1979); and Kuhn Loeb Lehman Brothers International, Lazard Frères et al., and S. G. Warburg & Co., Ltd., The Republic of Indonesia (1979), p. 21.

20. Calculated from Indonesia Development News 3 (March 1980).

21. From a flow of approximately $500 million in 1975 to less than $300 million in 1978: "Indonesian Survey," supplement to Euromoney, January 1979, p. 4.

22. Asia Yearbook, 1978 (Hong Kong: Far Eastern Economic Review, 1979), p. 206. Presidential decrees in 1977 (numbers 53, 54) streamlined the bureaucratic procedures for processing investment and modified the incentives offered, both in an attempt to strengthen the investment climate.

23. ASEAN Briefing 10 (May 1979).

24. J. Panglaykim, "Economic Cooperation: Indonesian-Japanese Joint Ventures," Asian Survey 18 (March 1978): 247-60; Steven Kohlhagen, "Host Country Policies and the Flow of Direct Foreign Investment in the ASEAN Countries," in International Business in the Pacific Basin, ed. Hal Mason (Toronto: D. C. Heath, 1978), pp. 100-1.

25. Far Eastern Economic Review, March 10, 1978, pp. 45–47.

26. Asia Research Bulletin, July 31, 1979, p. 587.

27. Charles Morrison, "Southeast Asia in a Changing International Environment: A comparative Foreign Policy Analysis of Four ASEAN-Member Countries" (Ph.D. diss., Johns Hopkins University, 1976), pp. 277–87; and Weinstein, "Multinational Corporations and the Third World."

28. The date 1969 was suggested as the origin of this concern. Author interview, Indonesian Embassy, Ottawa, May 1980.

29. Soedjatmoko, "Problems and Prospects for Development in Indonesia," Asia 19 (Autumn 1970): 20–21.

30. New Nation, July 15, 1974.

31. Author interview, Indonesian Embassy, Ottawa, May 1980.

32. H. S. Kartadjoemena, The Politics of External Economic Relations: Indonesia's Options in the Post-Détente Era (Singapore: Institute of Southeast Asian Studies, 1977), p. 112; and Far Eastern Economic Review, February 23, 1979, pp. 37–39.

33. Indonesia Development News 2 (September 1978).

34. Louis Wells and V'Ella Warren, "Developing Country Investors in Indonesia," Bulletin of Indonesian Economic Studies 15 (March 1979): 69–84.

35. "Indonesian Survey," supplement to Euromoney, January 1979, p. 10.

36. Callis, Foreign Capital, p. 52.

37. Nikar Sarkar, Foreign Investment and Economic Development in Asia (Bombay: Orient Longman, 1976), table 5.2, p. 90; and Jayaratnam Saravanamuttu, "A Study of the Content, Sources, and Development of Malaysian Foreign Policy, 1957-1975" (Ph.D. diss., University of British Columbia, 1976), pp. 48–57.

38. Tun Ismail, quoted in Far Eastern Economic Review, August 29, 1975 (referring to petroleum).

39. Tengku Razaleigh, Straits Times (Malaysia), July 7, 1975.

40. Wong, ASEAN Economies, pp. 62–67; and P. Arudsothy, "Malaysia," in The Economic Development of East and Southeast Asia, ed. Shinici Ichimura (Honolulu: University Press of Hawaii, 1975), pp. 116–17.

41. Malaysia, Third Malaysia Plan, 1976–1980 (Kuala Lumpur: Government Printers, 1976), p. 275.

42. Foreign Affairs Malaysia 8 (December 1975): 60–68.

43. Malaysia, Third Malaysia Plan, p. 56.

44. Malaysia, Second Malaysia Plan, 1971–1975 (Kuala Lumpur: Government Printers, 1971), p. 92.

45. The effectiveness of Malaysian and Singaporean free-trade zones have stimulated a "second generation" of imitations in the region: Far Eastern Economic Review, May 18, 1979, pp. 76–78; and

the United Nations Industrial Development Organization (UNIDO) singled out Malaysia of all the countries it surveyed as the only one where
industrial estates made a "major contribution" to industrialization
and employment: UNIDO, The Effectiveness of Industrial Estates in
Developing Countries (New York: UNIDO, 1978), pp. 10-11.

46. Malaysia, Third Malaysia Plan, p. 86.

47. On investment policies, see Allen, "Policies of ASEAN
Countries"; Kohlhagen, "Host Country Policies," pp. 101-2; and the
author also conducted interviews with Malaysian Industrial Development Authority officials to clarify several points.

48. From 1968 until April 1979 the agency was known as the
Federal Industrial Development Authority (FIDA).

49. Malaysia, Federal Industrial Development Authority, Annual Report, 1977 (Kuala Lumpur: Government Printers, 1978), p.
172.

50. On the New Economic Policy, see R. S. Milne, "The Politics of Malaysia's New Economic Policy," Pacific Affairs 49 (Summer 1976): 235-62; and R. S. Milne and Diane Mauzy, Politics and
Government in Malaysia (Vancouver: University of British Columbia
Press, 1978), pp. 321-51.

51. Malaysia, Second Malaysia Plan, p. 40.

52. Straits Times (Malaysia), February 21, 1974.

53. Asia Research Bulletin, July 31, 1978, p. 468; and 30 percent of equity must be reserved for Malay ownership; in 1976 and 1977
more than 40 percent was actually reserved: Malaysia, Annual Report, 1977, p. 183.

54. The share of Malay individuals is expected to remain quite
small, only 7.4 percent in 1990, leaving 22.6 percent for government
investment funds: Third Malaysia Plan, p. 87; however in 1976 private interests took up just over 50 percent of joint venture bumiputra
shares: Malaysia, Annual Report, 1977, p. 183.

55. R. S. Milne, "The Politics of Malaysia's New Economic
Policy," pp. 243-50.

56. Malaysia, Third Malaysia Plan, p. 184; and lagging Chinese
investment led to an increase in the planned foreign share for 1976-
80: Linda Lim, "The Political Economy of Foreign Investment in
Malaysia" (Paper presented to the Association for Asian Studies,
Washington, D.C., March 1980), p. 14.

57. Malaysia, Third Malaysia Plan, p. 273.

58. Tun Razak, reported in Straits Times (Malaysia), February
21, 1974.

59. By late 1979, 70 percent to 80 percent of firms were registered: author interview, Malaysian Industrial Development Authority,
October 1979. See Asia Research Bulletin, May 31, 1975, pp. 87-
88; June 30, 1975 p. 98; July 31, 1977, pp. 345-48; and Milne and
Mauzy, Politics and Government, pp. 344-41.

60. Louis Kraar and Stephen Blank, "Malaysia: The High Cost of Affirmative Action," Asia (March/April 1980), pp. 6-9.

61. Malaysia, Annual Report, 1977, pp. 153, 157; and Far Eastern Economic Review, August 3, 1979, pp. 36-37.

62. See the report on Minister of Trade and Industry Datuk Hamzah giving such assurances to Swiss investors in Malaysian Digest, October 15, 1977, p. 4.

63. ASEAN Briefing 16 (November 1979); Far Eastern Economic Review, August 3, 1979, pp. 36-37; and Milne and Mauzy, Politics and Government, pp. 348-50.

64. Asian Wall Street Journal, September 6, 1979.

65. Far Eastern Economic Review, June 16, 1978, pp. 46-47, and February 23, 1979, pp. 41-44; and Tadoyoshi Yamada, "Foreign Investment in the ASEAN Region," in ASEAN and a Positive Strategy for Foreign Investment, ed. Lloyd Vasey (Honolulu: University Press of Hawaii, 1978), p. 106.

66. Author interview, Malaysian Industrial Development Authority, October 1979.

67. Malaysia, Third Malaysia Plan, p. 89.

68. Callis, Foreign Capital, p. 22 (1936). Another 20 percent was from Spain.

69. See Renato Constantino and Letizia Constantino, The Philippines: The Continuing Past (Quezon City: Foundation for Nationalist Studies, 1978), pp. 269-311; Teodora Agoncillo and Milagros Guerrero, History of the Filipino People, 5th ed. (Quezon City: R. P. Garcia, 1977), pp. 563-68; Amado Castro, ed., "The Philippines," in The Economic Development of East and Southeast Asia, ed. Shimichi Ichimura (Honolulu: University Press of Hawaii, 1975), pp. 181-82, 221-22; and David Rosenberg, ed., Marcos and Martial Law in the Philippines (Ithaca, N.Y.: Cornell University Press, 1979), p. 290.

70. Ferdinand Marcos, "Redefining the Role of Foreign Investment in a Developing Economy," in ASEAN and A Positive Strategy for Foreign Investment, ed. Lloyd Vasey (Honolulu: University Press of Hawaii, 1978), p. 48.

71. See, for example, Robert Stauffer, "The Political Economy of a Coup: Transnational Linkages and Philippine Political Response," Journal of Peace Research 11 (1974): 161-77.

72. Cesar Virata, "Foreign Investment in Developing Countries: The Philippines," in Direct Foreign Investment in Asia and the Pacific, ed. John Drysdale (Toronto: University of Toronto Press, 1972), p. 259.

73. World Bank, The Philippines: Priorities and Prospects for Development (Washington, D.C.: World Bank, 1976); there was a net outflow of $380 million, 1955-70, p. 338.

74. Specific investment areas are listed in the annual "Investment Priorities Plan."

75. In 1977, 70 percent of firms registered for incentives were export-oriented: Board of Investments, Export Bulletin 5 (April 1977); and in 1974 official emphasis shifted to promotion of export industries: Republic of the Philippines, Four-Year Development Plan, FY 1974-1977 (Manila: National Economic and Development Authority, 1973), p. 66.

76. Marcos, "Redefining the Role," p. 48.

77. Investment Incentives Act, 1967; Foreign Business Regulation Act, 1968; and Export Incentives Act, 1970. All were amended by presidential decree in 1973. The policy on joint ventures is set out in Republic of the Philippines, Five-Year Philippine Development Plan, 1978-1982 (Manila: National Economic and Development Authority, 1977), p. 404.

78. Far Eastern Economic Review, February 23, 1979, pp. 52-53.

79. Virata, "Foreign Investment in Developing Countries," p. 259.

80. Republic of the Philippines, Four-Year Development Plan, pp. 42, 69.

81. Calculated from Board of Investments figures.

82. Republic of the Philippines, Five-Year Philippine Development Plan, p. 398.

83. Far Eastern Economic Review, March 10, 1978, pp. 47-48.

84. Mamoru Tsuda, A Preliminary Study of Japanese-Filipino Joint Ventures (Quezon City: Foundation for Nationalist Studies, 1978), pp. 3-7.

85. Board of Investments, Export Bulletin 3 (January 1975); Straits Times, April 4, 1977; Far Eastern Economic Review, February 23, 1979, pp. 52-55; and Asia Week, March 7, 1980, pp. 38-39.

86. Author interview, ASEAN director (Philippines), Manila, October 1979.

87. Marcos announcement, Straits Times (Malaysia), May 3, 1973, and New Nation, May 3, 1973; Board of Investments reports in Export Bulletin (August 1973 to December 1977); and Asia Research Bulletin, May 31, 1978, pp. 443-44.

88. Republic of the Philippines, Five-Year Philippine Development Plan, p. 406.

89. Policy coordinating staff, National Economic and Development Authority, Manila, October 1979.

90. Lim Joo-Jock, "Foreign Investment and Industrialization in Singapore: Adaptive Policies and Responses in an Internationally Competitive Situation," in Foreign Investment in Singapore: Some Broader Economic and Socio-political Ramifications, ed. Lim Joo-Jock (Singa-

pore: Institute of Southeast Asian Studies, 1977), p. 16; the opposition position is from personal discussions with an active member of Barisan.

91. Lee Soo-Ann, Industrialization in Singapore (Melbourne: Longmans, 1973); and Wong, ASEAN Economies, pp. 71-76.

92. Officially, these workers number 40,000, but there are many more working illegally, perhaps as many as 100,000.

93. Chia Siow Yue, "Singapore's Trade Strategy and Industrial Development, with Special Reference to the ASEAN Common Approach to Foreign Economic Policy" (Paper presented to the Tenth Pacific Trade and Development Conference, Canberra, 1979), p. 20.

94. 1963 figures are from Singapore, Economic Development Board (EDB), Annual Report 1963 (Singapore: EDB, 1964), p. 85; and 1972 calculated from Kunio Yoshihara, Foreign Investment and Domestic Response (Singapore: Eastern Universities Press, 1976), table S.10, pp. 244-47.

95. Yoshihara, Foreign Investment, p. 148.

96. The division between local and foreign capital is reflected in their organizations. International companies are represented in the International Chamber of Commerce, while the Chinese Chamber of Commerce is composed of local, smaller, mostly commercial interests: interview with the secretary-general of the Federation of Chambers of Commerce and Industry, Singapore, September 1979.

97. Hwang Peng Yuan, reported in Singapore, Economic Development Board, Annual Report 1977-78 (Singapore: EDB, 1978). An interview with an EDB official confirmed that his role as the head of the EDB's London office had prepared his secondment and that he retained active links to the EDB, Singapore, September 1979.

98. Except for the Singapore government's holdings, which have now been transferred to the administration of Ministry of Finance, Inc.

99. Information on the current policy is drawn from a review of Economic Development Board (EDB) annual reports and from interviews with an official of the EDB, Singapore, September 1979.

100. Chia Siow Yue, "Singapore's Trade Strategy," p. 9.

101. A minimum of Singaporean $250,000 was required. Much of the investment listed as originating in Hong Kong is derived from this program, as many of the owners took residence status in Singapore as insurance against future political developments in Hong Kong: interview, Economic Development Board, Singapore, September 1979.

102. Singaporean $49 million of government funds by mid-1978: Singapore, Annual Report 1977-78, pp. 22-24.

103. Chua Wee Meng, "The Singapore Economy: Past Performance, Current Structure and Future Growth Prospects," in Southeast Asian Affairs, 1977, ed. Kernial Sandhu (Singapore: Institute of Southeast Asian Studies, 1978), pp. 222-23.

104. Far Eastern Economic Review, May 12, 1978, pp. 40-41, and October 19, 1979, pp. 81-83; and Asian Wall Street Journal, September 6, 1979.

105. Interview with the secretary-general of the Singapore Federation of Chambers of Commerce and Industry, Singapore, September 1979.

106. Business Times (Singapore), September 1, 21, 1979.

107. The Philippines has several joint ventures in Indonesia in raw-materials projects; Philippine planners envision considerable economic complementarity with the eastern portion of Indonesia: Board of Investments (Philippines), Export Bulletin 5 (January 1977). Some of these funds may in fact come ultimately from U. S. sources.

108. Interview, Economic Development Board, Singapore, September 1979.

109. Twenty-three from non-European Economic Community Europe, 1 from Canada, 12 from newly industrialized countries, and 19 from Australia; Singapore, Economic Development Board, Major International Companies Manufacturing in Singapore (Singapore: EDB, 1979.

110. Singapore, Economic Development Board, Annual Report, 1977-78, p. 33.

111. Ibid. , two additional Economic Development Board officers were transferred to Japan to support this effort.

112. Labor Minister Ong Pong Boon, Straits Times, October 3, 1973.

113. Lim Joo-Jock, Foreign Investment in Singapore, pp. 10, 218-19.

114. Callis, Foreign Capital, p. 70.

115. James Ingram, Economic Change in Thailand, 1850-1970 (Stanford, Calif.: Stanford University Press, 1971), pp. 229-32; and Ker Sin Tze, Public Enterprise in ASEAN (Singapore: Institute of Southeast Asian Studies, 1978).

116. Prachoom Chomchai, "Thailand," in The Economic Development of East and Southeast Asia, ed. Sinichi Ichimura (Honolulu: University Press of Hawaii, 1975), pp. 140-72; and Wong, ASEAN Economies, pp. 76-79.

117. Ingram, Economic Change, p. 299.

118. Sarkar, Foreign Investment, p. 62.

119. Asia Research Bulletin, September 30, 1978, p. 488, quoting Phisit Pakkassem, director of the National Economic and Social Development Board (Thailand).

120. Figures from the 1960s calculated from Ingram, Economic Change, p. 291; for the 1970s from the Board of Investments data gathered by author; 1970: 33.4 percent, 1974: 30.8 percent, 1977: 27.0 percent, and 1978: 27.4 percent.

121. Details in Allen, "Policies of ASEAN Countries," pp. 77-78.

122. Amnuay Viravan, "Foreign Investment in Developing Countries: Thailand," in Direct Foreign Investment in Asia and the Pacific, ed. Peter Drysdale (Toronto: University of Toronto Press, 1972), p. 234. Amnuay was chairman of the Thai Board of Investments.

123. Weinstein, "Multinational Corporations," pp. 387-96; Canadian Embassy informants say that the laws are often ignored, that delays produce widespread bribery, and that approvals often hinge on factional gain calculations: interview, Bangkok, October 1979.

124. G. A. Marzouk, Economic Development and Policies: Case Study of Thailand (Rotterdam: Rotterdam University Press, 1972), pp. 230-34; Straits Times, January 26, 1977; and Asia Yearbook 1978 (Hong Kong: Far Eastern Economic Review, 1978), p. 326.

125. Straits Times, September 22, 1979; and Asia Research Bulletin, January 31, 1979.

126. Far Eastern Economic Review, February 23, 1979, pp. 52-53.

127. Sarasin Viraphol, Directions in Thai Foreign Policy (Singapore: Institute of Southeast Asian Studies, 1976), pp. 35-36; Seiji Naya and Narongchai Akrasanee, "Thailand's International Economic Relations with Japan and the U.S.: A Study of Trade and Investment Interactions," in Cooperation and Development in the Asia/Pacific Region: Relations between Large and Small Countries, ed. Leslie Castle and Frank Holmes (Tokyo: Japan Economic Research Center, 1976), pp. 94, 121.

128. Amnuay Viravan, "Foreign Investment," pp. 236-37.

129. Far Eastern Economic Review, April 11, 1980, p. 44.

130. Sarasin Viraphol, Thai Foreign Policy, p. 36; and Straits Times, August 26, 1976.

131. Far Eastern Economic Review, February 23, 1979, pp. 51-53.

132. Far Eastern Economic Review, March 10, 1978, p. 39.

133. The most convenient summary of the various dialogues is Association of Southeast Asian Nations, 10 Years ASEAN (Jakarta: ASEAN Secretariat, 1978), pp. 220-29.

134. Far Eastern Economic Review, June 9, 1978, p. 30 (interview with Rajaratnam).

135. Reports on the conference are contained in New Straits Times, August 8, 1977, and August 24, 1978; Straits Times, November 6, 1978; Far Eastern Economic Review, November 24, 1978, pp. 44-47; and Allen, "ASEAN Report," vol. 2, pp. 101-2.

136. This section is based on interviews with Canadian diplomatic personnel in the ASEAN countries and Ottawa and with the Canadian International Development Agency (CIDA) officials in Ottawa; see also CIDA, Industrial Cooperation with Developing Countries (Ottawa: CIDA, 1977).

137. Sinnathamby Rajaratnam, "Opening Address," in Economic Relations between West Asia and Southeast Asia, ed. Lee Soo Ann (Singapore: Institute of Southeast Asian Studies, 1978) (Papers of a conference held November 14-16, 1977); and Far Eastern Economic Review, March 31, 1978, pp. 36-40.

138. Straits Times, April 8, 1977; and Economist, November 25, 1978, p. 60.

139. Reports on the latter conference: ASEAN Business Quarterly 3 (1979): 24-25; V. Kanapathy, "Investments in ASEAN: Perspectives and Prospects," United Malayan Banking Corporation, Economic Review 15 (1979): 29; Far Eastern Economic Review, February 23, 1979, pp. 37-38 and March 16, 1979, p. 117; and Asian Finance (Hong Kong) 5 (April 1979): 18.

140. Far Eastern Economic Review, December 1, 1978, p. 57.

141. "ASEAN and EEC: Working toward a Growth Pact," Asian Finance 5 (February 1979): 113-15.

142. Far Eastern Economic Review, February 23, 1979, p. 37.

143. Far Eastern Economic Review, May 30, 1968, p. 46.

144. So far only a 70 percent share of the Indonesian urea projects has been agreed to, about $300 million of the $1 billion eventually expected: Indonesia Development News 3 (November 1979).

145. Straits Times, August 8, 1977.

146. Asia Research Bulletin, March 31, 1972, p. 823.

147. ASEAN Briefing 18 (January 1980).

148. New Straits Times, July 6, 1977; Malaysian Digest, September 15, 1977; and Far Eastern Economic Review, September 23, 1977, pp. 124-29.

149. U.S., Department of State, Bulletin, September 18, 1978, pp. 19-25; Indonesia Development News 1 (August 1978); and representatives of the Overseas Private Investment Corporation and the Export-Import Bank of the United States were sent through the region to publicize U.S. interest in the investment.

150. Straits Times, July 25, 1979; and ASEAN Briefing 10 (May 1979) and 13 (August 1979).

151. Ministry of Trade, Philippines, October 1979.

152. Far Eastern Economic Review, August 19, 1977, p. 28, and September 30, 1977, p. 51.

153. New Nation, August 8, 1977; and Straits Times, May 30, 1978.

154. New Straits Times, May 11, 1978.

155. Asiaweek, August 3, 1979.

156. Interview, Malaysian Industrial Development Authority, Kuala Lumpur, October 1979.

157. Allen, "ASEAN Report," vol. 2, p. 25.

158. ASEAN Briefing 17 (December 1979); and Far Eastern Economic Review, August 13, 1982, pp. 113-16.

159. A particular limitation with the data from the Philippines is that statistics were collected for the first time in 1968 and only for new investment from that time, leaving the bulk of U. S. investment in place before that date unrecorded.

160. Malaysia, Department of Statistics, Census of Manufacturing Industries, 1968 (Kuala Lumpur: Government Printers, 1968), table 30. Reproduced in Nikar Sarkar, ed., Foreign Investment and Economic Development in Asia (Bombay: Orient Longman, 1976), p. 90.

161. As previously noted, these figures may understate the U. S. role. Stauffer, "The Political Economy of a Coup," p. 166, cites estimates that 80 percent of foreign investment in 1970 was from the United States, compared with government figures of 55.4 percent.

162. See Stephen Korbin, "Foreign Enterprise and Forced Divestment in the LDCs," International Organization 34 (Winter 1980): 65-88.

163. The Christian Science Monitor, September 20, 1979, published Business International's comparative ratings for 1976-79; and the Dow-Jones assessment for 1979 was published in Allen, The ASEAN Report, vol. 1, p. 142.

6

DEPENDENCE AND
GLOBAL ORGANIZATIONS

AN APPROACH TO POWER IN
GLOBAL ORGANIZATIONS

The Importance of Organization

It is a commonplace observation that developing countries lack an adequate measure of organization through which to mobilize their resources, compared with more developed nations. As Marshall Singer points out in discussing the disparity in power between industrialized and developing areas: "impotence—lack of wealth, organization, and status—tends to generate still further impotence. Hence, the tendency is for the more powerful countries to get still more powerful, while the weaker countries get relatively weaker."[1] However, Singer goes on to point out that altering any one of these variables provides the opportunity to change the disparity. Better organization can be a tool to increase relative power. Samuel Huntington shares this emphasis on domestic organization as an element of power, but his observation is applicable to the international arena as well: "In the modernizing world he controls the future who organizes its politics."[2]

As was pointed out in Chapter 2, writers on international political economy are concerned with the issue of participation in international organizations. Interdependence writers advocate the use of international "regimes" (formal or informal organizations) to manage the effects of exchanges among countries, while dependency writers support the creation of institutional arrangements among developing countries to bolster their ability to bargain with the industrial countries. Increasing memberships in international institutions on a selective basis presumably augments the ability of nations to exercise control over their international relationships.

Perhaps most immediately relevant to control is the role played by global organizations in making information available. As O'Brien and Helleiner have pointed out,[3] developing countries are relatively disadvantaged in their bargaining with more developed countries because of differential access to up-to-date information of all sorts.[4] Information sharing through international institutions may equalize bargaining resources. Where one gets information may also be of significance. As Huntington has pointed out, the degree of control exercised by governments over access to their nationals structures influence, with external actors predominating where governments remain passive.[5] An example of this is provided by the observation of a diplomat in Singapore that formerly it was the case that a bureaucrat encountering a problem would direct his inquiry to London, whereas now it is much more common that another ASEAN official in a similar capacity would be contacted. As a result of this shared information, local solutions may be developed with the help of contacts made through the regional organization. This changes the structure of influence between developed and developing countries by altering its institutional basis.

There are several different types of global organizations. The most visible, but fewest in number, are formal intergovernmental organizations (IGOs), such as the United Nations. There are many more nongovernmental international organizations (NGOs), composed of members acting in a private capacity (even if they are agents of a government); these tend to be less visible, but they do not necessarily lack influence, as Amnesty International demonstrates. Possibly the largest in number, but the least visible, are informal personal relationships between individuals of one nation and individuals of another. Informal networks are thought to be quite important, and some, such as Chinese societies and family groups, are reputed to be influential in channeling trade, investment, and other economic resources throughout Asia. Unfortunately, few effective means to research these organizations exist, owing to the secrecy surrounding them; thus, these will have to be largely excluded from analysis. I therefore focus on IGOs and NGOs—only a part of the organizational system.

Third World participation in the international networks of IGOs and NGOs is relatively small, although apparently growing. Membership in intergovernmental organizations is concentrated in the more economically developed regions, particularly Europe and North America, and is sparser in Africa and Asia; the propensity to join IGOs is thought to be closely related to the level of economic development.[6] NGO membership is similarly skewed. As of 1966, more than one-half of all NGO memberships were from the developed Western countries, while noncommunist Asia was quite underrepresented.[7] Table 6.1 shows that the ASEAN states are members of far fewer global or-

TABLE 6.1

ASEAN Representation in Global Organizations
(in percent)

	1960	1966	1977
Indonesia	16.7	13.9	18.2
Malaysia	10.6	14.0	17.8
Philippines	18.9	21.2	22.1
Singapore	5.2	6.3	14.1
Thailand	13.1	13.7	18.1
For comparison			
France	83.8	79.4	75.3
United States	57.6	57.3	57.4
Japan	38.9	43.2	45.6
Total number of global organizations	1,165	1,596	2,112

Source: Union of International Associations, Yearbook of International Organizations, 1978 (Brussels: UIA, 1978), statistical summary, table 4.

ganizations than are the developed countries; although they are closing the gap, it is so large that the ASEAN countries are not likely to catch up in the near future. An increase in participation through membership would appear to be the first step in augmenting the influence of developing countries.

However, participation is not necessarily the equivalent of effective influence. As Cox and Jacobson have documented for the cases of some of the more important international organizations, the stratification of influence has consistently favored the rich Western countries, giving them predominance even in organizations with a universal membership.[8] Simple participation, even with the active involvement of the government,[9] is an inadequate measure of the structure of influence.

How, then, can we approach strategies of change in global organizations in a manner consistent with the emphasis on reducing dependence? Short of studying each organization and recommending specific policies to improve the performance of each country, there are two ways, both related to diversification through regionalism. First, members of a regional organization can create institutional ties among groups with a similar focus throughout the region, to allow them to act as bargaining units with external actors. These regional nongovernmental international organizations (RNGOs) can rely on information-sharing and group-negotiating activities to increase their influence. Second, governments of a regional organization can ensure that their potential influence is maximized by all being members of the same IGOs and by acting as a bloc on matters of mutual interest.[10] This treats the deficiencies of simple participation by extending the examination to the structure of memberships.

Both strategies would increase the potential influence of developing countries in global organizations. That is not to say that their actual influence in particular organizations and on all issues will increase. In some kinds of IGOs, governmental memberships introduce criteria of influence external to the organization itself, derived from the power of the members, while informal networks seem to be quite influential in other organizations.[11] This approach sidesteps the issue of decisional power, which would have to be based on research into cases of decision making to address the issue of potential influence, or of structural power, which is based on the aggregate pattern of relationships and which influences decisional power in a probabilistic fashion.

This chapter examines how ASEAN governments and groups have changed the pattern of their involvement in global organizations from several perspectives. First, the pattern of memberships in IGOs is examined to determine whether potential influence has increased. Second, the patterns of membership of ASEAN individuals and groups in NGOs are described. Third, the growth of RNGOs and their activities are described; since these organizations are closely connected with economic activities in the ASEAN area, greater detail is provided to supplement previous discussions of trade and investment issues and to complete the investigation of international political economy in the ASEAN area. Since reliable information on memberships in the RNGOs is not available, RNGOs are not included in the statistical descriptions of IGOs and NGOs. Finally, I return to the issues of diversification and dependence.

A Note on Methods

In examining the structure of memberships in IGOs, I have adopted a modified version of social-network theory. Since this approach derives from social anthropology rather than from any common political science literature, some preliminary explanation is necessary.

Social-network theory conceives of a social system as a structured set of relationships, much like a spider web or a family tree, which determines which actors can interact directly, which only indirectly, and which not at all. [12] The pattern of interconnection channels the flow of communication, access, and in a political situation, the flow of influence. Different internal structures channel influence in different ways. A hierarchically structured network, such as a military command structure, determines influence relations precisely and channels information only vertically, not laterally. A loose hierarchy with diffuse "clusters" of authority, such as a clientele system, provides greater local influence to the central actors in the clusters, while leaving overall coordination to negotiation among the leaders of the factions. [13] A relatively egalitarian structure, such as an association, spreads influence and access widely, while requiring coalition politics for the exercise of control. [14] In global organizations, a colonial system might approximate the hierarchical network; regional organizations, the clustered network; and NGOs, the egalitarian network. [15]

The ability of governments to act in unison in IGOs is a function of their relative closeness in the network. The preferred strategy discussed here is for them to maximize this closeness. Network theory provides a set of measures of closeness within a network that can be applied to this situation. [16] These are range, density, and centrality.

Before closeness within the network can be described by these measures, the network itself must be defined. Since the object here is to examine changes in the memberships of the ASEAN states in IGOs, the network consists of IGOs, each IGO being a separate element of the total network; membership by an ASEAN state will constitute a direct connection with that element. As we are interested in the structure of ASEAN linkages in the network, not all IGOs qualify for the network, only those with at least one ASEAN member. The universe of IGOs with at least one ASEAN member constitutes the ASEAN IGO network; this provides the base for subsequent calculations. Obviously, the size of the network changes as ASEAN states join IGOs that are new to them, so all relationships are expressed as percentages, standardizing the measures over time.

The range of an ASEAN member is simply that proportion of the whole network to which the state is connected by membership. It is derived by dividing a given state's memberships by the universe of qualifying IGOs in the network. A range of 50 percent would indicate that state A belongs to exactly one-half of the IGOs having some ASEAN member; a range of 100 percent would mean that state A belongs to every IGO that has any ASEAN member—no other state could be the only ASEAN member. A small range establishes a direct constraint over potential influence; you cannot (normally) exercise influence in an organization to which you do not belong. As a measure of closeness, range provides a preliminary assessment of state A's access and ability to act as a bloc member—in 50 percent of ASEAN IGOs, for example.

Density measures the actual degree to which memberships are shared. It is derived by dividing the number of shared memberships for state A by the potential number that could be shared, given state A's range of membership. For example, if state A is a member of 10 IGOs and if there is one other ASEAN member in each, the actual shared memberships are 10; all 4 other ASEAN states could potentially be members, so the potential is 40; density is 25 percent. Density is the measure of closeness from the perspective of each state's potential bloc activity. Low density means that state A has few opportunities to work in unison with other ASEAN members in the IGOs to which it belongs, while high density indicates a large potential for joint action. If a particular ASEAN state is to reduce dependence through collective action in international organizations, the density of that country's network should be high or increasing.

Centrality is a comparative measure of the density of each state's network in the whole ASEAN network. It is derived by dividing the number of memberships shared by state A with other ASEAN states by the potential that could be shared in the entire ASEAN network (not in each state's network, as in density). For example, state A is a member of 10 IGOs and shares 10 memberships; there are 15 IGOs to which some ASEAN state belongs, so there are 60 potentially shared memberships (if state A had joined all IGOs); centrality is 16.7 percent. There are two points to be derived from measures of centrality. First, the more central actors in a network have more potential influence than the less central through their greater ability to manage the flow of information within the network and through their potential to act as intermediaries on behalf of actors less well connected.[17] Comparing the measures of centrality indicates whether some of the ASEAN states have more potential influence than their partners and, if so, which ones do. Second, centrality is the most important indicator of ASEAN's collective potential to act as a bloc in international organizations. The higher the centrality scores, the greater the potential ability of the group to bring collective muscle to bear in international organizations. If the ASEAN states are to reduce their dependence through collective action in international organizations, centrality scores should be high or increasing.

These network measurements allow some degree of precision in analyzing how the pattern of ASEAN memberships in IGOs has changed. Membership data have been collected from standard sources[18] for the years 1967, 1972, and 1977, and are compared. In addition, data for ASEAN memberships in NGOs for the year 1977 are presented as a comparison to IGO memberships and as a prelude to the description of RNGOs. Changes in the nature of the IGO network provide some indication as to whether the ASEAN states have acted, consciously or unconsciously, to increase their potential to reduce dependence through organizational ties, by diversifying memberships to each other. As Charles Pentland points out, membership in international organizations "reflects the member's determination to crystallize certain of their relationships into a more codified pattern of rules and procedures."[19] These network measures reflect that determination.

ASEAN IN INTERGOVERNMENTAL ORGANIZATIONS

It has been pointed out that the pattern of memberships in international organizations composed of the Asian states has changed over the past decade to focus on the ASEAN states. Michael Haas, in chronicling the growth of Asian international organizations, notes that the Association of Southeast Asian Nations "has had such a profound impact that it has 'ASEANized' the international relations of Asian countries."[20] By acting as a bloc in Asian regional international organizations and by creating subregional institutions for themselves, the ASEAN states have come to play a more decisive role in the Asian regional international system. One of Haas's students, James Schubert, provides additional evidence of this trend. Using a form of small-space analysis to depict the memberships of a number of Asian intergovernmental organizations, he argues that the ASEAN states form a distinct cluster within the Asian system, that they join regional IGOs twice as frequently as other Asian states, and that the most recent growth of the Asian IGO system has tended to exclude outside states entirely.[21] These observations underline the importance of the ASEAN states in international organizations, but by focusing on the Asian regional system, they say little about the role of the ASEAN states in the global system or about the internal structure of the apparent ASEAN cluster.

The ASEAN states have extended their memberships in global organizations. As Table 6.1 shows, their memberships in both IGOs and NGOs have grown faster than the system itself, with only the Philippines failing to double the system's rate of growth. In the case of IGOs, expansion is also quite evident, from 56 in 1967 to 78 in 1977 (Table 6.2). The ASEAN states are represented more widely than ever in the international community.

Within this base of IGOs to which some ASEAN state belongs, the ASEAN members' ranges vary widely. No state is a member of all of the organizations, as some IGOs are specialized to the degree that membership criteria exclude some; Malaysia, for example, could join the Organization of Petroleum Exporting Countries (OPEC) with Indonesia, but the other ASEAN members could not. Still, these two states belong to a very large proportion of the ASEAN IGO network (Table 6.2), while Singapore (the least involved) belongs to more than one-half. The expectation, then, would be that Indonesia and Malaysia are the most influential members of ASEAN in the world of IGOs, as they have connections to a larger number, while Singapore's influence would be relatively restricted by fewer memberships; the Philippines and Thailand fall closer to the more influential end of the spectrum. The ASEAN members' potential to act as bloc members corresponds to this ranking, except that, given the relatively high range scores, only Singapore stands out as significantly less capable of joining its ASEAN partners in joint action in IGOs.

The changes in range scores reinforce this conclusion. Expansion of the ASEAN network was led by Indonesia and Malaysia, each adding 23 IGOs to the total over ten years, while the other three states joined new (to them) IGOs at a lower rate. Still, each state did expand its memberships in IGOs, increasing its range in the process. Each of the ASEAN states is more capable of joining in collective action in IGOs in 1977 than was the case in 1967.

Collective action is based on shared membership in organizations. Table 6.3 provides the details of the number of memberships each country has in common with each other ASEAN member. Again, Indonesia and Malaysia have the most memberships shared with their ASEAN partners, while Singapore has the least. The expansion of memberships on the part of Indonesia and Malaysia is evident in their large increases in shared memberships, particularly in the period from 1967 to 1972; these two states were joining IGOs with their regional partners. However, changes between 1972 and 1977 resulted in slower growth in common memberships for the larger states and in large increases for Singapore. It would appear that in the period from 1967 to 1972, the four large ASEAN states consolidated their common memberships, while Singapore entered the shared system in the later period. The most significant point is the most obvious from the table: every ASEAN member has increased its number of shared memberships, in every dyad, for each time period. The base capability for joint action has clearly increased in each case by a significant margin.

The potential ability of a state to muster help for its objectives in the IGOs to which it belongs is indicated by the density of that state's shared memberships. Scores for 1977, for example (Table 6.4), indicate that Singapore (with the highest density) could call on 3.4 ASEAN comrades in its average IGO, while Indonesia (lowest density) would have only 2.9 other ASEAN members in its average IGO. This measure converts shared memberships into an indicator of potential

TABLE 6.2

Range of Memberships in ASEAN Intergovernmental Organization Network

	1967		1972		1977	
	Number	Percent	Number	Percent	Number	Percent
Indonesia	42	75	51	81	65	83
Malaysia	38	68	49	78	61	78
Philippines	37	66	44	70	53	68
Singapore	28	50	33	52	45	58
Thailand	39	70	47	75	56	72
Average	37	66	45	71	56	72
Total intergovernmental organization (ASEAN network)	56	—	63	—	78	—

Note: Range equals actual memberships for each state divided by total memberships (ASEAN network).

Source: Compiled by author.

149

TABLE 6.3

Shared ASEAN Memberships in Intergovernmental Organizations

| | Shared with | | | | | | | | | | | | | | |
| | Indonesia | | | Malaysia | | | Philippines | | | Singapore | | | Thailand | | |
Memberships of	1967	1972	1977	1967	1972	1977	1967	1972	1977	1967	1972	1977	1967	1972	1977
Indonesia	—	—	—	29	41	52	32	41	49	24	30	40	31	42	50
Malaysia	29	41	52	—	—	—	27	36	44	26	32	43	28	39	47
Philippines	32	41	49	27	36	44	—	—	—	21	26	36	34	41	47
Singapore	24	30	40	26	32	43	21	26	36	—	—	—	20	26	38
Thailand	31	42	50	28	39	47	34	41	47	20	26	38	—	—	—

Total shared memberships	1967	1972	1977
Indonesia	116	154	191
Malaysia	110	148	186
Philippines	114	144	176
Singapore	91	114	157
Thailand	113	148	182
Total	544	708	892

Source: Compiled by author.

TABLE 6.4

Density of Shared Memberships in Intergovernmental Organizations, Country Intergovernmental Organization Networks
(in percent)

	1967	1972	1977
Indonesia	69	75	73
Malaysia	72	76	76
Philippines	77	86	87
Singapore	81	86	87
Thailand	72	79	81
Average	74	79	80

Note: Density equals actual shared memberships for each country divided by the potential for sharing in that country's intergovernmental organization network (its intergovernmental organization memberships multiplied by four).

Source: Compiled by author.

TABLE 6.5

Centrality of ASEAN Members in ASEAN Intergovernmental Organization Network
(in percent)

	1967	1972	1977
Indonesia	52	61	61
Malaysia	49	59	60
Philippines	51	57	56
Singapore	41	45	50
Thailand	50	59	58
Average	49	56	57

Note: Centrality equals actual shared memberships for each country divided by the potential for sharing in the ASEAN network (ASEAN network size times four).

Source: Compiled by author.

coalitions, although obviously not all organizations have the same potential nor are all organizations equally important. Still, it is significant that density scores for all of the ASEAN members are high, and that each has increased. Each ASEAN state has more opportunity to collaborate with regional partners than was formerly the case. Isolation, one disadvantage of developing countries in IGOs, has been countered by a greater potential for collaboration.

In comparing the density scores, several points are evident. The states with the highest density are those with the lower range of memberships in the ASEAN network; this is particularly notable in the case of Singapore. Although they have joined fewer IGOs than some of the other ASEAN members (particularly Indonesia and Malaysia), Singapore, Thailand, and the Philippines have apparently focused their memberships in organizations with a high rate of ASEAN membership. Indonesia and Malaysia have apparently expanded their range of IGO memberships in a manner more independent of the other ASEAN members. Looking at the IGOs with a single ASEAN member confirms this. In 1977 there were nine such IGOs (of 78): five involved Indonesia, all of which were commodity organizations (OPEC, the Intergovernmental Council of Copper-Exporting Countries, the International Coffee Organization, the International Bauxite Organization, and the International Tea Committee); Malaysia alone belonged to two Commonwealth organizations (the Commonwealth Advisory Aeronautical Research Council and the Commonwealth Agricultural Bureaux); the remaining two were Thailand's (the Permanent Court of Arbitration and the International Sericultural Commission). There would not appear to be an explanation of this in the type of IGO, as there are four Commonwealth organizations that have more than one ASEAN member (Malaysia and Singapore) and eight commodity organizations with shared memberships. But looking at the IGOs with five ASEAN memberships shows where the states with higher density scores have concentrated. These fall into two groups, the UN family and Asian regional IGOs, although only one-half of the latter group draws all five members of ASEAN. The ASEAN states have the highest potential for joint action in universal organizations and Asian regional organizations, both arenas of general political importance, while Indonesia and Malaysia have expanded their separate interests into IGOs concerned with technical and commodity issues.

While density indicates the potential for particular states to pursue collective goals in the IGOs to which they belong, centrality refers to their potential to act as a bloc in that portion of the global IGO network that has some ASEAN membership. It is a more general indicator of the degree to which ASEAN IGO memberships constitute a cluster with potential joint-bargaining capabilities. These scores (Table 6.5) are considerably lower than those for density, and although they are increasing, ASEAN as a group is certainly less formidable than are the individual states in a potential to pursue joint action. The average centrality score indicates that in 1977 ASEAN could muster just over three members in the hypothetical average IGO. Although ASEAN's potential to act as a bloc in the international community is increasing, it is a modest one. The ASEAN states do appear as a cluster, but not as a tight and cohesive one.

Another aspect of centrality is the ability of some states to act as intermediaries through their memberships that are not shared by other states. Indonesia and Malaysia score the highest in centrality and should more frequently have this opportunity. One example of this type of activity was the active role of Indonesia and Malaysia in the Islamic Conference, attempting to resolve the Philippines' conflict with the Moro National Liberation Front through negotiated settlements. Another instance involved Indonesia's efforts to increase the flow of OPEC oil to Thailand and to the Philippines during the Gulf War in late 1980.[22] It may be a coincidence that the recipients of assistance have lower centrality scores than the providers, but it does conform to theory.

The analysis of the memberships of ASEAN states in IGOs points to consistent changes that increase their potential influence in the international system. They have extended the range of their memberships; more of these memberships are shared; each state has a high potential to muster other ASEAN members for joint objectives; ASEAN as a group is emerging as a membership cluster of moderate cohesion in the international system. The existence of an ASEAN cluster in the global system is a recent phenomenon. It was not detected by Wallace in his study of data up to 1964; on the contrary, the only identifiable clusters involving Southeast Asian nations were those of the Commonwealth and of security-treaty systems with the United States.[23] Although Wallace did point to a loosening of ties to Europe throughout the Third World, no replacement in Southeast Asia was apparent. ASEAN has emerged to fill this vacuum with an influence center focused on local states, completing the erosion of colonial and great-power dominance in institutional ties.

Another change in the structure of Southeast Asian memberships in the international system is the emergence of Indonesia and Malaysia as the dominant "joiners" of IGOs. In the period 1960-64, Thailand and the Philippines had the lead in IGO memberships,[24] perhaps as a result of a relatively longer independent existence. Malaysia was just emerging from colonialism, and Indonesia was still wracked by domestic instability; however, these two states now lead their ASEAN partners in the range of their IGO networks and in the number of memberships shared with them. Malaysia and Indonesia are now the two states most central to the new ASEAN cluster and are the most probable leaders in global organizations.

A final note on the ASEAN IGO network is that it has a marked orientation toward economic affairs. Almost one-half (35 of 78) of these IGOs were substantively concerned with economic affairs in 1977, ranging from the Indo-Pacific Fisheries Council to the Islamic Development Bank. This reinforces the point made by Schubert's analysis of Asian regional IGOs: one source of inspiration for cooperation was found in a concern for independent development.[25] Memberships in intergovernmental organizations appear to reflect the emphasis in ASEAN affairs generally on cooperation in external economic affairs toward the end of independent economic development. If the potential identified in the structure of memberships is realized, the ASEAN states should be more capable of attaining this end.

NONGOVERNMENTAL INTERNATIONAL ORGANIZATIONS

As was pointed out, NGOs in the international system are more numerous and generally less visible than IGOs. They are also likely to be less authoritative than organizations composed solely of governments; only governments are able to commit domestic actors through legislative action, for example. It is not necessarily the case, however, that all NGOs are less influential than all IGOs. Certain NGOs have formalized consultative status with the UN Economic and Social Council and specialized agencies of the United Nations or with other IGOs, which provide them with a platform for articulating policy preferences. Some NGOs have access to technical expertise in specialized fields through their membership, which allows them to function as pressure groups and as implementing agencies with some success. Other NGOs are formed of the domestic groups regulated by IGOs, and they serve to extend the domain of an international organizational network; they may articulate the aggregate subnational interests to the governmental members of IGOs or even directly to the international level. Although the degree of their influence may be limited and their method of exercising it indirect, the vast proliferation of functionally specialized NGOs since World War II would make an assumption of lack of influence problematic.[26]

In this section, I briefly describe the structure of ASEAN membership in global NGOs for 1977. The character of these NGOs is indicated, and the nature of the network of NGOs is compared with that of IGOs.

The first thing that strikes the researcher about NGOs is their incredible variety. The Union of International Associations (UIA) classifies NGOs into 20 categories; they have been reclassified into 8 for the purposes of this research.[27] As can be seen in Table 6.6,

TABLE 6.6

ASEAN Memberships in Nongovernmental International
Organizations, 1977, by Type of Organization

	Number	Percent	Average Number of ASEAN States
Religion, ethics	43	7	2.79
Sport, recreation	80	13	3.26
Education, youth	44	7	3.09
Medicine, health	103	17	2.82
Professional, science	230	37	2.58
Labor	18	3	3.06
Politics, development	28	5	2.58
Commerce, industry	64	10	2.56
Other	5	1	3.80
Total	615	100	
Average			3.00

Source: Compiled by author.

their substance covers the gamut of human interests, and their numbers far exceed those of IGOs. There was some ASEAN membership
in 615 NGOs in 1977, compared with only 78 IGOs.

The largest group of NGOs are professional societies other than
educational or commercial. Those outside of medical fields account
for 37 percent (230) of the ASEAN NGO network and include such associations as the World Poultry Science Association, the International
Union of Physiological Sciences, and the International Union of Prehistoric and Protohistoric Sciences. The other major group of professional societies comprises those concerned with medicine and
health, such as the International Society of Tropical Dermatology, the
World Psychiatric Association, and the International Association for
the Study of Pain; these account for another 17 percent, bringing the
total for professional societies to over one-half of the total (333).
These NGOs are composed of individuals and national professional
associations, and they tie ASEAN nationals into the international grid
of professional identity. Headquarters are overwhelmingly located in
Europe and the United States (probably the centers of membership),
with only a few (eight) NGOs in these categories headquartered in the
ASEAN area. To the extent that these organizations create or rein-

force an identity, it is not a Southeast Asian one, but it is also apparent that professionals in these developing countries are not entirely isolated from developments in their disciplines: to the contrary, they appear to account for the majority of transnational linkages.

The next largest number of NGOs are those concerned with social and cultural issues. These include sports, recreation, and leisure, and range from the United Nations of Yoga to the World Bridge Federation and the International Society of Money Box Collectors. Only two, the Asian Badminton Confederation and the World Airlines Clubs Associations, list ASEAN as their home. Religious groups account for a relatively small proportion of NGOs (7 percent); one from each major world tradition is located in the ASEAN area: the World Fellowship of Buddhists, the Christian Conference of Asia, and the International Islamic Organization. Roughly equal in numbers are educational and youth groups, such as the World Council on Curriculum and Instruction or the International Youth Hostel Federation; there are five Asian regional educational NGOs with headquarters in ASEAN countries. Together, these three groups account for another 27 percent of the ASEAN NGO network, and they are centered outside of the ASEAN region in the vast majority of cases, although proportionately less than were professional societies. In total, more than three-quarters of all NGOs with ASEAN membership are concerned with presumably nonpolitical subjects. Prior to the Moscow Olympics, one might have dismissed such groups as politically insignificant (Ping-Pong diplomacy notwithstanding), but they are potentially influential.

Fewer than one-fifth of all NGOs in ASEAN are directly concerned with politics, commerce, or labor. The 18 labor NGOs are largely global organizations of trade unions or their Asian regional association, such as the Textile Workers' Asian Regional Organization and the International Confederation of Free Trade Unions Asian Regional Organization; only the Manila-based Brotherhood of Asian Trade Unionists is located in the region and is composed of local members. The groups focused on politics and development are also relatively few in number, and as is the case generally with NGOs, they often appear to work at cross-purposes (the Socialist International and the World Anti-Communist League provide a clear example). Two, the Asian Development Center and the Asian Cultural Forum on Development, have ASEAN homes.

Only 10 percent of the NGOs are commercial or industrial, and these are distributed generally in the same manner as the ASEAN economies are structured. More than 40 percent (26) are groups from the service sectors, such as transport, banking, tourism, and hotels; one-quarter (16) are concerned with agricultural commodities and production; one-quarter are manufacturers' associations; the rest

(5) are Chambers of Commerce and employers' associations. In contrast to other types of NGOs, relatively more of these NGOs have their headquarters in the ASEAN region (12.5 percent), such as the Southeast Asia Iron and Steel Institute, the Federation of ASEAN Shippers' Council, and the Asian and Australasian Hotel and Restaurant Association.

I have provided a comparative statistic on the distribution of membership in NGOs in Table 6.6 by indicating the average number of ASEAN states represented in each type of organization. The types of NGOs that have a larger ASEAN membership tend to be those in sports, education, and labor, while politics and commerce tend to have a less inclusive ASEAN membership. Given that labor is not generally strong and independent in Southeast Asia, all of the more commonly shared NGOs are politically innocuous. Especially in commerce and industry, the globally based NGOs would appear to be relatively peripheral to common ASEAN interests; the same measure for IGOs in 1977 is much higher (3.59 compared with 2.56 for commerce NGOs). The pattern of memberships supports the conclusion that these NGOs are less relevant to political and economic interests in Southeast Asia.

All of the network measures presented in Table 6.7 reflect the more diffuse nature of NGO memberships in the ASEAN region compared with IGOs. The average range of ASEAN members in the total NGO network is just over one-half (55 percent), indicating much less common support for similar interests; as was shown in Table 6.2, the average range of state involvement in the IGO network for the same year is 16 percent higher. The pattern of ranges in NGOs also differs from that of IGOs. The Philippines has the largest NGO range, followed by Thailand. Indonesia and Malaysia, the two states with the widest IGO memberships in 1977, rank third and fourth, respectively, in their NGO range. Only Singapore stands in the same relative position—last—in NGO and IGO range. Perhaps by coincidence, this relative ranking in NGO participation closely resembles that for IGOs in the early 1960s, raising the possibility that, as Indonesia and Malaysia further develop, their relative standings will change, as did their IGO standings. Also, if one assumes that IGO memberships reflect government interests while NGOs represent private interests, it may be the case that the ASEAN governments perceive their interests in a more common framework than do their respective private sectors.

The figures for density of the national NGO networks also indicate that each country is relatively more independent of its ASEAN partners than was the case for IGOs. Thailand, Malaysia, and Indonesia each share roughly the same number of relationships and have similar ranges, producing a set close in density. But none of the ASEAN members has a density in the NGO network approaching that

TABLE 6.7

ASEAN Nongovernmental International Organization Network, 1977

| | Range | | Shared | | |
	Number	Percent	Memberships	Density (percent)	Centrality (percent)
Indonesia	339	55	832	61	34
Malaysia	331	54	861	65	35
Philippines	420	68	850	51	35
Singapore	265	43	621	59	25
Thailand	342	56	881	64	36
Average	339	55	809	60	33

Source: Compiled by author.

of IGOs. Private interests in global organizations appear to be much more divergent than are government interests.

The most extreme case of individual interests is found in the NGOs to which only a single ASEAN member belongs. These account for almost one-quarter of the NGOs (151 of 615), compared with only 12 percent of IGOs (9). The Philippines and Indonesia together account for two-thirds of these single memberships, and Singapore the fewest (58, 38, and 14, respectively); by substance, professional societies form the majority (57 percent) of the single memberships, with the only other notable group being commercial associations. Filipinos, for example, belong to a number of commercial NGOs alone and to a number of religious groups that are mostly Catholic; the supposed link to Latin America is present, but only in three organizations (the Hispano-Luso-American-Philippine Assembly on Tourism, for example). Most of the individual interests are professional ties of Filipinos and Indonesians.

The opposite extreme, ASEAN-wide NGOs, adds to the picture of a lack of common interests. The proportion of NGOs with all five ASEAN states represented is particularly low compared with IGOs; only 16.7 percent of NGOs are totally shared, while this group of IGOs was almost one-half of the total (41 percent). At present, it is quite apparent that private groups in the ASEAN states find fewer common interests in the global network of NGOs than do their governments in intergovernmental organizations. The opportunity for social integration through communication in the network of transnational private organizations is curtailed by a diversity of interests.

Comparing centrality scores for NGOs with those of IGOs, it is evident that there is no real cluster of ASEAN memberships in world NGOs. The average NGO centrality is far below that for IGOs. Furthermore, there is no single country that is markedly more connected to the NGO world than the others, and only Singapore stands out as less connected. This reinforces the image of NGO memberships being much more diffuse than is true for IGOs; private bodies in the ASEAN area do not share common interests to a substantial degree.

In general, the structure of the NGO network is quite different from that of the IGO network. It is much more diffuse in national memberships and is largely composed of professional societies. Mutual interests seem to focus on sport and social activities, rather than on political or economic fields. There is little convincing evidence that nationals of the ASEAN states compose anything resembling the cluster of IGOs that their governments have forged. There is one close similarity: the vast majority of central offices of both types of transnational organization are located outside of the region.

ASEAN REGIONAL NONGOVERNMENTAL ORGANIZATIONS

The relatively less cohesive structure of ASEAN participation in the network of global NGOs is in part a product of incomplete data. The standard reference on international organizations, which has been the primary source of information for the analysis up to this point, includes entries for only two ASEAN regional NGOs;[28] as I have followed this source in the classification of international organizations while using its data base, I have chosen to present information on organizations excluded by the UIA separately.

The formation of regional international organizations has generally been followed by the development of regional, private pressure groups. The European Economic Community (EEC) is the most developed in this regard, with more than 400 such groups[29] that function to provide communications channels between private-sector interests and the national governments or regional organization.[30] Latin American regionalism has also spawned many industry and trade groups,[31] as have some African regional efforts. Table 6.8 presents the names and, where available, the dates of establishment of the parallel set of organizations under the ASEAN umbrella. There are approximately 50 ASEAN private transnational associations.[32]

In contrast with the relative emphasis in membership in global NGOs in professional and noneconomic fields, the ASEAN NGOs are predominantly in economic fields. Only the first 14 regional nongovernmental organizations listed in the table are concerned with social,

TABLE 6.8

ASEAN Regional Nongovernmental International Organizations
(by type, with some dates of establishment)

Social, cultural, and professional
  ASEAN Interparliamentary Organization
  ASEAN Council of Museums
  Federation of ASEAN Public Information Organizations
  ASEAN Trade Union Council (1976)
  Committee for ASEAN Youth Cooperation
  ASEAN Council of Japan Alumni
  ASEAN Federation of Women
  Federation of ASEAN Economics Associations
  Confederation of ASEAN Journalists
  ASEAN Federation of Accountants (1977)
  ASEAN Federation of Jurists
  ASEAN Pediatric Federation (1976)
  ASEAN College of Surgeons
  ASEAN Cardiologists' Federation
  ASEAN Karate Federation (1978)
  ASEAN Public Relations Federation (1977)
Commerce, industry, and finance
  ASEAN Business Council
  ASEAN Tours and Travel Association
  ASEAN Motion Picture Producers' Association
  ASEAN Consumers' Protection Agency
  Federation of ASEAN Newspaper Publishers
  Association of Southeast Asian Publishers (1972)
  Confederation of ASEAN Chambers of Commerce and Industry (1972)
  ASEAN Council of Petroleum Cooperation (1975)
  ASEAN Timber Producers' Association (1974)
  ASEAN Insurance Council (1975)
  Federation of ASEAN Shippers' Council (1975)
  Federation of ASEAN Shipowners' Association (1975)
  ASEAN Port Authorities' Association (1976)
  ASEAN Banking Council (1976)
  ASEAN Central Bank Group (1967)
  ASEAN Tin Research and Development Center (1977)
  ASEAN Marketing Association (1977)
  ASEAN Reinsurance Corporation (1979)

Commerce, industry, and finance (continued)
  Federation of ASEAN Stock Exchanges (1979)
  ASEAN Steel Action Group (1975)
Regional industry clubs
  ASEAN Automotive Federation (1976)
  ASEAN Federation of Electrical, Electronic and Allied Industries
    (1977)
  Rubber Industries Association of Southeast Asian Nations (1977)
  ASEAN Federation of Glass Manufacturers (1977)
  ASEAN Federation of Cement Manufacturers (1977)
  ASEAN Chemical Industries Club (1977)
  ASEAN Federation of Food Processing Industries (1978)
  ASEAN Iron and Steel Federation (1978)
  ASEAN Pulp and Paper Industry Club (1978)
  ASEAN Agricultural Machinery Federation (1978)
  ASEAN Federation of Furniture Manufacturers (1978)
  ASEAN Federation of Textile Industries (1978)
  Ceramics Industry Club of ASEAN (1979)
  ASEAN Plywood Federation (1980)
  ASEAN Leather-Based Products Club (in formation)
  ASEAN Musical Instruments Club (in formation)
  ASEAN Air Transport Manufacturers' Club (in formation)
  ASEAN Cordage, Rope and Twine Manufacturers' Club (in forma-
    tion)
  ASEAN Power Generation Club (in formation)
  ASEAN Shipbuilders and Ship Repairers' Club (in formation)
  ASEAN Metallic Mineral Products Club (in formation)
  ASEAN Non-Electrical Machinery Manufacturers' Club (in forma-
    tion)
  ASEAN Aluminium Industry Club (in formation)
Regional commodity clubs
  ASEAN Sugar Business Club (1979)
  ASEAN Pepper Business Club (1980)
  ASEAN Coffee Business Club (1980)
  ASEAN Fruits and Vegetables Business Club (1980)
  ASEAN Livestock Business Club (1979)

Source: Compiled by author.

cultural, or professional matters; the others are private business associations. The RNGOs have filled the niche left most open by NGOs.

Most of the RNGOs are relatively recent in origin and, undoubtedly, are still developing. The oldest for which a date of establishment is available, the Confederation of ASEAN Chambers of Commerce and Industry (ASEAN CCI or ACCI), is only ten years old.[33]
Most of the RNGOs were formed in the period from 1976 to 1978, following the increased emphasis on economic cooperation expressed at
the summit meetings in Bali and Kuala Lumpur in 1976 and 1977.
In part, the formation of these groups is a response to the recommendation of the UN Study Team report, which encouraged the establishment of business-sector groups to support efforts at economic integration by providing information and reactions to government initiatives; the regional industry clubs are the most direct result of this
approach.[34]

The exact configuration of membership is not available, but it
would appear that it is now quite widely based in each of the ASEAN
states and will be almost universal in the next few years.

The RNGOs in the social, cultural, and professional fields operate much in the same manner as their counterparts around the world.
The Federation of ASEAN Economics Associations, for example,
meets periodically and publishes papers just like any other academic
association. However, even though these organizations may contribute
to social integration among their ASEAN members and may provide a
boost to the acceptance of ASEAN as a meaningful region, it is the
purpose here to highlight the activities of a number of commercial
RNGOs, particularly as they influence the rate and direction of ASEAN
economic integration and development. These organizations offer the
potential for the development of regional business networks that would
compete with existing ties to the major economic powers.

One of the most active RNGOs has been the ASEAN Banking Council. Formed in 1976 with strong support from Singapore, the banking
group has made numerous proposals aimed at strengthening regional
cooperation, but it is also directed toward a stronger ASEAN role internationally. At the formation meeting, Singapore's Finance Minister Hon Sui Sen urged greater cooperation with this rationale: "This
will strengthen our bargaining position in trade and finance negotiations
at international forums."[35]

Proposals of the ASEAN Banking Council have ranged widely,
but they focus on creating more commonality of services available
within the region and on supplanting the role of foreign banks with local
ones. Programs such as the exchange of desk officers among ASEAN
banks to promote intraregional trade, the creation of a regional training school, preferential loan schemes for regional projects, the creation of a regional bankers' acceptance market to facilitate ASEAN finan-

cial transactions, and most recently, an ASEAN Export-Import Bank and an ASEAN Finance Corporation have been advanced.[36] The momentum of the Banking Council has been so continuous that it has effectively displaced the ASEAN-CCI Committee on Banking as the center for coordination in this sector.[37] Of course, support for regional buildup of banking services has had a fillip from both Singapore and Manila, each with its own aspirations as a financial center for ASEAN and beyond.

In the area of shipping, three RNGOs formed a joint secretariat in 1978 to coordinate and develop regional services, largely with the ultimate aim of freeing Southeast Asia from the predominant influence of foreign shipping conferences. These are the ASEAN Port Authorities Association, the Federation of ASEAN Shipowners' Association, and the most active group, the Federation of ASEAN Shippers' Council (FASC). The FASC was formed in 1975, after a concerted lobbying effort on the part of Singapore and the Philippines and after a UN Economic and Social Commission for Asia and the Pacific study, to formalize and extend preexisting cooperative efforts with the ASEAN governments.[38] It has had some success in challenging rate and tonnage increases set by the major group operating in Asia, the Far Eastern Freight Conference.[39] One objective is to form a regional common market in shipping,[40] but the major effort to date has been in the area of strengthening regional bargaining power in international shipping conferences through coordination with each other and with other developing Asian countries.[41] In the longer term, it is hoped that an effective infrastructure of shipping services among the ASEAN countries will develop to permit greater trade integration, a situation that does not now exist. This group of RNGOs has also usurped the ASEAN-CCI committee concerned with shipping.

The ASEAN Timber Producers' Association has focused on relations with export partners. Set up in late 1974, the association moved quite quickly to regulate maximum levels of lumber exports.[42] More recently, it has weakened the fixed-price monopoly of the Japan Lumber Importers' Association, which was based on long-term supply contracts, and has pushed for a greater degree of downstream processing in the region. Taiwan was pressed into signing a price-stabilization agreement in late 1979, and ASEAN import houses in Japan are being considered as a means of undermining the external monopoly in marketing held by the Japanese.[43] Japan, Taiwan, and Korea have been "warned" by the Sabah chief minister (through the lumber association) that they are almost completely dependent on ASEAN for their lumber imports[44] and must accede to ASEAN demands, a point that might be disputed by some Canadians.

One final group in this category of RNGOs that deserves mention is the ASEAN Council of Petroleum Cooperation (ASCOPE). As in other

RNGOs, early emphasis was placed on collecting basic data, in this case on energy and petrochemical capabilities in the region. However, ASCOPE has gone considerably further by helping to coordinate national plans, working on common pricing and marketing strategies, and pushing an emergency-sharing agreement through ASEAN in early 1977 whereby 80 percent of Indonesia's and Malaysia's net exportable surplus will be channeled to the other ASEAN members when needed. [45]

Although not all of the RNGOs are as active as the ones mentioned, these do provide the flavor of the purposes of the well-established ones. Regional coalitions of business leaders from a particular sector have first established mutual interests through exchange of information and have then proceeded to challenge actors external to the region who were perceived to be placing limits on the growth and profitability of operations of local interests, sometimes with confrontation tactics. In much the same manner that the major common ventures of the intergovernmental organization of ASEAN have focused on countering foreign positions that disadvantage local interests, it would appear that the common focus of private transnational associations is also on attempts to boost the relative bargaining position of ASEAN private actors. In a secondary way, this mutuality of interests focuses on speeding economic integration among the members of ASEAN; this is a lower priority because individual interests still form the basis of cooperation.

ASEAN Chambers of Commerce and Industry

Expanding on the basis of private cooperation is the primary function of the most important RNGO in ASEAN, the Confederation of ASEAN Chambers of Commerce and Industry, which is essentially the interface between the ASEAN intergovernmental structure and the private sectors of the five countries. This organization ties together the national peak groups of the five members: the National Chamber of Commerce and Industry of Malaysia, the Philippines Chamber of Commerce and Industry, the Singapore Federation of Chambers of Commerce and Industry, the Joint Standing Committee on Commerce and Industry of Thailand, and the Indonesian Chambers of Commerce and Industry (KADIN). Although the umbrella ACCI was established in 1972, as late as 1974 it was reported that the national members were themselves less than unified and organized, and real efforts to strengthen the organization did not appear until 1975. [46] In that year the ACCI revamped its internal organization to parallel that of the ASEAN intergovernmental structure by setting up working groups on all major areas, of which the Working Group on Trade (WGT) and the Working Group on Industrial Complementation (WGIC) have been the most significant. [47] The general aims of the ACCI are to effect private-sector cooperation within ASEAN, to maintain close relations with regional and international organizations having similar aims, and to act as the major liaison between the private sectors of the ASEAN members and their governments. [48]

There are three major paths followed by the ACCI in coordinating private-sector efforts toward greater economic integration. The first two of these correspond to the efforts by ASEAN in the areas of trade liberalization and industrial complementation and are directed by the two working groups mentioned. The third is in encouraging the formation of industry and commodity clubs, and in coordinating their activities, as the primary instruments in achieving the first two goals.

The Working Group on Trade, originally named the Working Group on the Preferential Trade Agreement, reports recommendations and provides information to the ASEAN intergovernmental Committee on Trade and Tourism through the ACCI Council. Organized in mid-1975 to provide lists of products for the Preferential Trade Agreement negotiations (signed in early 1977), it was to have been finished with its task by mid-1977, [49] but the continuing business of gradually lowering tariff barriers through quarterly ASEAN meetings has required continuous WGT support. The process of providing specific items and suggested reductions in tariff levels is conducted primarily at the national level and is coordinated by national trade ministries in consultation with private groups. Although the level of consultation in the Philippines is perhaps more extensive than in some other ASEAN members, it is illustrative of the process. [50] Public hearings are conducted by the Tariff Board, with representation invited from, but not limited to, industry clubs and the chamber of commerce. Specific items are proposed by both the government and by private business, representations are invited from other ASEAN governments, and then a package is sent to cabinet for approval or rejection. The industry clubs occasionally act like lobbying groups in this process, but they are often ill-prepared; however, some suggestions are transmitted from one country's chamber of commerce to another's for inclusion in that country's list. Governments retain control over the final product, which is derived from proposals by the private sector, with the WGT mobilizing the private effort.

The WGT has also focused on other related issues, such as non-tariff barriers, customs procedures, trade statistics, and commercial arbitration, attempting to push for more unified practices in each ASEAN country. [51] One imaginative proposal was for the creation of private cooperatives to buy and sell products in more economical quantities for the region as a whole, to avoid transfer-price abuses by multinational corporations. [52] Any trade-related issue is within the legitimate purview of the WGT, but the governments, of course, remain supreme.

The Working Group on Industrial Complementation is the primary agent between the governments and the private sectors in efforts to rationalize industrial projects among the five countries. This working group develops proposals from individual industry club members and transmits them to the intergovernmental ASEAN Committee on Industry, Minerals, and Energy, which refers them to the Economic Ministers Meeting for approval. The initiative comes from the private sector, in line with the UN Team recommendation.[53] This task was enthusiastically undertaken by the WGIC, which in 1975 and 1976 churned out 25 specific proposals spanning the whole range of industrial sectors and which proposed a detailed set of guidelines for this type of ASEAN project.[54] However, the initiative of the private sector soon snagged on the caution of the governments, with the result that none of these, or the following proposals, were approved until 1980, and then only as test cases.[55]

The long delay revolved around a lack of agreement among the governments on philosophical issues as well as around a lack of coordination between the governments and the private sectors. The major issues preventing agreement were the allowable degree of participation of foreign investors and the degree to which each project was to be granted a semimonopoly status in the region. Both are critical parts of the guidelines on complementation. Malaysia and Indonesia have been adamant on 51 percent ASEAN ownership on any project granted incentives; Thailand and the Philippines (the latter with reservations) were willing to go along with this, but not Singapore, with its more heavily international industrial base. Singapore in 1979 unexpectedly vetoed the guidelines over this issue, but it apparently conceded in 1980.[56] Singapore was also the most reluctant to see the emergence of semimonopolies in products manufactured for the ASEAN market, which would reduce their international competitiveness, but this was resolved in Singapore's favor, after threats of nonparticipation, by allowing voluntary participation on a project-by-project basis.[57] With the governments in disagreement, the private sector was unable to "get a clear idea of official thinking,"[58] which forced the complementation proposals to go through several revisions, killing much of the previous momentum.[59] The start-and-stop nature of the private-sector participation has stimulated the ACCI to undertake a major study reviewing its role in economic cooperation, aimed toward regaining the lost impetus.[60]

The second general purpose of the ACCI is to establish and maintain contact with international organizations and actors on behalf of the private sectors of ASEAN. This theme was elaborated at the first meeting of the ACCI in 1972. Guidelines were established for joint trade missions to develop new export markets, for participation in international trade fairs, and for drawing new foreign investment. [61] Little appears to have been accomplished in this direction through 1975; however, by 1976 the issue was rekindled, and initiatives were taken to establish relations with the International Chamber of Commerce, the International Organization for Standardization, and the Pacific Basin Economic Cooperation Council (an organization of business executives from the more industrialized countries of the Pacific). [62] A wide range of contacts is now maintained independently of the ASEAN governmental network.

Under the purview of the ASEAN governmental structure, a number of important international connections have been established. Early international participation was on an informal basis. The ACCI was granted observer status in ASEAN negotiations with the EEC, and the courtesy was returned by allowing observers from Japan, the EEC, and Hong Kong to attend biannual ACCI conferences. [63] However, with the increasing institutionalization of economic relations between ASEAN and its major partners in the form of "dialogues" and "forums," the private sector has been brought into the process on a more regular basis. The ACCI now has permanent links to the United States in the form of the ASEAN-US Business Council and the American-ASEAN Trade Council, which includes efforts to increase trade and identify smaller U.S. companies to be encouraged to invest and trade with the ASEAN countries. [64] These are purely private-sector transnational organizations composed of the respective chambers of commerce. Similar organizations tie the ACCI to other partners: the ASEAN-Japan Business Conference links the ACCI to the Japanese Federation of Economic Organizations and to the Japanese Chamber of Commerce and Industry; [65] the Australia-ASEAN Business Council provides a common forum for private groups from both areas, and it is undertaking a study of trade and investment relations to prepare the way for more harmonious cooperation. [66] Following the large industrial cooperation conference between ASEAN and the EEC, talks got under way to establish a permanent ASEAN-EEC Economic Council to perform a similar role with the European countries, but this has yet to be formally established. [67] With these foreign policy linkages to the major economic partners, the ACCI is entering more into the world of diplomacy. Common positions are prepared for negotiations with external partners, future relations with the major industrial nations are considered at ACCI conferences, and collective trade arrangements with the industrial countries have been considered as a means of strengthening ASEAN regional bonds. [68] International private-sector contacts organized by the ACCI are emerging as a major supplement to intergovernmental relations, particularly in the fields of trade and investment.

However close relations with other governments are becoming, it is not entirely clear that issues between the ACCI and the five ASEAN governments have been resolved. The area of liaison between the private sector and governments does not satisfy the ACCI members. There are supposed to be strong links between the ACCI working groups and their counterparts in the intergovernmental structure. Some of these, such as shipping, banking, and tourism, are actually between governmental committees and the specialized RNGOs, rather than with the ACCI working groups concerned. [69] But the major active ACCI working groups, those on trade and industrial complementation, have repeatedly requested closer links to their intergovernmental counterparts, the Committee on Trade and Tourism (COTT) and the Committee on Industry, Minerals and Energy (COIME), respectively. [70] Only in mid-1980 were invitations to attend government meetings extended to these two groups, [71] despite expressions of support for their work by governmental leaders over the past several years. [72] Formerly, contact between the ACCI and the ASEAN governments was either informal, or as in the case of the November 1977 "dialogue" between private and government sides, it took the form of a diplomatic conference. [73] The ACCI was apparently caught in a cross fire: on the one flank it was encouraged to speed up ASEAN economic cooperation, [74] while on the other it faced governmental intransigence to implement any of its proposals. Expressions of private-sector dissatisfaction peaked in late 1979 and early 1980, [75] which may have assisted the governments in breaking their own deadlock over issues of private-sector cooperation. [76]

At the national level, private coordination with the five governments is varied, but no less problematic. [77] As is the case in other regional organizations, contact at the national level is much more extensive than that at the regional level, but in ASEAN the overlap between the governments and the private sector is more marked, compounding the problem. The Philippines was early in organizing national associations of all types, virtually forcing industry groups that desired contact with the government to join the national chambers of commerce. The former minister of industry, Vincente Paterno, was personally influential in organizing business into national peak groups, with the rationale that a unified front of Philippine business groups was the only effective way to deal with better-organized and more informed foreign delegations. The government makes clear what is allowed and desirable; it briefs and debriefs delegates to private meetings of the ACCI; and both sides attend many of the other's meetings. [78] Several sources in other ASEAN countries commented on how well organized the delegations from the Philippines were and on the constant rotation between government and private-sector personnel. The Indonesian delegations to the ACCI are also reported to be well organized and to be "mostly generals" who are quite assertive and capable of scuttling proposals not to their liking. One source claimed that papers the Indonesians presented at ACCI meetings were obviously prepared by the government; with the prevailing interconnections between the military and private business and with the chair of the Indonesian section of the ACCI in the hands of former government members during several periods,[79] the opportunity for coordination should be extensive. The Indonesian government justifies close private-government interrelations because of the need, arising from the colonial period, for government leadership; although it maintains that there is no government membership in the private sector, a government representative always attends association meetings.[80] Thai delegations to the ACCI are also reported to be heavily staffed by government members, but in this case, bureaucrats mainly from the Board of Investment and the Ministry of Finance make up the delegations. Both public and private sides are invited to each other's meetings, with the private sector reportedly participating equally. In addition, the private industry groups have become influential in domestic economic matters since their organization in 1976.[81] One Singaporean plaintively remarked that the overlap between governments and private sectors in these three countries was so great that sometimes it was difficult to tell to whom he was talking. Another source pointed out the paradox that as these delegations were so close to their governments, one would expect easy progress, but the result was, in fact, to make them more inflexible and unable to compromise their governments' instructions.

Singapore's own set of connections between the chambers of commerce and the Ministry of Trade and Economic Development Board are close, but informally based on "old boy" networks. No formal consultation takes place, but coordination is nonetheless effective on most issues. The Malaysian government had little contact with private business groups before 1978, but then it started to model its efforts on those of the Philippines. It is now committed to developing close and regular contact between the government, particularly the Malaysian Industrial Development Authority (MIDA), and the various ethnic chambers of commerce in order to supplement the existing links to the Federation of Malaysian Manufacturers; by late 1979 MIDA officials were reporting that the bottleneck in communication had been broken. Although Malaysia was formerly reputed to be similar to Indonesia and Thailand in terms of government's role in supposedly private-sector matters, it is now moving to coordinate rather than simply to impose its will, possibly a consequence of generally better relations with non-Malay business groups. Nevertheless, the national ACCI groups are properly seen as less coherent extensions of the ASEAN governmental structure in many ways.

The regional chamber of commerce has become influential in the coordination and initiation of economic cooperation, both in the region and with major outside economic partners. Although forging close and regular links among the ACCI, the ASEAN structure, and national members has proved difficult, these problems seem to be less critical now than five years ago. Placed in perspective, the extension of the ASEAN organizational structure downward to include private business has not proved more difficult, nor more fractious, than the lateral coordination among the five governments. The ACCI appears to be on the way to becoming a full partner in ASEAN economic cooperation and a vocal advocate of faster and more meaningful integration.

The Regional Industry and Commodity Clubs

The detailed work of economic cooperation takes place at a level below the national and ASEAN chambers of commerce. Following suggestions from the ASEAN Economic Ministers' Meeting in 1976, the ACCI decided to set up associations of specific industries to facilitate exchanges across ASEAN borders.[82] The result was the identification of 29 industry groups that covered the spectrum of ASEAN economic activities. [83] The formation of regional industry clubs (RICs) in these sectors was to be encouraged, with the Philippines leading the way and convincing the other ASEAN governments of their utility. [84] This is the deepest level of the ASEAN economic organization's penetration, linking specialized groups of businesses together across national borders.

Formation of these groups, in contrast with most of the rest of the ASEAN structure, is from the bottom up. At the national level, relevant business leaders first organize national industry clubs (NICs), applying for recognition as a regional industry club when at least three such NICs exist; this allows them to participate in ACCI activities on a formal basis. The RICs fit into the ACCI organization as subunits of the Working Group on Industrial Complementation. The decision to parallel the RICs in commodity fields was made by the Working Group on Trade in 1978;[85] the regional commodity clubs (RCCs) fall under the WGT rather than under the WGIC and have a slightly different set of purposes. The rules for the clubs stipulate that the members of the governing body of the RICs and RCCs must be ASEAN nationals, but international companies are allowed to participate fully, and they may even cast a vote in meetings if they are represented by an ASEAN national. [86]

The objective of the regional clubs is to enhance both ASEAN economic cooperation and international cooperation in the industries sponsoring them. The major activity of the RICs is to propose specific projects for industrial complementation, which then have the support of local business managers. However, some have also proposed joint marketing efforts in external trade, common standards for products, joint training and research efforts, joint materials supply, and other activities of particular interest to specific industries.[87] The commodity clubs are concerned with controlling competition within ASEAN among different producers of similar products, establishing common standards for foreign-trade purposes, and promoting joint international marketing efforts;[88] buffer stocks of some commodities have also been mooted, to offset potential shortages in the region.[89] The original ideas were to rationalize industries in the same general field of production in different ASEAN countries, to end wasteful competition by directing development before it was too late, and to increase the bargaining position of each sector with international traders and investors through a greater degree of unification.[90] Since all of these organizations are relatively new, it is premature to attempt to evaluate their achievements in attaining these goals, but a few examples provide indications of their activity.

The ASEAN Automotive Federation is the oldest and best established of the RICs and, so far, is the only one to have industrial-complementation projects accepted by the ASEAN governments. Extending back to informal cooperation between Thai and Philippine planners in the early 1970s, aimed at rationalizing national automobile industries,[91] the present club is attempting to work toward an integrated ASEAN automobile industry, suggested in 1971.[92] By 1978 the automobile federation had detailed plans for sharing parts manufacturing, and it had consulted with the Japan Auto Parts Industrial Association informally (since most automobiles in the ASEAN countries are of Japanese manufacture).[93] In early 1979 the ACCI approved the scheme, passed it to the governments, which approved the first stage in 1980, and then started consideration of a second stage.[94] Complementation in the automobile industry is often portrayed as a test case for the wider ambitions of other sectors; it is the first to be attempted because foreign-exchange savings could be significant and the governments are concerned to preserve this sector.[95] Still, it would appear that this goal of the RICs will be slow in materializing, unless the ten years required to move to implementation in the automobile plan are considerably shortened.

The other, newer clubs have made less progress, but are hardly inactive. Almost all have made proposals for complementation, although none of these has been approved by the governments, and for tariff reductions.[96] The textile club has set up a data bank, organized a trade fair, considered methods to combat protectionism in external markets, and issued guidelines for government negotiations with third countries.[97] At least the Singapore textile club has also been active in the negotiation of international textile agreements.[98] The steel club has taken over the work of the United Nations Industrial Development Organization project on standardization.[99] Furniture makers jointly accepted an order too large for any one of them, while polyvinylchloride producers have set up joint purchases of supplies by the shipload.[100] These sorts of activities have undoubtedly benefited ASEAN manufacturers, but so far fall short of the ultimate goals of the clubs.

A number of interviews pointed to a problem common to all of the clubs that was impeding greater progress.[101] Since they are funded by their own industries, available resources are low; they rely on voluntary expertise within the industry and generally have a loose organization. The result is that they are often unprepared to present viable proposals to their governments, sometimes are ignorant of information provided by the governments, and therefore make little progress even with repeated meetings. The short-term investment for long-term gain is difficult to mobilize, even in the clubs not characterized as "talk shops" by observers. Most of the clubs are underdeveloped in staff, funding, and will.

Despite their shortcomings, benefits are to be reaped. The most simple is the gain in familiarity among business leaders in each country of others' procedures and problems through contact and informal exchanges. Some participants pointed to an increase in intra-ASEAN trade and investment as opportunities were turned up by meetings. As Morrison points out,[102] involvement of the clubs may speed integration by allowing a veto to each industry over projects that might otherwise flounder before implementation, but after considerable effort had been expended. From the perspective of the structure of organizations in the region, it is apparent that the regional clubs are providing the basis for closer links among ASEAN actors, are allowing the development of common interests, and are providing the structural means for greater bargaining ability with external actors.

In addition, participation in these transnational associations has produced a sizable stock of individuals with a genuine, informed ASEAN outlook, located at the strategic nexus of private business and government. Indeed, given the considerable overlap of private and public sectors in the ASEAN countries, it is a safe assumption that this ASEAN socialization will have a significant effect on public policies. While it may be premature to proclaim the emergence of an ASEAN capitalist class, it is likely that regional interests have come to rival wider, and preexisting, international interests (whether or not these are identical to those of the center countries) for a significant social group with wide economic influence. This socialization effect is, in large part, derived from the regional nongovernmental organizations.

The regional NGO network supplements both the IGO network and the global NGO network, providing depth to IGOs and a local base for private transnational activity. The focus of the IGO network on independent economic development is extended downward to the private sector of each country by the RNGOs, assisting the efforts of the governments by involving the private sector in economic development led by international linkages. Yet, these are not completely autonomous organizations, as the degree of government tutelage and control seems high. At the same time, the RNGOs form a dense cluster of transnational economic linkages centered in the ASEAN region, which compensates for the diffuse structure of NGOs generally and increases the centrality of the ASEAN national actors in nongovernmental transnational networks. The addition of several layers of regional transnational organizations provides the network infrastructure for increased influence of ASEAN actors in NGO affairs: increased potential communication, increased range in a variety of important substantive areas, and increased common centrality in political-economic organizations.

CONCLUSION

In considering structural power as expressed through transnational organizations, this segment of the study has applied social-network theory as a research guide. The purpose has been to analyze changes in the structure of organizational networks that would provide clues as to how bargaining positions might be expected to change between the members of ASEAN and the wider international system.

In both intergovernmental organizations and nongovernmental international organizations there has been considerable diversification of memberships so that the ASEAN members are more closely connected. The emergence of an ASEAN cluster of IGOs, based on large increases in shared memberships, provides a greater potential for joint action in reference to other governments. Individual ASEAN countries have focused on organizations concerned with economic development, giving substance to their increased potential bargaining power. Purely regional NGOs have been formed where the wider NGO network was the most diffuse and lacking: in economic affairs. These RNGOs have been active in forging closer ties among the private sectors of the ASEAN states, assisted by their governments in many cases. Joint bargaining and other collective ventures have been the focus of their activities, with some success. Without being able to apply the same statistical evidence to the RNGOs as was available for IGOs, it would appear that RNGOs also constitute a cluster of increasing closeness. In both intergovernmental and nongovernmental international organizations, the ASEAN states have increased their potential influence through diversification. In the arenas of global organization, the ASEAN states are becoming potentially more influential, countering a manifestation of dependence.

NOTES

1. Marshall R. Singer, Weak States in a World of Powers: The Dynamics of International Relationships (New York: Free Press, 1972), pp. 70-74, 368 (emphasis added).

2. Samuel Huntington, Political Order in Changing Societies (New Haven, Conn.: Yale University Press, 1968), p. 461.

3. Rita Cruise O'Brien and G. K. Helleiner, "The Political Economy of Information in a Changing International Economic Order," International Organization 34 (Autumn 1980): 445-70.

4. This point was made in reference to multinational corporations by Richard Barnet and Ronald Müller, Global Reach (New York: Simon & Schuster, 1974), pp. 193-94.

5. Samuel Huntington, "Transnational Organizations in World Politics," World Politics 25 (1973): 355.

6. Harold K. Jacobson, Networks of Interdependence: International Organizations and the Global Political System (New York: Alfred Knopf, 1979), p. 54 and table 3.5, p. 55.

7. Kjell Skjelsbaek, "The Growth of International Nongovernmental Organization in the Twentieth Century," International Organization 25 (Summer 1971): 430-32.

8. Robert Cox and Harold Jacobson, eds., The Anatomy of Influence: Decision Making in International Organization (New Haven, Conn.: Yale University Press, 1974), p. 423.

9. As Peter Busch pointed out, joining an organization may simply create a convenient overseas post for an undesirable, whether the prime minister's stupid brother or a political rival.

10. "One of the most significant indices is the degree of shared participation in international organizations, which may operate either toward cohesion or power," Louis Cantori and Steven Spiegel, The International Politics of Regions (Englewood Cliffs, N.J.: Prentice-Hall, 1970), p. 38.

11. Cox and Jacobson, The Anatomy of Influence, pp. 437-43, include five variables in their stratification of power index (GNP, per capita GNP, population, nuclear capability, prestige), which are external to the organization; William Averyt, "Eurogroups, Clientela, and the European Community," International Organization 29 (1975): 949-72; Peter Busch, "Germany in the European Economic Community: Theory and Case Study," Canadian Journal of Political Science 11 (1978): 545-74, provides examples of elite networks.

12. Jeremy Boissevain, Friends of Friends: Networks, Manipulators, and Coalitions (Oxford: Basil Blackwell, 1974); and J. Clyde Mitchell, ed., Social Networks in Urban Situations (Manchester: Manchester University Press, 1969).

13. Steffan Schmidt, James Scott, Carl Landé, and Laura Guasti, eds., Friends, Followers and Factions: A Reader in Political Clientelism (Berkeley and Los Angeles: University of California Press, 1977).

14. Johan Galtung, "A Structural Theory of Integration," Journal of Peace Research 4 (1968): 375-95.

15. See Todd LaPorte, ed., Organized Social Complexity (Princeton, N.J.: Princeton University Press, 1975), for a parallel discussion.

16. Boissevain, Friends of Friends, pp. 36-42.

17. Ibid. I have modified the method of computing centrality to fit complex networks.

18. The data for this section were gathered primarily from Union of International Associations (UIA), Yearbook of International Organizations (Brussels: UIA, 1967, 1972, 1977). I have also benefited from comparison of this data with that collected and updated by Michael Wallace for the Correlates of War Project. My data differ slightly from his, as I have followed UIA's definition of intergovernmental organization.

19. Charles Pentland, "International Organizations," in World Politics, ed. James N. Rosenau, Kenneth W. Thompson, and Gavin Boyd (New York: Free Press, 1976), p. 626.

20. Michael Haas, "The ASEANization of Asian International Relations," Asia-Pacific Community 6 (Fall 1979): 73, 85.

21. James N. Schubert, "Toward a 'Working Peace System' in Asia: Organizational Growth and State Participation in Asian Regionalism," International Organization 32 (Spring 1978): 425-62.

22. Lela G. Noble, "Ethnicity and Philippine-Malaysian Relations," Asian Survey 15 (May 1975): 453-72; and Far Eastern Economic Review, November 21, 1980, p. 9.

23. Michael D. Wallace, "Clusters of Nations in the Global System, 1865-1964," in Explaining War, ed. J. David Singer (Beverly Hills, Calif.: Sage, 1979), p. 267; nor did 1962 data show commonality of membership: Bruce M. Russett, International Regions and the International System (Chicago: Rand McNally, 1967), pp. 103-8.

24. Michael D. Wallace and J. David Singer, "Intergovernmental Organization in the Global System, 1816-1964: A Quantitative Description," International Organization 24 (Spring 1970): table 2, p. 269.

25. Schubert, "Toward a 'Working Peace System,'" p. 457.

26. The Union of International Associations (UIA) listed 832 NGOs as of 1951, and 2,401 as of 1976. UIA, Yearbook of International Organizations, 1977.

27. Data for this section were collected from ibid.

28. The Federation of ASEAN Shippers' Council and the Association of Southeast Asian Publishers; there are also a number of NGOs headquartered in the ASEAN region with membership drawn from other countries as well (Association of Pediatric Societies of the Southeast Asian Region, Southeast Asian Society of Soil Engineering, Southeast Asia Iron and Steel Institute, Association of Southeast Asian Institutes of Higher Learning), which are not included in this section.

29. Jacobson, Networks of Interdependence, p. 127.

30. Leon Lindberg, "Interest Group Activities in the EEC," in Regional International Organizations: Structures and Functions, ed. Paul Tharp (New York: St. Martin's Press, 1971), pp. 11-20.

31. Philippe Schmitter, "Bureaucratic Political Activism in LAFTA," in Regional International Organizations, ed. Tharp, pp. 21-35.

32. The sources used in compiling this list are wide, but started from the list presented in Association of Southeast Asian Nations, 10 Years ASEAN (Jakarta: ASEAN Secretariat, 1978), p. 239f. References in newspaper articles, ASEAN Chamber of Commerce and Industry documents, and other sources have been checked and added. This list is probably incomplete, particularly in sociocultural and professional groups, which receive little publicity. I know, for example, that there must be a coordinating committee for the ASEAN Games similar to the Olympic Committee, but no reference to it has been discovered.

33. The ASEAN Central Bank Group was formed, with ASEAN, in 1967, but it appears to have been absorbed by the ASEAN Bankers' Association.

34. "Economic Cooperation among Member Countries of the Association of South East Asian Nations: Report of a United Nations Team," Journal of Development Planning 7 (1974): 239-40.

35. Quote from ASEAN Review, September 4, 1976, p. 29. See also reports in Straits Times, March 1, 1976; and July 9, 1976; and New Nation, June 2, 1976. More generally, see Michael Skully, ASEAN Regional Financial Cooperation: Developments in Banking and Finance (Singapore: Institute of Southeast Asian Studies, 1979).

36. New Nation, January 7, 1978; ASEAN Briefing, April 1979; July 1979; February 1980; and Far Eastern Economic Review, February 1, 1980, pp. 34-36; and February 15, 1980, pp. 60-61.

37. Skully, ASEAN Regional Financial Cooperation, p. 12; and Business International Asia, ASEAN: Challenges of an Integrating Market (Hong Kong: BIA, 1979), p. 42.

38. Straits Times (Malaysia), September 24, 1973; October 19, 1973; and July 2, 1975; and New Straits Times, April 17, 1975.

39. Straits Times, September 27, 1977; Far Eastern Economic Review, February 23, 1979, pp. 98-99; and ASEAN Briefing, November 1980.

40. Straits Times, June 27, 1977; and ASEAN Briefing, April 1980.

41. Korea was admitted as an associate member in mid-1979, and Hong Kong and Taiwan reported considering similar moves to institutionalize present levels of cooperation: ASEAN Briefing, July 1979. See also Thomas Allen, The ASEAN Report, vol. 2 (Hong Kong: Dow-Jones, 1979), pp. 96-97.

42. New Straits Times, November 19, 1974; and April 26, 1975.

43. Far Eastern Economic Review, May 12, 1978, pp. 36-38.

44. Asia Research Bulletin, vol. 8, no. 8 (January 31, 1979).

45. Straits Times, May 25, 1976; Asia Research Bulletin, vol. 6, no. 11 (April 30, 1977); and Abdul Rahman bin Haji Yusof, "Effective Program for ASEAN Industrial Cooperation, 1978-1983" (Paper presented at the Third Conference of the Federation of ASEAN Economics Associations, Kuala Lumpur, 1978), p. 6.

46. Straits Times, December 18, 1974, reporting on remarks of the chairman of the ASEAN Permanent Committee of Commerce and Industry.

47. ASEAN Business Quarterly 3 (1979): 26-27.

48. Interview, Lee Ong Pong, secretary-general of the Singapore Federation of Chambers of Commerce and Industry, Singapore, September 1979; see also the constitution of the ASEAN Chambers of Commerce and Industry, reproduced in Allen, ASEAN Report, p. 31; and Association of Southeast Asian Nations, Chambers of Commerce and Industry (ASEAN-CCI), ASEAN-CCI Handbook, 1981 (Singapore: ASEAN-CCI, 1901).

49. New Straits Times, November 25, 1975; and Straits Times, November 27, 1976.

50. This information is based on interviews in the Ministry of Trade, Republic of the Philippines, October 1979.

51. New Nation, November 23, 1976.

52. Fibers, paper, and milk powder, for example. "The Worm Turns," Commerce (Manila), November 25, 1975, pp. 10-15. To some degree this has materialized in the commodity clubs, discussed below.

53. Journal of Development Planning 7 (1974): 57-58.

54. New Straits Times, July 17, 1975; and Straits Times, July 1, 1976; and November 27, 1976.

55. Reports of approval. See ASEAN Briefing, May 1980; and Far Eastern Economic Review, October 10, 1980, pp. 78-79.

56. Association of Southeast Asian Nations, Chambers of Commerce and Industry (ACCI), Report of the First Plenary Meeting of the ASEAN-CCI Working Group on Industrial Complementation (Singapore: ACCI, June 30, 1976), pp. 23, 27, 50, 58-66; and author interview, Malaysian Industrial Development Authority, Kuala Lumpur, October 1979.

57. Far Eastern Economic Review, October 10, 1980, p. 78; and author interview, Singapore Federation of Chambers of Commerce and Industry, September 1979.

58. Then chairman of the ASEAN Chambers of Commerce and Industry, Kamarul Ariffin, quoted in New Straits Times, June 29, 1976.

59. Proposals were changed in 1978 and again in 1979. ASEAN Business Quarterly 4 (1978): 48; Straits Times, February 27, 1979; Asian Wall Street Journal, January 27, 1979; and ASEAN Briefing, September 1979.

60. ASEAN Briefing, July 1980.

61. Edward Janner Sinaga, "ASEAN: Economic, Political and Defense Problems, Progress and Prospects in Regional Cooperation with Reference to the Role of Major Powers in Southeast Asia" (Ph.D. diss., George Washington University, 1974), p. 117.

62. Straits Times, November 27, 1976.

63. Reports in Asia Research Bulletin, April 30, 1972; and New Straits Times, October 24, 1977.

64. ASEAN Briefing, May 1979; August 1979; and June 1980.

65. M. L. Prachaksilp Tongyai reports on one meeting of the organization in "Japanese Silence: ASEAN Noise," Asia-Pacific Community 4 (Spring 1979): 63-65; and Far Eastern Economic Review, December 28, 1979, p. 32.

66. ASEAN Briefing, August 1980; and September 1980.

67. ASEAN Business Quarterly 1 (1979): 24; and ASEAN Briefing, October 1980.

68. Straits Times, May 30, 1978; and June 17, 1978.

69. The ASEAN Tours and Travel Association is the active private organization in that sector.

70. Far Eastern Economic Review, December 8, 1978, pp. 47-49; Straits Times, November 14, 1978; Business Times, December 5, 1978; and New Straits Times, November 5, 1978.

71. ASEAN Briefing, April 1980; and Far Eastern Economic Review, July 18, 1980, p. 51.

72. For example: Razak, Foreign Affairs Malaysia, vol. 8, no. 3 (September 1975); Marcos, Straits Times, November 4, 1977; Lee, Straits Times, December 13, 1978; and Kriangsak, New Nation, February 15, 1978.

73. New Straits Times, October 24, 1977.

74. Straits Times, June 20, 1979.

75. Far Eastern Economic Review, December 28, 1980, pp. 31-32; and July 18, 1980, pp. 51-52; and ASEAN Briefing, January 1980.

76. Singapore was reluctant to go along with complementation schemes because it was feared that preferred products would be more expensive, reducing their global competiveness: interview, chairman, Federation of Singapore Chambers of Commerce and Industry, September 1979. The other governments were unwilling to emasculate the schemes, but made participation voluntary in October 1980: Far Eastern Economic Review, October 10, 1980, p. 78.

77. Unless otherwise indicated, this section is based on interviews with officials in the Malaysian Industrial Development Authority, the National Economic and Development Authority (Philippines), the Singapore Federation of Chambers of Commerce and Industry, and a former ASEAN Chambers of Commerce and Industry official.

78. ASEAN Chambers of Commerce and Industry, Report of the Proceedings, Fifth Council Meeting (Singapore: ACCI, November 26, 1976), annex O.

79. Harold Crouch, The Army and Politics in Indonesia (Ithaca, N. Y.: Cornell University Press, 1978), p. 283, notes that the former head of Kostrad, General Sofjar, was the general chairman of the Indonesian Chamber of Commerce until 1973. A former Ministry of Foreign Affairs official, Abdul Hamid, was listed as the chair in 1977.

80. Azis Saleh, "Mechanisms in Indonesia for Communication in Government and Private Sectors," in Report of the First Plenary Meeting, ASEAN Chambers of Commerce and Industry, p. 53.

81. Business International Asia, ASEAN, pp. 45-46.

82. Straits Times, June 28, 1976.

83. ASEAN Briefing, prepublication issue.

84. ASEAN Business Quarterly 1 (1979): 26-27.

85. Straits Times, April 18, 1978.

86. Business International Asia, ASEAN, p. 36.

87. H. Edward English, "ASEAN's Quest for Allocative Efficiency in Manufacturing" (Paper, Canadian Asian Studies Association, Montreal, May 1980), pp. 12f.

88. Interview, Ministry of Trade, Republic of the Philippines, October 1979.

89. Straits Times, July 1, 1979.

90. Interview, former official of the ASEAN Chambers of Commerce and Industry, Manila, October 1979.

91. Interview, former Thai government economist, Singapore, September 1979.

92. Asia Research Bulletin, October 31, 1971.

93. Association of Southeast Asian Nations, ASEAN-CCI Handbook 1978, p. 57; and Far Eastern Economic Review, December 28, 1979, p. 32.

94. Far Eastern Economic Review, February 15, 1980, p. 48; and October 10, 1980, pp. 78-79; and Asian Wall Street Journal, January 29, 1979.

95. English, "ASEAN's Quest," pp. 17-23, considers the economic effect and problems of automobile complementation.

96. Association of Southeast Asian Nations, ASEAN-CCI Handbook, pp. 58-90, lists some proposals; Business International Asia, ASEAN, pp. 38-42, lists others.

97. New Nation, November 4, 1978; and Business Times, October 18, 1978.

98. Interview, Canadian High Commission, Singapore, September 1979.

99. Straits Times, April 18, 1976.

100. Asian Wall Street Journal, December 23, 1978.

101. Based on interviews in Singapore, Kuala Lumpur, and Manila.

102. Charles Morrison, "The ASEAN Governments and Transnational Relations" (Paper, International Studies Association, Washington, D.C., 1979), p. 14.

7

DEFENSIVE REGIONALISM
AND THE LIMITS
OF DEPENDENCE

The preceding chapters have examined in some detail an array of specific policies and historical changes in the patterns of international interactions of the ASEAN countries. The theoretical basis for this study focused attention on patterns of trade relations, investment relations, and participation in international organizations as the variables to be examined. As was pointed out, the pattern of these three types of international transactions indicates something about the strength or weakness of the states considered; particularly, that asymmetrically concentrated trade and investment relations and diffuse international participation are likely to be associated with dependence. It has been argued that certain of the policies of the five Southeast Asian states, including those directed through ASEAN, constitute a defensive strategy to reduce the degree of dependence; these policies have attempted to diversify trade and investment relations and to build the organizational basis for concerted international action through several types of international organizations.

In order to clarify the relationships between ASEAN and the international system, I reintroduce the theoretical issues raised in Chapter 2 and then summarize and evaluate the effectiveness of the ASEAN strategy.

INTERNATIONAL ECONOMIC-POLICY ORIENTATIONS

It is necessary to characterize the various policy approaches in the global economic system if the ASEAN strategy is to be placed in a comparative context. The three major approaches were discussed in Chapter 2 as they related to diversification, but now they must be related to each other in a schematic sense.

TABLE 7.1

Global Economic Policy Orientations and Available Developing
Country Strategies

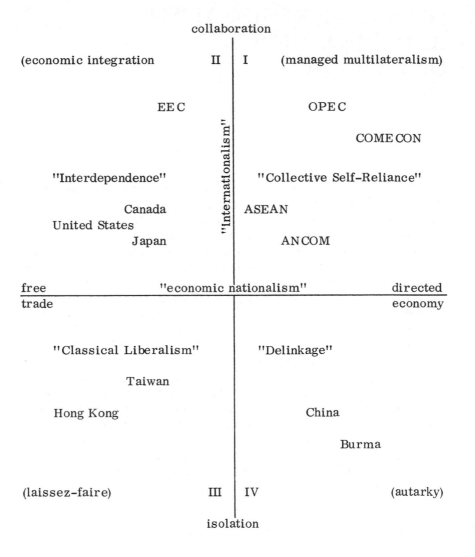

collaboration

(economic integration   II | I   (managed multilateralism)

EEC   OPEC

COMECON

"Interdependence"   "Collective Self-Reliance"

Canada   ASEAN
United States
Japan   ANCOM

free   "economic nationalism"   directed
trade   economy

"Classical Liberalism"   "Delinkage"

Taiwan

Hong Kong   China

Burma

(laissez-faire)   III | IV   (autarky)

isolation

"Internationalism" (vertical axis label)

Note: Placement of individual examples is impressionistic and
only for illustrative purposes.

Source: Compiled by the author.

Treatments of approaches to international political economy vary in complexity, but tend to array the different theories along a single continuum. This philosophical continuum extends from liberal free trade, at one extreme, to Marxism, at the other end, with economic nationalism and neomercantilism somewhere in between;[1] Walleri adds to this convention a position he labels "internationalism," essentially as a variant of economic nationalism.[2] Although this scheme does differentiate important aspects of associated foreign policy behavior clearly according to the political inclinations of the leaders of states, there is a second dimension that is left implicit and undeveloped.

Each of the major approaches to international political economy contains, explicitly or implicitly, a prescription for the extent of multilateral collaboration, governmental and transnational, in the global economy. The terms and style of how a nation should cooperate with others in achieving its economic goals differ according to the approach selected as a model for policy. If we develop this second dimension of "economic nationalism," the result is a four-cell characterization of major approaches, as in Table 7.1.

On the left side of Table 7.1, toward "free trade," government intervention is low, leaving transnational actors, such as trading companies, multinational corporations, and international banks, free to operate; national government regulation of transnational actors increases as the policy model moves toward a "directed economy." This is the common dimension of economic nationalism as it affects the international political economy; governments buffer international forces through national legislation. However, governments also differ in how much they cooperate with each other. At the bottom of Table 7.1, this cooperation is minimal ("isolation"), and it increases, moving upward ("collaboration"), both in intergovernmental cooperation through international organizations (General Agreement on Tariffs and Trade [GATT]) and in transgovernmental activity (as occurs at many levels in the European Economic Community [EEC]) to coordinate policy. Here, governments control the effects of relatively free transnational activity through collaboration (interdependence) or collectively regulate transnational forces (collective self-reliance).

Classical liberalism would, in pure form, result in an international economic system controlled by markets rather than by states. Although the volume of transactions would presumably be high, political cooperation would not be necessary—any intervention in the market is seen as undesirable. States can remain politically isolated from one another in economic matters and can allow factor endowments to structure transnational economic flows. Of course, to Adam Smith any manifestation of economic nationalism, and particularly mercantilism, was purely anathema.[3] Thus, economic nationalism and internationalism would both be low; this is represented by quadrant III in Table 7.1. Although few states actually practice this approach, support in rhetoric is not so rare.

Research into transnational politics and into the resulting interdependence points to a conceptually distinct variety of economic liberalism. Policy is portrayed as set, not so much by states as unitary actors, or by markets, but by transnational networks of government and private actors, acting to coordinate policies by combinations of formal and informal collaboration, through and around institutional settings. The complete development of this variant would be global integration through policy harmonization.[4] The reality of most major industrial states is modified economic liberalism, with a high degree of interdependence managed by decentralized political collaboration. Thus economic nationalism is relatively low and internationalism relatively high, as represented by quadrant II.

The growing body of dependency theories, drawing on a historical interpretation of capitalist development in the "world system," depicts the present state of Third World impoverishment and underdevelopment as a direct result of penetration. The only strategy, then, that would halt further elaboration of this process is withdrawal from the international economic system, or at least from the capitalist portion of it. This is variously referred to as "delinking" or "self-reliance," and it involves partial or whole disengagement from the international system of economic relations, followed at a later date by selective restructuring of trade relations to avoid any concentrated links with dominant states.[5] Normally a socialist revolution is seen as the intrinsic domestic component of this policy set. This combines a high degree of economic nationalism with dramatically reduced internationalism; the logical extreme would be autarky. Few states have successfully practiced this policy, with the notable examples of Burma and China now appearing to abandon the extremes of isolation. Table 7.1 encompasses this alternative in quadrant IV.

Maldistribution of global wealth is also the starting point for the fourth major policy orientation, that of collective self-reliance. Numerous attempts have been made to alter the structure of economic relations between the South and the North through some type of collective action. Regional organizations of developing states are the most pervasive example of this orientation, aimed at increasing the scope for their trade through collective action and tariff reductions, following the advice of the UN Economic Commission for Latin America under Raul Prebisch.[6] Commodity organizations, such as the Organization of Petroleum Exporting Countries (OPEC), have raised the expectations of other exporting nations for a shift in control over prices and revenues. The United Nations Conference on Trade and Development (UNCTAD), in calling for a new international eco-

nomic order, is the most diffuse example of what Mortimer refers to
as "the idea of empowerment through solidarity and collective action."[7] The label "collective self-reliance" is a contradiction in
terms only at first glance; the meaning of acquiring effective control
over one's own resources through internationalism in opposition to the
dominant economic powers is quite clear when viewed from a Third
World perspective. The full development of this policy orientation
would result in a system of managed multilateralism through which
nationally defined economic goals would be sought through international coalitions. This high degree of internationalism with economic
nationalism constitutes quadrant I in Table 7.1.

The main line of debate over which policy orientation is the
most appropriate for developing countries focuses on liberalism versus
socialist delinking. The advocates of liberalism urge greater opening
of national economies to international trade and investment, and participation in the interdependent system of more highly industrialized
states.[8] The dependistas counter that this was precisely what fostered underdevelopment in the first place and that cutting links with
this system is the only remedy. The literature on interdependence
partially supports this contention as, for small states, vulnerability
is likely to be highly asymmetrical rather than mutual, resulting in
substantial differences in bargaining resources and power to the disadvantage of the small state. On the other hand, a substantial degree
of autarky has neither proved in practice to be the route to economic
growth for China or Burma, nor has it been easily achieved by Tanzania.[9] It would appear that the developing countries, following a
liberal policy and relying less on economic nationalism, would be
forced to follow the classical liberal option rather than interdependence as they lack the organizational resources to participate fully
and effectively in an interdependent option. At the same time, when
even the largest nation attempting to remain self-reliant has failed to
achieve a degree of economic growth that satisfies domestic aspirations, a policy of delinkage appears inordinately expensive to even
smaller nations. The real choice is between peripheral liberalism
and collective self-reliance for the developing countries; this is particularly the case if domestic economic policies are predicated on
increasing welfare through economic growth rather than through redistribution of existing resources.

From this perspective, the debate has been over the wrong two
policy orientations. A peripheral position in a liberal international
economic system is an unstable one; planning for domestic economic
growth can only be a series of responses to unstable commodity
prices and shifts in comparative advantage in the wider global system.
Even if the arguments of unfair exchange between developed and developing countries were incorrect and could be remedied through

mechanisms of interdependence, this uncertainty is a major disadvantage. It would appear that this is a major reason for the growing interest among developing countries in schemes of collective self-reliance and for the selection of Economic Cooperation among Developing Countries (ECDC) as the preferred strategy of the Group of 77;[10] it is significant that the shift to ECDC came only after the perceived failure of another internationalist strategy, UNCTAD, part of the New International Economic Order.

However attractive as this strategy might appear as a means of shifting the pattern of global resource distribution, there are few examples of success. Increasing the level of economic nationalism has some undesirable effects, for example in decreasing the flow of foreign investment, but this would not appear to be the major obstacle. Political collaboration has been the difficult element to introduce. Rivalry for leadership in regional organizations of Third World states and commodity organizations has been rife (OPEC provides an instructive example), leading to fragmentation and stagnation. If liberalism is undesirable, collective self-reliance appears unattainable.

The ASEAN strategy is one variant of collective self-reliance. It combines political collaboration through a regional organization with domestic policies designed to reduce dependence. In order to assess the success of, and preconditions for, this variant of a collective self-reliance strategy, I review the findings of the previous chapters.

ASEAN AS DEFENSIVE REGIONALISM

At the core, the idea of reducing the imbalance of power of the local states relative to the large industrial states, often also former colonial powers, is endemic to the regional organization's members. However, the examination of policies in prior chapters reveals a more complex pattern, which was separated here into issues of trade, foreign investment, and international organizations.

In the area of trade policy, there has for some time been concern over concentrated relations with a single great-power partner. Following independence, Malaysia moved fairly rapidly to reduce the preponderance of British trade; likewise, the Philippines expressed concern over continuing expressions of U.S. economic dominance.[11] Awash in a Malay sea, Singapore made the shift to a globally oriented trading state after its separation from Malaysia. This postcolonial concern was reinforced by the resurgence of Japan as an economic power in the region in the early 1970s.

The result has been a substantial shift toward a policy of trade diversification. Singapore formally adopted this policy in 1965, but implemented it in a series of phases culminating in a large-scale trade diversification drive in 1976. Malaysia refocused attention on the disadvantages of concentrated trade with the rise of concern over the increasing role of Japan in 1972 and again in the past few years. Thailand also experienced anti-Japanese sentiment by 1972, but in large measure the government failed to formulate concrete policy until 1977 and 1978. Anti-Japanese riots in Indonesia in 1974 prompted some efforts to diversify away from an overpresence of Japanese trade, but continued support for this policy flagged in the mid-1970s, only to re-emerge with Repelita III, the economic plan for 1979-83. The Philippines initiated a far more active trade policy after 1972, with the explicit goal of reducing the relative role of the United States; within a few years Japan, the partner selected to balance the United States, was the target of concern in its own right, and policy now focuses on courting Europe. Singapore and the Philippines appear to have the most elaborate policies for diversification, with the others largely responding with ad hoc measures as domestic sentiment peaks, occasionally followed by a lapse of attention; Indonesia may now be joining the consistent diversification planners as well.

Although the major impetus to policies of trade diversification was the threat of overdependence on a single large economic power, more general diversification was also sought. The concern about the role of the single largest trading partner led each country to attempt to develop a counterweight from one of the other global trading powers. As this policy's effects became obvious, in that another dependency could replace the first, a greater emphasis emerged on reducing the combined role of the major industrial powers. This is particularly evident in the Philippines, Singapore, and Malaysia, with Indonesia apparently arriving at the same conclusion by 1979. The result is that trading partners among the smaller industrial countries, including those of Eastern Europe, have been sought to provide the same goods with less political baggage. Other Third World countries have also become the focus of trade efforts, particularly with the shift of emphasis in UNCTAD from bargaining with the large industrial countries to Economic Cooperation among Developing Countries. These two trends are quite evident, again, in the policies of the Philippines and Singapore, with Thailand and Indonesia also eyeing the Third World trade, and Malaysia actively cultivating smaller industrial countries. The thrust of trade diversification has shifted to encompass other developing countries and smaller industrial nations.

In terms of dependence, the desire is to reduce specific vulnerabilities. By spreading trade over a wider base, no particular influence accrues to any specific partner. By exerting more national control over the pattern of trade, it is slowly restructured to reduce political dependence. This policy is entirely in line with that advocated

by the delinkage school in its political goal, but it differs in that the
total volume of trade is expected to increase, rather than decrease,
over time. Trade diversification represents an increase in economic
nationalism as a policy orientation.

In addition to the rise of economic nationalism as the informing
element of national policy, there has been an increase in internationalism. The regional organization has been used as a tool of trade
policy in several ways. Specific bilateral trade issues with the dialogue partners have been channeled through ASEAN, trade promotion
has been a central concern, and particularly desirable partners in
the counterbalancing act have been courted as a group effort. These
efforts would appear to contribute directly to national trade diversification. In addition, the relative influence of each ASEAN member has
been increased as the group has behaved more as a bloc; a bloc of
Southeast Asian nations is far more significant to outside trading
partners than any one individually. This to some degree redresses
the imbalance of sensitivity between the ASEAN members and the
larger trade partners; the major nations have been more responsive
to ASEAN than they were to its members. Thus, specific vulnerabilities have been the target of increasing economic nationalism, and
general sensitivity has been the province of the increase in internationalism.

Policies of trade diversification have had some effect. All countries except Indonesia showed a lower level of trade concentration in
1979 than in 1967; even Indonesia was less concentrated than was the
case at the peak of 1974 (refer to Tables 4.3-4.7). Here, too, another point is clarified. The universal rise in concentration in the
period from 1968 to 1970 is due largely to a rapid growth rate in trade
with Japan; for Indonesia and the Philippines, this trend lasted into
1974. Correspondence with the rise of anti-Japanese sentiments is
almost exact, as is the shift to a policy of diversification. Diversification appears to have continued beyond the anticolonial phase as a
response to Japanese economic penetration in the 1970s.

In addition to the pattern of general geographical diversification,
specific reductions in sensitivities and vulnerabilities were achieved.
Each member of ASEAN reduced the proportion of trade with the large
industrial countries as a group: the Philippines, Singapore, and
Thailand by significant margins, and Malaysia and Indonesia by small
increments. Overall sensitivity to the interconnected system of the
major industrial economies was reduced, which decreases the asymmetry of general economic relations (refer to Table 4.2). Singapore,
Malaysia, and Indonesia reduced the role of their predominant partners in Europe, which reduced a source of vulnerability; unfortunately,
Indonesia became newly vulnerable to Japan for no net gain. The role
of Japan was similarly eroded in Singapore, Thailand, and the Philip-

pines. Philippine vulnerability to the United States, its primary concern, was quite strikingly reduced. The only country that did not shift the pattern of vulnerability and sensitivity in its favor was Indonesia. Each of the other four increased its structural power through trade diversification.

The results of diversification follow rather closely from policy expressions summarized earlier, reducing the likelihood that this is simply a serendipitous trend. Post-1972 concern in the Philippines, post-1974 anxiety in Indonesia, post-1972 policies in Malaysia, domestic concern in Thailand after 1972, and Singapore's 1976 trade drive are all apparent in the most diffuse measure of geographical concentration presented here. States can indeed influence the pattern of their structural relations in trade, even with the invincible giants.

In the second major issue area, that of direct foreign investment, there is also a pattern of policy evolution that fits the guidelines of collective self-reliance. The pattern of concern over the role of foreign investors closely parallels that previously discussed in regard to dominance of particular trade partners, and it will not be repeated here except to note that the apparent causes of concern are again the role of the former colonial powers and then the resurgence of Japan in the 1970s. If anything, the degree of alarm has been more acute over investment than over trade, which is understandable given the more permanent presence of investment.

Policy regarding foreign investment has gone through three analytical stages, following a commitment on the part of all five ASEAN members to use it extensively in their economic growth plans. Although none of these stages is necessarily chronologically distinct, and each has to some degree been present during the whole of the countries' postindependence history, one stage has appeared to be dominant at any given time and has structured the strategy of policy.

From the 1960s through the 1970s, the states of Southeast Asia attempted to exert increasing control over the terms of entry and participation of foreign capital. The precise conditions vary somewhat from state to state, but they include several major elements. Participation of foreigners is generally limited, outside of purely export-oriented projects, to some fraction that mandates that most projects will be joint ventures with locals. This is the case in Thailand, the Philippines, and Indonesia, with Singapore approximating the result without a formal policy; Malaysia's New Economic Policy, although requiring joint ventures only in specific areas, in effect requires joint ventures with the quasi-government holding agencies through the bumiputra preference system. In some cases, the length of time a foreign interest can maintain majority control is also limited, particularly in the Philippines and Indonesia. Each of the ASEAN states guides foreign investment into particular economic sectors through incentives; since most foreign-investment entry requires approval, this in effect screens proposals for desirability and excludes investment in areas designated as preserves for domestic entrepreneurs, or in the case of Singapore, areas considered to be too technology-poor. In industries considered to involve the use or exploitation of scarce resources, such as mining, forestry, or petroleum products, the nature of the allowable contract has become consistently more restrictive: for example, Indonesia's several generations of mining contracts, Malaysia's Petroleum Development Act, or Thailand's ban on the export of unprocessed teak. Plans for increasing local processing or for diversifying product lines are also important elements in approval, particularly in Singapore and Malaysia and increasingly so in Indonesia and the Philippines. These exercises in economic nationalism have come to characterize each of the ASEAN states to a fairly high degree.

Increasing economic nationalism, however, contributed to a second stage in policy evolution. In combination with recession in the major investing countries in the mid-1970s, these policies resulted in a sharp downturn in investment inflow. The resulting concern over the domestic investment climate, considered by foreign (and some local) business managers to be too restrictive, generated a flurry of backtracking in controls and efforts to promote investment wherever possible. Malaysia relaxed the Industrial Coordination Act and emphasized its pragmatism; Thailand rescinded portions of the Alien Business Act; many high government leaders doubled as investment solicitors; export processing zones, industrial estates, and other subsidized facilities blossomed in the jungles. It became apparent that the limits of economic nationalism had been reached if foreign investment growth was also to be attained.

An international strategy was adopted to continue efforts to control the political effects of foreign investment, while allowing continued absolute expansion. Diversification of the sources of foreign investment has become the dominant strategy of the ASEAN states. Policies in the 1950s and early 1960s included this element, but it was largely directed at the former colonial power. Singapore supposedly followed this policy from independence, and Thailand in the early 1970s attempted to discourage any particular country from overcontrol of specific industries, but the Philippines in the mid-1970s was the first to explicitly incorporate diversification as a goal of national policy. Both Thailand and Singapore have, in the past few years, exhibited a greater degree of interest in actually diversifying. Indonesia has long been concerned with the implications of excessive foreign investment from any one country for the independence of its foreign policy, but, with Malaysia, it has eschewed what might be interpreted

as inflammatory rhetoric by the major investing countries it depends
upon. As Olsen points out in a different context, a lack of publicity
is a definite advantage to the effectiveness of attempts to manipulate
economic relations;[12] the low-key Malaysian and Indonesian approach
may be the most appropriate tactic. By the end of the 1970s, each
ASEAN country cited diversification as a primary part of the invest-
ment-control strategy.

Although this strategy is primarily one directed separately by
each ASEAN member, the ASEAN organization has been a significant
part of the policy process, largely in the same manner as is true for
trade diversification, previously discussed. ASEAN's most direct
contribution to investment diversification has been through a number
of bilateral activities carried on between ASEAN and major external
economic partners; these include several industrial cooperation conferences with EEC members, mediation of a number of specific problems regarding external partners' investment policies, and the creation of private business associations to link investors in the industrial countries to potential partners in ASEAN. In a more indirect
fashion, ASEAN's internal economic activities have contributed to a
stronger perception of a healthy investment climate in the region.
Constant publicity surrounding the major regional industrial projects
has drawn interest from potential investors, as have the more limited-
scale industrial complementation programs; some freeing of regional
trade through negotiated tariff reductions has also been held up to
foreign investors as beneficial to their market accessibility should
they invest in the region. Finally, the incessant haggling over the
permissible role of foreign investment in ASEAN projects has raised
the specter of a common set of investment guidelines for foreigners,
which would lessen the current element of shopping for the best bargain among several countries. To some degree, the indirect contribution has been expounded as creating a "get in now, while you can"
atmosphere for foreign investment. [13] Although the major thrust of
ASEAN activities in investment has been to increase the flow, the particular targets are carefully selected so as to contribute to diversification of the regional pool.

In terms of dependence, these policy orientations are consistent
with the model of collective self-reliance. By increasing the level of
economic nationalism, not only are more of the benefits of foreign investment presumably channeled to domestic groups, but state control
over the type and level of investment is increased, allowing for more
coherent planning of economic growth. This element of policy is quite
in line with that advocated by the delinking school, although it would,
in theory, be pursued further to outright nationalization in many cases.
The element of policy that differentiates this strategy is the focus on
internationalism. Not only do the ASEAN states pursue parts of their

control strategy through the regional organization, but their emergent focus on diversification is predicated on the notion of political vulnerability inherent in concentrated investment relations. Delinkage would aim at reducing the overall level of foreign investment, while diversification intends to allow absolute increase in levels of investment while controlling the political effects. It could be argued that delinkage is more sensitive to the domestic effects of foreign investment, while diversification is primarily targeted at associated international political effects.

The general level of geographical concentration of investment has declined for most of the ASEAN members (refer to Tables 5.2-5.6). Indonesia and the Philippines have diversified substantially from initially very high levels of concentration, while Singapore has diversified somewhat from a similarly high level. Malaysia has also achieved some diversification of the investment pool, but starting from a lower level of concentration; the most recent trend, however, is in the opposite direction. Only Thailand has increased its level of concentration, but it started from a very diversified initial position. Of the five states, Singapore stands out as the least diversified, with the other four at similar levels of diversification in the late 1970s. This points to a contrast with the case of trade, as policy seems to be less directly related to the movement of the index of concentration of investment. Singapore, with a longstanding concern, remains rather more concentrated than Thailand, which only tentatively adopted investment diversification in the late 1970s; fewer direct parallels with policy can be made in yearly movements in the other ASEAN cases, also. Despite substantial evidence of diversification among the ASEAN states, there is less evidence of a sensitivity of the flow of foreign investment to government policy.

The reason for this may be partially clarified by changes in the more specific goals of diversification. Each ASEAN member reduced the role of its largest investor, with the exception of Thailand, which remained vulnerable to Japan over the entire period. U. S. predominance in Indonesia and the Philippines was substantially eroded, although Indonesia later became vulnerable to Japan's large investment role; and Britain's position of preeminence disappeared in Malaysia and Singapore. The pattern of specific vulnerability has changed with diversification; an international political strategy has had some positive effect. However, the degree of concentration on the major industrial nations has not been reduced substantially; overall proportions of investment from the United States, Europe, and Japan have been relatively constant with rather minor fluctuations. Sensitivity to the major powers of the international economic system for investment remains high. One possible conclusion is that the international market for capital is in fact oligopolistic and that variations in investing nations' attention account for a large portion of changes in host country flows. In foreign investment, a strategy of diversification may be limited to balancing a few major investors rather than encompassing wider geographical dispersion.

These two elements of ASEAN international economic policy—trade diversification and investment control and diversification—rely largely on domestic economic nationalism for their adoption and implementation. To the degree that they are also informed by internationalism, it is of a largely noninstitutional nature. Trade and investment missions are sent to a wide variety of other countries, which requires a broadening of diplomatic relations but few formal organizations. The ASEAN regional organization is, of course, used, and its network of organizational contacts with outside states is tapped. But diversification largely involves states responding to political effects of the international economic system, in an attempt to reduce undesirable results of dependence. In this sense, diversification is also informed by political internationalism.

The more conventional conception of internationalism revolves around intergovernmental organizations, transnational organizations, diplomatic coalitions, and international conventions. This element is also evident in the case of ASEAN. Memberships in intergovernmental organizations has increased since 1967 by a substantial margin, indicating a wider base for substantive international negotiations for the ASEAN states. Perhaps of more significance, the number of these memberships that are shared, rather than independent of the other ASEAN members, has increased (by 65 percent, refer to Table 6.3), providing the basis for more and wider behavior as a bloc; the ASEAN states have become, since the early 1960s, an identifiable cluster in the system of intergovernmental organizations. As was pointed out in discussing the development of ASEAN, there is considerable evidence of collaboration within the region in preparation for meetings with outside actors, which indicates that this cluster actually behaves in a cohesive fashion.

In the realm of private transnational organizations (NGOs), an ASEAN bloc is not evident, with a very important exception. ASEAN involvement in the more universal NGOs is quite diffuse, with far fewer cases of shared memberships. This provides little opportunity for collaborative activity. However, a well-developed network of purely regional NGOs (RNGOs) has been established; it is both densely shared among the ASEAN members and provides considerable evidence of collaborative activity. This collaboration is not only among the ASEAN members but it is also between the ASEAN members as an organized bloc and external actors.

The focus of activity in these areas of organized political internationalism is on economic affairs. One-half of the intergovernmental

organizations (IGOs) are substantively concerned with international
economic affairs, as are three-quarters of the RNGOs, while only
one-tenth of the NGOs have this focus. ASEAN's involvement in the
network of international economic affairs is heavily weighted toward
economic development.

There is, then, a substantial element of organized political internationalism among the ASEAN members. This has taken the forms
of wider involvement in existing networks of intergovernmental structures as a bloc and of the creation of new, nominally private, regional associations. In both cases, the opportunity for collaboration
among the ASEAN states has increased in two significant ways:
greater occasion for exchanges of information within the regional
grouping exists and more opportunities for acting as a bloc in reference
to actors external to the region are created. In terms of dependence,
the development of networks of state and private international organizations has occurred in such a manner as to reverse the structural
imbalance between these developing countries and their largely developed economic partners by creating the basis for bloc action with
developed countries and by shifting more organizational ties toward
other developing countries.

International organizations provide the infrastructure of internationalism. For the ASEAN states to collaborate in attaining common goals in the international system, a cohesive set of organizations
must exist. The governments of the ASEAN states have joined the
same organizations to a greater degree now than was the case in
1967; by doing so, they have acquired the ability to behave as bloc when
their common interests dictate or when one member is able to mobilize
the other members to its cause. Within the region, the governments
have fostered the formation of RNGOs that tie local interests together;
often, this is in opposition to external interests. The RNGOs sub-
stitute regional ties for unorganized contacts with outside agents who
have access to more powerful organizations, such as multinational
corporations. For the private sectors of the ASEAN members, these
RNGOs may be the most significant aspect of the ASEAN organization;
by sharing information and by providing forums for collective negotiation, they may eventually result in a decisive shift of bargaining
power. The structural basis for internationalism has been created
around ASEAN.

The economic policy orientation of the ASEAN states, then, relies heavily on a combination of economic nationalism and internationalism, an orientation broadly categorized as collective self-reliance. It seems apposite to describe the ASEAN policy orientation
as "defensive regionalism." Few would expect that these states will
become a significant power center in the international system, but
their policies seem to aim at increasing their local influence and

autonomy through changes in the structure of economic influence in the fields of trade, investment, and international organizations. This strategy has met with modest success: the structural changes are moderate, but are clearly in the direction of reducing dependence.

DEFENSIVE REGIONALISM AND
THE LIMITS OF DEPENDENCE

Establishing precise boundaries for a transition from dependence to autonomy seems unhelpful. Any quantitative demarcation implies that the phenomenon of dependence is discrete: a given state is either dependent or autonomous. This does not correspond to reality, where states are more or less dependent or interdependent in particular issue areas and at given times, as their relative power positions change. Also, in a "through the looking glass" world, a precise cutoff point means what you want it to mean; because there is a baseline figure, Singapore changes its status from developing to developed frequently, depending on the skill of its staticians in manipulating national-income figures for international banks. What would appear to make some sense is in showing in what direction a set of indicators of dependence is moving: toward increased dependence or toward increased autonomy.

It has been argued that the ASEAN states are moving toward increased autonomy in the specific issue areas examined. Trade relations have become generally more diversified and specifically less concentrated on a single partner; investment sources have become more diversified generally by balancing the formerly major partners with one or two others; ASEAN participation in international organizations has become more characterized by bloc membership and by locally centered transnational associations. The structure of power is being altered away from continued dependence.

While I think that the evidence clearly supports this conclusion, it also seems prudent to indicate what I am not contending. Caporaso has argued for a distinction between "dependence" as a characteristic of a state's position in the international sphere and "dependency" as a syndrome of domestic distortions of development resulting from a pattern of penetration.[14] Nothing in this book addresses the latter question: the states of ASEAN may well continue to suffer from dependency. Second, I have followed the distinction between structural power and decisional power, and I have not argued that changes in the structural pattern of power indicate that the outcomes of specific bargains have been more favorable; that is an empirical question that rests on a different type of research. Lessened dependence leads to the expectation that, over the long term, better bargains will result, but it does not, in itself, prove that they have. Third, I have not attempted to join the fray on the question of whether dependent states are diplomatic followers of their hegemons; the growing body of literature on this issue is both ambiguous and contradictory.[15] A state's votes in international forums probably result from a more sophisticated judgment than a simple tallying of dependence ties, anyway. Finally, I have not argued that the ASEAN states are no longer dependent; clearly, the balance of relative power still lies on the side of the great powers. The size of the gap may have been reduced, but more powerful states still are capable of imposing their will.

In a sense, the responses of the larger powers have permitted the ASEAN states to reduce their dependence. Although it would not be in the economic power interests of the larger global economic powers to facilitate the ASEAN states' quest for less dependence through defensive regionalism, other considerations have been present. Japan is itself concerned lest too high a profile in Southeast Asia damage wider interests, and it has sought a degree of diversification to other areas, although ASEAN remains highly important; ASEAN's demands have been met with a more solicitous response rather than with opposition. The EEC has responded enthusiastically to ASEAN courting, after having been a target of earlier anticolonial sentiment; diversification toward Europe represents an opportunity to reestablish an economic presence that was lost in Southeast Asia. U.S. security interests in Asia have again increased, leading to more diplomatic attention to the area and to responsiveness to economic requests. Should these great power needs change, the maneuverability of the ASEAN states may be constrained. For example, if increasing protectionism leads Japan to abandon the global markets for a regional one, increased Japanese economic pressure could reverse the course of trade and investment diversification. Weaker states inevitably operate within the boundaries set by larger powers.

Other limitations have already been raised. Trade diversification is restricted by economic structure, by the generally higher costs of alternate sources, and by the difficulty of penetrating new markets. Investment diversification is limited by the fact of a global market in which only a few large states export significant amounts of capital. However, the organizational part of ASEAN's strategy has not been constrained by the internal power struggles characteristic of other regional groupings; in the 1970s the ASEAN members avoided internal dissension quite well, perhaps as a result of the perception of common external threats to their security and economic well-being. The limitations of dependence have not been so great as to defeat visible progress toward greater autonomy.

The ASEAN case may be unique among Third World states in some ways, but its strategy of defensive regionalism offers another variant of collective self-reliance, which has had some success. Particularly in light of the lack of substantive change in the international economic system through universal organizations, a strategy that relies primarily on the initiative of individual states through a regional organization has a clear advantage. Few Third World states can expect to eliminate dependence, but even small reductions should be welcomed.

NOTES

1. See Joan Spero, The Politics of International Economic Relations (New York: St. Martins Press, 1977); Ronald Chilcote and Joel Edelstein, eds., Latin America: The Struggle with Dependency and Beyond (Cambridge: Schenkman, 1974), pp. 1-88; Robert Gilpin, U.S. Power and the Multinational Corporation: The Political Economy of Foreign Direct Investment (New York: Basic Books, 1975); and Helio Jaguaribe, Political Development: A General Theory and a Latin American Case Study (New York: Harper & Row, 1973).

2. R. Dan Walleri, "The Political Economy Literature on North-South Relations," International Studies Quarterly 22 (December 1978): 587-624.

3. Jacob Oser and William Blanchfield, The Evolution of Economic Thought, 3rd ed. (New York: Harcourt Brace Jovanovich, 1975), pp. 68-72.

4. For a treatment of these literatures as a single body, see Robert O. Keohane and Joseph S. Nye, "International Interdependence and Integration," in Handbook of Political Science, ed. Fred Greenstein and Nelson Polsby, vol. 8 (Reading, Mass.: Addison-Wesley, 1975).

5. In addition to the references cited in Chapter 2, see Samuel Parmar, "Self-Reliant Development in an 'Interdependent' World," in Beyond Dependency, ed. Guy Erb and Valeriana Kallab (New York: Praeger, 1975), pp. 3-27.

6. Raul Prebisch, Toward a New Trade Policy for Development (New York: United Nations, 1964).

7. Robert Mortimer, The Third World Coalition in International Politics (New York: Praeger, 1980), p. 5.

8. Chilcote and Edelstein, Latin America; and David Blake and Robert Walters, The Politics of Global Economic Relations (Englewood Cliffs, N.J.: Prentice-Hall, 1976), pp. 168-71.

9. Thomas Biersteker, "Self-Reliance in Theory and Practice in Tanzanian Trade Relations," International Organization 34 (Spring 1980): 229-64.

10. Mortimer, The Third World, describes the evolution of this strategy.

11. Benito Legarda, Jr., and Roberto Garcia, "Economic Collaboration: The Trading Relationship," in The United States and the Philippines, ed. Frank Golay (Englewood Cliffs, N.J.: Prentice-Hall, 1966), pp. 139-43.

12. Richard Olsen, "Economic Coercion in World Politics: With a Focus on North-South Relations," World Politics 31 (July 1979): 471-94.

13. This was expressed clearly to the author in interviews with economic development officials in several countries.

14. James Caporaso, "Dependence, Dependency, and Power in the Global System: A Structural and Behavioral Analysis," International Organization 32 (Winter 1978): 22.

15. For a review of some of the more recent literature, see Walleri, "The Political Economy Literature," pp. 613-20; Neil Richardson and Charles Kegley, Jr., "Trade Dependence and Foreign Policy Compliance: A Longitudinal Analysis," International Studies Quarterly 24 (June 1980): 191-222; Michael Dolan, Brian Tomlin, Maureen Molot, and Harald Von Riekhoff, "Foreign Policies of African States in Asymmetrical Dyads," International Studies Quarterly 24 (September 1980): 415-49; and Neil Richardson, "Economic Dependence and Foreign Policy Compliance: Bringing Measurement Closer to Conception" (Paper, International Studies Association, Los Angeles, March 1980).

SELECTED BIBLIOGRAPHY

BOOKS AND ARTICLES

Agoncillo, Theodora, and Milagros Guerrero. History of the Filipino People. 5th ed. Quezon City: R. P. Garcia, 1977.

Allen, Thomas. The ASEAN Report. 2 vols. Hong Kong: Dow-Jones, 1979.

_____. "Policies of the ASEAN Countries toward Direct Foreign Investment." In Asian Business and Environment in Transition, edited by A. Karpoor. Princeton, N.J.: Darwin Press, 1976.

Amnuay Viravan. "Foreign Investment in Developing Countries: Thailand." In Direct Foreign Investment in Asia and the Pacific, edited by Peter Drysdale. Toronto: University of Toronto Press, 1972.

Ariff, Mohamed. "Development of Malaysia's Trade Policy." In ASEAN Cooperation in Trade and Trade Policy, edited by Seiji Naya and Vinyu Vichit-Vadakan. Bangkok: UN Asian and Pacific Development Institute, 1977.

_____. Malaysia and ASEAN Economic Cooperation. Bangkok: UN Asian and Pacific Development Institute, 1978.

Ariff, Mohamed, Fong Chan Onn, and R. Thillainathan, eds. ASEAN Cooperation in Industrial Projects. Kuala Lumpur: Malaysian Economic Association, 1977.

Arndt, Hanna W. "ASEAN Industrial Projects." Asia-Pacific Community 2 (Fall 1978): 117-28.

Arndt, Hanna W., and Ross Garnaut. "ASEAN and the Industrialization of East Asia." Journal of Common Market Studies 17 (March 1979): 191-212.

Arudsothy, P. "Malaysia." In The Economic Development of East and Southeast Asia, edited by Shinici Ichimura. Honolulu: University Press of Hawaii, 1975.

Axline, W. Andrew. "Underdevelopment, Dependence and Integration: The Politics of Regionalism in the Third World." International Organization 31 (Winter 1977): 83-105.

Barnet, Richard, and Ronald Müller. Global Reach: The Power of the Multinational Corporations. New York: Simon & Schuster, 1974.

Baumgartner, Thomas, and Thomas R. Burns. "The Structuring of International Economic Relations." International Studies Quarterly 19 (June 1975): 126-59.

Berendsen, B. S. M. Regional Models of Trade and Development. Leiden: Martinus Nijhoff, 1978.

Bergsten, C. Fred. "The Threat Is Real." Foreign Policy 14 (Spring 1974): 84-90.

Biersteker, Thomas J. "Self-Reliance in Theory and Practice in Tanzanian Trade Relations." International Organization 34 (Spring 1980): 229-64.

Blake, David, and Robert Walters. The Politics of Global Economic Relations. Englewood Cliffs, N.J.: Prentice-Hall, 1976.

Boissevain, Jeremy. Friends of Friends: Networks, Manipulators and Coalitions. Oxford: Basil Blackwell, 1974.

Boyce, Peter. "The Machinery of Southeast Asian Regional Diplomacy." In New Directions in the International Relations of Southeast Asia: The Great Powers and Southeast Asia, edited by Lau Teik Soon. Singapore: Singapore University Press, 1973.

Busch, Peter. "Germany in the European Economic Community: Theory and Case Study." Canadian Journal of Political Science 11 (1978): 545-74.

Busch, Peter, and Donald Puchala. "Interests, Influence and Integration." Comparative Political Studies 9 (October 1976): 235-54.

Business International Asia. ASEAN: Challenges of an Integrating Market. Hong Kong: Business International Asia, 1979.

Caldwell, Malcolm. "ASEANization." Journal of Contemporary
Asia 4 (1974): 36-70.

Callis, Helmut. Foreign Capital in Southeast Asia. New York: Institute of Pacific Relations, 1942.

Cantori, Louis, and Steven Spiegel. The International Politics of Regions. Englewood Cliffs, N.J.: Prentice-Hall, 1970.

Caporaso, James. "Dependence, Dependency, and Power in the Global
System: A Structural and Behavioral Analysis." International
Organization 32 (Winter 1978): 13-44.

_____. "Methodological Issues in the Measurement of Inequality,
Dependence and Exploitation." In Testing Theories of Economic
Imperialism, edited by Steven Rosen and James Kurth. Toronto:
Lexington Books, 1974.

Castro, Amado. "The Meaning of Economic Cooperation in ASEAN."
In ASEAN Trader, pp. 35-36. Manila: ASEAN Trade Fair,
1978.

_____. "Regional Cooperation in Southeast Asia: Implications for
World Leadership." In Southeast Asia, An Emerging Center
of World Leadership? Economic and Resource Considerations,
edited by Wayne Raymond and K. Mulliner. Athens: Ohio University Center for International Studies, 1977.

Castro, Amado, ed. "The Philippines." In The Economic Development of East and Southeast Asia, edited by Shinici Ichimura.
Honolulu: University Press of Hawaii, 1976.

Chee, Stephen. "Malaysia's Changing Foreign Policy." In Trends
in Malaysia II, edited by Yang Mun Cheong. Singapore: Singapore University Press, 1974.

Chia Siow Yue. Singapore and ASEAN Economic Cooperation. Bangkok: UN Asian and Pacific Development Institute, 1978.

Chilcote, Ronald. "Dependency: A Critical Synthesis of the Literature." Latin American Perspectives 1 (Winter 1974): 4-29.

Chilcote, Ronald, and Joel Edelstein, eds. Latin America: The
Struggle with Dependency and Beyond. Cambridge, Mass.:
Schenkman, 1974.

Choucri, Nazli. "International Political Economy: A Theoretical Perspective." In Change in the International System, edited by Ole Holsti, Randolph Siverson, and Alexander George. Boulder, Colo.: Westview Press, 1980.

Chua Wee Meng. "The Singapore Economy: Past Performance, Current Structure and Future Growth Prospects." In Southeast Asian Affairs, 1977, edited by Kernial Sandhu. Singapore: Institute of Southeast Asian Studies, 1978.

Constantino, Renato, and Letizia Constantino. The Philippines: The Continuing Past. Quezon City: Foundation for Nationalist Studies, 1978.

Cooper, Richard N. "Economic Interdependence and Foreign Policy in the Seventies." World Politics 24 (January 1972): 159-81.

_____. The Economics of Interdependence: Economic Policy in the Atlantic Community. New York: McGraw-Hill, 1968.

_____. "Trade Policy Is Foreign Policy." Foreign Policy 9 (Winter 1972): 18-36.

Corea, Ernest. "ASEAN: The Road from Bali." In Development and Underdevelopment in Southeast Asia, edited by Gordon Means. Ottawa: Canadian Council for Southeast Asian Studies, 1976.

Cox, Robert W., and Harold Jacobson. The Anatomy of Influence: Decision Making in International Organizations. New Haven, Conn.: Yale University Press, 1974.

Crouch, Harold. The Army and Politics in Indonesia. Ithaca, N.Y.: Cornell University Press, 1978.

Diaz-Alejandro, Carlos. "Delinking North and South: Unshackled or Unhinged?" In Rich and Poor Nations in the World Economy, edited by Carlos Diaz-Alejandro. New York: McGraw-Hill, 1978.

Dolan, Michael, Brian Tomlin, Maureen Appel Molot, and Harald von Riekhoff. "Foreign Policies of African States in Asymmetrical Dyads." International Studies Quarterly 24 (September 1980): 415-49.

Drysdale, Peter, ed. Direct Foreign Investment in Asia and the Pacific. Toronto: University of Toronto Press, 1972.

"Economic Cooperation among Member Countries of the Association of Southeast Asian Nations: Report of a United Nations Team." Journal of Development Planning 7 (1974): 1-260.

Fifield, Russell. "ASEAN: Image and Reality." Asian Survey 19 (December 1979): 1199-1208.

_____. National and Regional Interests in ASEAN. Singapore: Institute of Southeast Asian Studies, 1979.

Funnell, Victor. "China and ASEAN: The Changing Face of Southeast Asia." World Today 31 (July 1975): 299-306.

Galtung, Johan. "A Structural Theory of Integration." Journal of Peace Research 4 (1968): 375-95.

Ghazali bin Shafie and Tan Sri Muhammad. "ASEAN's Response to Security Issues in Southeast Asia." In Regionalism in Southeast Asia. Jakarta: Centre for Strategic and International Studies, 1975.

Gilpin, Robert. U.S. Power and the Multinational Corporation: The Political Economy of Foreign Direct Investment. New York: Basic Books, 1975.

Goh Keng Swee. "Some Lessons of Recent Development Experience of ASEAN Countries." Australian Outlook 29 (December 1975): 270-78.

Golay, Frank, ed. "Economic Collaboration: The Role of American Investment." In The United States and the Philippines, edited by Frank Golay. Englewood Cliffs, N.J.: Prentice-Hall, 1966.

_____. "Economic Underpinnings of Southeast Asia." In Southeast Asia, An Emerging Center of World Influence? Economic and Resource Considerations, edited by Wayne Raymond and K. Mulliner. Athens: Ohio University Center for International Studies, 1977.

_____. "National Economic Priorities and International Coalitions." In Diversity and Development in Southeast Asia, edited by Guy Pauker, Frank Golay, and Cynthia Enloe. New York: McGraw-Hill, 1977.

_____. Underdevelopment and Economic Nationalism in Southeast Asia. Ithaca, N.Y.: Cornell University Press, 1969.

Gordon, Bernard. The Dimensions of Conflict in Southeast Asia. Englewood Cliffs, N.J.: Prentice-Hall, 1966.

Haas, Ernst B. "On System and International Regimes." World Politics 37 (January 1975): 147-74.

_____. "Turbulent Fields and the Theory of Regional Integration." International Organization 30 (Spring 1976): 173-212.

Haas, Michael. "The ASEANization of Asian International Relations." Asia-Pacific Community 6 (Fall 1979): 73-86.

Halliday, Jon, and Gavin McCormack. Japanese Imperialism Today. New York: Monthly Review Press, 1973.

Hill, H. Monte. "Community Formation within ASEAN." International Organization 32 (Spring 1978): 569-75.

Hirschman, Albert O. National Power and the Structure of Foreign Trade. Berkeley and Los Angeles: University of California Press, 1945.

Hoan, Buu. "Asia Needs a New Approach to the Multinationals." In ASEAN and a Positive Strategy for Foreign Investment, edited by Lloyd Vasey. Honolulu: University Press of Hawaii, 1978.

Holsti, K. J. "A New International Politics? Diplomacy in Complex Interdependence." International Organization 32 (Spring 1978): 513-30.

Horelick, Arnold. "The Soviet Union's Asian Collective Security Proposal: A Club in Search of Members." Pacific Affairs 47 (Fall 1974): 269-85.

Howell, Llewellyn, Jr. "Attitudinal Distance in Southeast Asia: Social and Political Ingredients in Integration." Southeast Asia 11 (Winter 1974): 577-608.

Hughes, Helen, and You Pok Seng, eds. Foreign Investment and Industrialization in Singapore. Madison: University of Wisconsin Press, 1969.

Huntington, Samuel. "Transnational Organizations in World Politics." World Politics 25 (April 1973): 333-68.

Indorf, Hans. ASEAN: Problems and Prospects. Singapore: Institute of Southeast Asian Studies, 1975.

Ingram, James. Economic Change in Thailand, 1850-1970. Stanford, Calif.: Stanford University Press, 1971.

Inkeles, Alex. "The Emerging Social Structure of the World." World Politics 27 (July 1975): 467-95.

Jabar, Tayseer. "Review Article: The Relevance of Traditional Integration Theory to Less Developed Countries." Journal of Common Market Studies 9 (1970): 254-67.

Jacobson, Harold K. Networks of Interdependence: International Organizations and the Global Political System. New York: Alfred Knopf, 1979.

Jaguaribe, Helio. Political Development: A General Theory and a Latin American Case Study. New York: Harper & Row, 1973.

James, Elijah M. "The Political Economy of Export Concentration." Journal of Economic Issues 15 (December 1980): 967-75.

Johnson, Harry. "A Theoretical Model of Economic Nationalism in New and Developing States." Political Science Quarterly 80 (June 1965): 169-85.

Jorgensen-Dahl, Arnfinn. "ASEAN 1967-1976: Development or Stagnation?" Pacific Community 7 (July 1976): 519-35.

_____. "Extra-Regional Influences on Regional Cooperation in S. E. Asia." Pacific Community 8 (April 1977): 412-29.

Kaiser, Karl. "Transnational Politics: Toward a Theory of Multinational Politics." International Organization 25 (Autumn 1971): 790-817.

Kanapathy, V. "Investments in ASEAN: Perspectives and Prospects." United Malayan Banking Corporation, Economic Review 15 (1979): 18-40.

Kartadjoemena, H. S. The Politics of External Economic Relations: Indonesia's Options in the Post-Detente Era. Singapore: Institute of Southeast Asian Studies, 1977.

Kegley, Charles, Jr., and Llewellyn Howell, Jr. "The Dimensionality of Regional Integration: Construct Validation in the Southeast Asian Context." International Organization 29 (Autumn 1975): 997-1020.

Keohane, Robert O., and Joseph S. Nye. "International Interdependence and Integration." In Handbook of Political Science, edited by Fred Greenstein and Nelson Polsby. Vol. 8, International Politics. Reading, Mass.: Addison-Wesley, 1975.

_____. Power and Interdependence: World Politics in Transition. Boston: Little, Brown, 1977.

_____. "Transgovernmental Relations and International Organizations." World Politics 27 (October 1974): 39-62.

_____. "World Politics and the International Economic System." In The Future of the International Economic Order: An Agenda for Research, edited by C. Fred Bergsten. Lexington, Mass.: D. C. Heath, 1973.

Keohane, Robert O., and Van Doorn Oms. "The Multinational Enterprise and World Political Economy." International Organization 26 (Winter 1972): 84-120.

Ker Sin Tze. Public Enterprise in ASEAN. Singapore: Institute of Southeast Asian Studies, 1978.

Khien Theeravit. "Trends and Problems in Thai Foreign Policy." In Trends in Thailand II, edited by Somporn Sangchai and Lim Joo-Jock. Singapore: Singapore University Press, 1976.

Khoman Thanat. "ASEAN: Problems and Prospects in a Changing World." In The ASEAN: Problems and Prospects in a Changing World, edited by Sarasin Viraphol, Amphan Manatra, and Masabide Shibusa. Bangkok: Institute of Asian Studies, Chulalongkorn University, 1976.

King, Frank H. H. "The Foreign Policy of Singapore." In The Other Powers: Studies in the Foreign Policies of Small States, edited by R. P. Barston. New York: Harper & Row, 1973.

Knorr, Klaus. The Power of Nations: The Political Economy of International Relations. New York: Basic Books, 1975.

Koh, T. T. B. "International Collaboration concerning Southeast Asia." The Annals 390 (July 1970): 18-26.

Kohlhagen, Steven. "Host Country Policies and the Flow of Direct Foreign Investment in the ASEAN Countries." In International Business in the Pacific Basin, edited by Hal Mason. Toronto: D. C. Heath, 1978.

Korbin, Stephen. "Foreign Enterprise and Forced Divestment in the LDCs." International Organization 34 (Winter 1980): 65-88.

Kraar, Louis, and Stephen Blank. "Malaysia: The High Cost of Affirmative Action." Asia (March-April 1980): 6-9.

Krasner, Stephen D. Defending the National Interest: Raw Materials Investments and United States Foreign Policy. Princeton, N.J.: Princeton University Press, 1978.

_____. "State Power and the Structure of International Trade." World Politics 28 (April 1976): 317-47.

LaPorte, Todd, ed. Organized Social Complexity: Challenge to Politics and Policy. Princeton, N.J.: Princeton University Press, 1975.

Lau Teik Soon. "ASEAN and the Bali Summit." Pacific Community 7 (July 1976): 536-50.

_____. "ASEAN and the Future of Regionalism." In New Directions in the International Relations of Southeast Asia: The Great Powers and Southeast Asia, edited by Lau Teik Soon. Singapore: Singapore University Press, 1973.

Lee Soo-Ann. Industrialization in Singapore. Melborne: Longmans, 1973.

Lee Soo-Ann, ed. New Directions in the International Relations of Southeast Asia: Economic Relations. Singapore: Singapore University Press, 1973.

Legarda, Benito, Jr., and Roberto Garcia. "Economic Collaboration: The Trading Relationship." In The United States and the Philippines, edited by Frank Golay. Englewood Cliffs, N.J.: Prentice-Hall, 1966.

Leifer, Michael. "The ASEAN States and the Progress of Regional Cooperation in Southeast Asia." In Politics, Society and Economy in the ASEAN States, edited by Bernard Dahm and Werner Draguhn. Wiesbaden: Otto Harrassowitz, 1975.

_____. "The ASEAN States: No Common Outlook." International Affairs 49 (October 1973): 600-7.

_____. Dilemmas of Statehood in Southeast Asia. Vancouver: University of British Columbia Press, 1972.

_____. "Regionalism, the Global Balance and Southeast Asia." In Regionalism in Southeast Asia. Jakarta: Centre for Strategic and International Studies, 1975.

Leonard, H. Jeffery. "Multinational Corporations and Politics in Developing Countries." World Politics 32 (April 1980): 454-83.

Lim, Robyn Abell. "The Philippines and the Formation of ASEAN." Review of Indonesian and Malay Affairs 7 (January 1973): 1-18.

Lim Chong Yah. "ASEAN's Package Deal Industrial Projects." Asia-Pacific Community 2 (Fall 1978): 129-39.

Lim Joo-Jock, ed. Foreign Investment in Singapore: Some Broader Economic and Socio-political Ramifications. Singapore: Institute of Southeast Asian Studies, 1977.

Lyon, Peter. "ASEAN and the Future of Regionalism." In New Directions in the International Relations of Southeast Asia: The Great Powers and Southeast Asia, edited by Lau Teik Soon. Singapore: Singapore University Press, 1973.

_____. "Regional Organization and Southeast Asia." Southeast Asian Spectrum 4 (April-June 1976): 33-42.

Manglapus, Raul. Japan in Southeast Asia: Collision Course. New York: Carnegie Endowment for International Peace, 1976.

Marcos, Ferdinand. "Redefining the Role of Foreign Investment in a Developing Economy." In ASEAN and a Positive Strategy for Foreign Investment, edited by Lloyd Vasey. Honolulu: University Press of Hawaii, 1978.

Marzouk, G. A. Economic Development and Policies: Case Study of Thailand. Rotterdam: Rotterdam University Press, 1972.

Mazrui, Ali A. "The New Interdependence." In Beyond Dependency: The Developing World Speaks Out, edited by Guy F. Erb and Valeriana Kallab. New York: Praeger, 1975.

Melchor, Alejandro, Jr. "Assessing ASEAN's Viability in a Changing World." Asian Survey 17 (April 1977): 422-34.

Millar, T. B. "Prospects for Regional Security Cooperation in Southeast Asia." In Conflict and Stability in Southeast Asia, edited by Mark Zacher and R. S. Milne. New York: Anchor Press, 1974.

Milne, R. S. "Impulses and Obstacles to Caribbean Political Integration." International Studies Quarterly 18 (September 1974): 291-316.

_____. "The Politics of Malaysia's New Economic Policy." Pacific Affairs 49 (Summer 1976): 235-62.

Milne, R. S., and Diane Mauzy. Politics and Government in Malaysia. Vancouver: University of British Columbia Press, 1978.

Mitchell, J. Clyde, ed. Social Networks in Urban Situations. Manchester: Manchester University Press, 1969.

Moertopo, Ali. Indonesia in Regional and International Cooperation: Principles of Implementation and Construction. Jakarta: Centre for Strategic and International Studies, 1973.

Morrison, Charles, and Astri Suhrke. "ASEAN in Regional Defense and Development." In Changing Patterns of Security and Stability in Asia, edited by Sudershan Chamla and D. R. Sardesai. New York: Praeger, 1980.

_____. Strategies of Survival: The Foreign Policy Dilemmas of Smaller Asian States. St. Lucia: University of Queensland Press, 1978.

Morse, Edward L. "Crisis Diplomacy, Interdependence and the Politics of International Economic Relations." World Politics 24 (Spring Supplement 1972): 123-50.

_____. Modernization and the Transformation of International Relations. New York: Free Press, 1976.

_____. "The Politics of Interdependence." International Organization 23 (Autumn 1969): 311-26.

_____. "The Transformation of Foreign Policies: Modernization, Interdependence and Externalization." World Politics 22 (April 1970): 371-92.

Mortimer, Robert. The Third World Coalition in International Politics. New York: Praeger, 1980.

Murakami, Atsushi. Exports from Developing Countries to Japan: Problems and Solutions. Bangkok: Economic Cooperation Center for the Asian and Pacific Region, 1975.

Mytelka, Lynn. "The Salience of Gains in Third-World Integrative Systems." World Politics 25 (January 1973): 236-50.

Narongchai Akrasanee. "Development of Trade and Trade Policies in Thailand and Prospects for Trade Cooperation with ASEAN." In ASEAN Cooperation in Trade and Trade Policy, edited by Seiji Naya and Vinyu Vichit-Vadakan. Bangkok: UN Asia and Pacific Development Institute, 1977.

Naya, Seiji, and Narongchai Akrasanee. "Thailand's International Economic Relations with Japan and the U.S.: A Study of Trade and Investment Interactions." In Cooperation and Development in the Asia/Pacific Region: Relations between Large and Small Countries, edited by Leslie Castle and Frank Holmes. Tokyo: Japan Economic Research Center, 1976.

Naya, Seiji, and Theodore Morgan. "The Accuracy of International Trade Data: The Case of Southeast Asian Nations." SEADAG Paper 41 (July 1968).

Neuchterlein, Donald. "Prospects for Regional Security in Southeast Asia." Asian Survey 8 (September 1968): 806-16.

Noble, Lela G. "Ethnicity and Philippine-Malaysian Relations." Asian Survey 15 (May 1975): 453-72.

O'Brien, Rita Cruise, and G. K. Helleiner. "The Political Economy of Information in a Changing International Economic Order." International Organization 34 (Autumn 1980): 445-70.

Olsen, Richard S. "Economic Coercion in World Politics: With a Focus on North-South Relations." World Politics 31 (July 1979): 471-94.

Osborn, James. "Resources for Development and Development of Resources in Southeast Asia." In Southeast Asia, An Emerging Center of World Influence? Economic and Resource Considerations, edited by Wayne Raymond and K. Mulliner. Athens: Ohio University Press, 1977.

Oser, Jacob, and William Blanchfield. The Evolution of Economic Thought. 3d ed. New York: Harcourt Brace Jovanovich, 1975.

Ott, Marvin. The Neutralization of Southeast Asia: An Analysis of the Malaysia/ASEAN Proposal. Athens: Center for International Studies, Ohio University, 1974.

Panglaykim, J. "Economic Cooperation: Indonesian-Japanese Joint Ventures." Asian Survey 18 (March 1978): 247-60.

Parmar, Samuel L. "Self-Reliant Development in an 'Interdependent' World." In Beyond Dependency: The Developing World Speaks Out, edited by Guy F. Erb and Valeriana Kallab. New York: Praeger, 1975.

Paterno, Vincente. "Address." In Regionalism in Southeast Asia. Jakarta: Centre for Strategic and International Studies, 1975.

Pentland, Charles. "International Organizations." In World Politics, edited by James N. Rosenau, Kenneth W. Thompson, and Gavin Boyd. New York: Free Press, 1976.

Pollard, Vincent. "ASA and ASEAN, 1961-1967: Southeast Asian Regionalism." Asian Survey 10 (March 1970): 244-55.

Prachaksilp Tongyai. "Japanese Silence: ASEAN Noise." Asia-Pacific Community 4 (Spring 1979): 63-65.

Prachoom Chomchai. "Thailand." In The Economic Development of East and Southeast Asia, edited by Sinichi Ichimura. Honolulu: University Press of Hawaii, 1975.

Prebisch, Raul. Toward a New Trade Policy for Development. New York: United Nations, 1964.

Rajaratnam, Sinnathamby. "ASEAN External Relations." ASEAN Trader. Manila: ASEAN Trade Fair, 1978.

_____. "Beyond Nationalism, More Nationalism." Solidarity (Manila) 4 (January 1969): 42-47.

_____. "Opening Address." In Economic Relations between West Asia and Southeast Asia, edited by Lee Soo Ann. Singapore: Institute of Southeast Asian Studies, 1978.

Richardson, Neil R. Foreign Policy and Economic Dependence. Austin: University of Texas Press, 1978.

Richardson, Neil, and Charles Kegley, Jr. "Trade Dependence and Foreign Policy Compliance: A Longitudinal Analysis." International Studies Quarterly 24 (June 1980): 191-222.

Robison, Richard. "Toward a Class Analysis of the Indonesian Military Bureaucratic State." Indonesia 25 (April 1978): 17-39.

Romulo, Carlos. "Filipino Foreign Policy." Ambassador 3 (February 1973): 26-32.

_____. "A Perspective on ASEAN." Asia-Pacific Community 2 (Fall 1978): 1-6.

Rosecrance, Richard, and Arthur Stein. "Interdependence: Myth or Reality?" World Politics 26 (October 1973): 1-27.

Rosenberg, David, ed. Marcos and Martial Law in the Philippines. Ithaca, N.Y.: Cornell University Press, 1979.

Rothstein, Robert. Global Bargaining: UNCTAD and the Quest for a New International Economic Order. Princeton, N.J.: Princeton University Press, 1979.

Russett, Bruce M. International Regions and the International System: A Study in Political Ecology. Chicago: Rand McNally, 1967.

Sadli, Mohammad. "Foreign Investment in Developing Countries: Indonesia." In Direct Foreign Investment in Asia and the Pacific, edited by Peter Drysdale. Toronto: University of Toronto Press, 1972.

Sarasin Viraphol. Directions in Thai Foreign Policy. Singapore: Institute of Southeast Asian Studies, 1976.

Sarkar, Nikar K., ed. Foreign Investment and Economic Development in Asia. Bombay: Orient Longman, 1976.

Schmid, Gregory. "Interdependence Has Its Limits." Foreign Policy 21 (Winter 1975/76): 188-97.

Schmidt, Steffan, James Scott, Carl Landé, and Laura Guasti, eds. Friends, Followers and Factions: A Reader in Political Clientelism. Berkeley and Los Angeles: University of California Press, 1977.

Schubert, James N. "Toward a 'Working Peace System' in Asia: Organizational Growth and State Participation in Asian Regionalism." International Organization 32 (Spring 1978): 425-62.

Seah Chee Meow. "ASEAN and Regionalism in Southeast Asia." Southeast Asian Spectrum 2 (April 1974): 1-6.

Shee Poon-Kim. "A Decade of ASEAN, 1967-1977." Asian Survey 17 (August 1977): 753-70.

Sherk, Donald. "Foreign Investment in Southeast Asia: A Reconsideration." In Conflict and Stability in Southeast Asia, edited by Mark Zacher and R. S. Milne. Garden City, N.Y.: Anchor Books, 1974.

Simon, Sheldon. "The ASEAN States: Obstacles to Security Cooperation." Orbis 22 (Summer 1978): 415-34.

_____. Asian Neutralism and U.S. Foreign Policy. Washington, D.C.: American Enterprise Institute for Public Policy Research, 1975.

Singer, Marshall R. Weak States in a World of Powers: The Dynamics of International Relationships. New York: Free Press, 1972.

Skjelsback, Kjell. "The Growth of International Nongovernmental Organization in the Twentieth Century." In Transnational Organizations and World Politics, edited by Robert O. Keohane and Joseph S. Nye. Cambridge, Mass.: Harvard University Press, 1972.

Skully, Michael. ASEAN Regional Financial Cooperation: Developments in Banking and Finance. Singapore: Institute of Southeast Asian Studies, 1979.

Sloan, John W. "The Strategy of Developmental Regionalism: Benefits, Distribution, Obstacles and Capabilities." Journal of Common Market Studies 10 (1971): 138-62.

Soedjatmoko. "Problems and Prospects for Development in Indonesia." Asia 19 (Autumn 1970): 7-21.

Somsakdi Xuto. Regional Cooperation in Southeast Asia: Problems, Possibilities and Prospects. Bangkok: Institute of Asian Studies, Chulalongkorn University, 1973.

Spero, Joan. The Politics of International Economic Relations. New York: St. Martin's Press, 1977.

Stauffer, Robert. "Philippine Authoritarianism: Framework for Peripheral 'Development.'" Pacific Affairs 50 (Fall 1977): 365-86.

_____. "The Political Economy of a Coup: Transnational Linkages and Philippine Political Response." Journal of Peace Research 11 (1974): 161-77.

Subhan, Malcolm. "ASEAN and the EEC: The Search for a Trade Relationship." Southeast Asian Spectrum 2 (April 1974): 7-11.

_____. "ASEAN-EEC Relations." In Southeast Asian Affairs, 1977, edited by Kernial Sandhu. Singapore: Institute of Southeast Asian Studies, 1977.

Suhadi Manghusuwondo. "Economic Interdependence: The Indonesian View." In New Directions in the International Relations of Southeast Asia: Economic Relations, edited by Lee Soo-Ann. Singapore: Singapore University Press, 1973.

Sumardi Reksoputranto. "Development of Trade Policies of Indonesia in the Context of ASEAN Cooperation." In ASEAN Cooperation in Trade and Trade Policy, edited by Seiji Naya and Vinyu Vichit-Vadakan. Bangkok: UN Asian and Pacific Development Institute, 1977.

Sumitro Djojohadikusumo. "Foreign Economic Relations: Some Trade Aspects." Indonesia Quarterly 1 (January 1973): 18-26.

Sutomo Roesnadi. "Indonesia's Foreign Policy." In Trends in Indonesia, edited by Yong Mun Cheong. Singapore: Singapore
University Press, 1972.

Tsuda, Mamoru. A Preliminary Study of Japanese Filipino Joint
Ventures. Quezon City: Foundation for Nationalist Studies,
1978.

van der Kroef, Justus. "ASEAN Security and Development: Some
Paradoxes and Symbols." Asian Affairs 9 (June 1978): 143-60.

_____. "ASEAN's Security Needs and Policies." Pacific Affairs
47 (Summer 1974): 154-70.

_____. "Indonesia's National Security: Problems and Strategy."
Southeast Asian Spectrum 3 (July 1975): 37-49.

Virata, Cesar. "Foreign Investment in Developing Countries: The
Philippines." In Direct Foreign Investment in Asia and the
Pacific, edited by John Drysdale. Toronto: University of Tor-
onto Press, 1972.

Wallace, Michael D. "Clusters of Nations in the Global System,
1865-1964." In Explaining War, edited by J. David Singer.
Beverly Hills, Calif.: Sage, 1979.

Wallace, Michael D., and J. David Singer. "Intergovernmental Organization in the Global System, 1816-1964: A Quantitative
Description." International Organization 24 (Spring 1970): 239-
87.

Walleri, R. Dan. "The Political Economy Literature on North-South
Relations." International Studies Quarterly 22 (December 1978):
587-624.

Waltz, Kenneth. Theory of International Politics. Reading, Mass.:
Addison-Wesley, 1979.

Weinstein, Franklin. "Indonesia." In Asia and the International System, edited by Wayne Wilcox, Leo Rose, and Gavin Boyd.
Cambridge, Mass.: Winthrop, 1972.

_____. Indonesian Foreign Policy and the Dilemma of Dependence:
From Sukarto to Soeharto. Ithaca, N.Y.: Cornell University
Press, 1976.

_____. "Multinational Corporations and the Third World: The Case of Japan and Southeast Asia." International Organization 30 (Summer 1976): 373-404.

Wells, Louis, and V'Ella Warren. "Developing Country Investors in Indonesia." Bulletin of Indonesian Economic Studies 15 (March 1979): 69-84.

Wilbur, Charles K., ed. The Political Economy of Development and Underdevelopment. New York: Random House, 1973.

Wilson, Dick. The Neutralization of Southeast Asia. New York: Praeger, 1975.

Wong, John. ASEAN Economies in Perspective: A Comparative Study of Indonesia, Malaysia, the Philippines, Singapore and Thailand. Philadelphia: Institute for the Study of Human Issues, 1979.

_____. "Southeast Asia's Growing Trade Relations with Socialist Economies." Asian Survey 17 (April 1977): 330-44.

Wriggins, W. Howard. "Third-World Strategies for Change: The Political Context of North-South Interdependence." In Reducing Global Inequities, edited by W. Howard Wriggins and Gunner Adler-Karlsson. New York: McGraw-Hill, 1978.

Yamada, Tadoyoshi. "Foreign Investment in the ASEAN Region." In ASEAN and a Positive Strategy for Foreign Investment, edited by Lloyd Vasey. Honolulu: University Press of Hawaii, 1978.

Yamakage, Susumu. "Extra-Regional Dependence of the ASEAN Region: The Transaction Analysis of Trade Flows, 1950, 1960, 1970." Discussion Paper 93. Kyoto: Center for Southeast Asian Studies, Kyoto University, 1977.

_____. "Interdependence of the ASEAN Region: The Transaction Analysis of Trade Flows, 1950, 1960, 1970." Discussion Paper 92. Kyoto: Center for Southeast Asian Studies, Kyoto University, 1977.

Yoshihara, Kunio. Foreign Investment and Domestic Response. Singapore: Eastern Universities Press, 1976.

UNPUBLISHED PAPERS AND MANUSCRIPTS

Ariff, Mohamed. "ASEAN's External Economic Relations—The Quest for a Common Approach." Paper, Malaysian Economic Association, Kuala Lumpur, 1979.

_____. "The New International Economic Order: ASEAN at the Crossroads." Paper presented at the Third Conference of the Federation of ASEAN Economic Associations, Kuala Lumpur, 1978.

bin Yusof, Abdul Rahman. "Effective Program for ASEAN Industrial Cooperation, 1978-1983." Paper presented at the Third Conference of the Federation of ASEAN Economic Associations, Kuala Lumpur, 1978.

Bucklin, William. "Regional Economic Cooperation in Southeast Asia: 1945-1969." Ph.D. dissertation, Michigan State University, 1972.

Chia Siow Yue. "Singapore's Trade Strategy and Industrial Development, with Special Reference to the ASEAN Common Approach to Foreign Economic Policy." Paper presented at the Tenth Pacific Trade and Development Conference, Canberra, 1979.

English, H. Edward. "ASEAN's Quest for Allocative Efficiency in Manufacturing." Paper, Canadian Asian Studies Association, Montreal, 1980.

Jorgensen-Dahl, Arnfinn. "Southeast Asia and Theories of Regional Integration." Ph.D. dissertation, Australian National University, 1975.

Lee, S. Y., and Ann Booth. "Towards an Effective Programme for ASEAN Cooperation from 1978 to 1983." Paper presented at the Third Conference of the ASEAN Federation of Economic Associations, Kuala Lumpur, 1978.

Lim, Linda. "The Political Economy of Foreign Investment in Malaysia." Paper, Association for Asian Studies, Washington, D.C., 1980.

Lim Chong Yah. "Singapore's Position in ASEAN Economic Cooperation." University of Singapore staff seminar paper, 1979.

Morrison, Charles. "The ASEAN Governments and Transnational Relations." Paper, International Studies Association, Washington, D. C., 1979.

_____. "Southeast Asia in a Changing International Environment: A Comparative Foreign Policy Analysis of Four ASEAN-Member Countries." Ph. D. dissertation, Johns Hopkins University, 1976.

Narongchai Akrasanee. "ASEAN and the New International Economic Order: A View from Thailand." Paper presented at the Third Conference of the ASEAN Federation of Economic Associations, Kuala Lumpur, 1978.

Richardson, Neil R. "Economic Dependence and Foreign Policy Compliance: Bringing Measurement Closer to Conception." Paper, International Studies Association, Los Angeles, March 1980.

Saravanamuttu, Jayaratnam. "A Study of the Content, Sources and Development of Malaysian Foreign Policy, 1957-1975." Ph. D. dissertation, University of British Columbia, 1976.

Sinaga, Edward Janner. "ASEAN: Economic, Political and Defense Problems, Progress and Prospects in Regional Cooperation with Reference to the Role of Major Powers in Southeast Asia." Ph. D. dissertation, George Washington University, 1974.

Snow, Robert T. "Southeast Asia and the World System: Origins and Extent of Export Oriented Industrialization in the ASEAN Countries." Paper, Association for Asian Studies, Washington, D. C., 1980.

Solidum, Estrella. "The Nature of Cooperation among the ASEAN States as Perceived through Elite Attitudes—A Factor for Regionalism." Ph. D. dissertation, University of Kentucky, 1970.

Wells, R. J. G. "ASEAN Commodity Trade Policies: Objectives and Strategies." Paper presented at the Third Conference of the Federation of ASEAN Economic Associations, Kuala Lumpur, November 24, 1978.

OFFICIAL PUBLICATIONS

Association of Southeast Asian Nations. 10 Years ASEAN. Jakarta: ASEAN Secretariat, 1978.

Association of Southeast Asian Nations, Chambers of Commerce and Industry. ASEAN-CCI Handbook, 1978. Bangkok: ASEAN Chamber of Commerce and Industry, 1978.

_____. Report of the First Plenary Meeting of the ASEAN-CCI Working Group on Industrial Complementation. Singapore: ASEAN Chambers of Commerce and Industry, 1976.

_____. Report of the Proceedings, Fifth Council Meeting. Singapore: ASEAN Chambers of Commerce and Industry, 1976.

Embassy of the Republic of Indonesia, Singapore. "Indonesia's Trade Policies." Singapore: Embassy of the Republic of Indonesia, 1971.

Malaysia. Second Malaysia Plan, 1971-1975. Kuala Lumpur: Government Printers, 1971.

_____. Third Malaysia Plan, 1976-1980. Kuala Lumpur: Government Printers, 1976.

Malaysia, Federal Industrial Development Authority. Annual Report, 1977. Kuala Lumpur: Government Printers, 1978.

Republic of the Philippines. Five-Year Philippine Development Plan, 1978-1982. Manila: National Economic and Development Authority, 1977.

_____. Four-Year Development Plan, FY 1974-1977. Manila: National Economic and Development Authority, 1973.

Republic of the Philippines, National Economic and Development Authority. Philippine Development Report, 1978. Manila: National Economic and Development Authority, 1979.

Republic of the Philippines, Philippine Army Civil Relations and Information Service. Guiding Principles of the New Society II. Manila: National Printing, 1978.

Singapore, Economic Development Board. Annual Report, 1960-1978. Singapore: Economic Development Board, various dates.

_____. Major International Companies Manufacturing in Singapore. Singapore: Economic Development Board, 1979.

United Nations, Industrial Development Organization. The Effectiveness of Industrial Estates in Developing Countries. New York: UNIDO, 1978.

World Bank. The Philippines: Priorities and Prospects for Development. Washington, D.C.: World Bank, 1976.

NEWSPAPERS AND PERIODICALS

ASEAN Briefing (Singapore).

ASEAN Business Quarterly (Singapore).

Asia Research Bulletin (Hong Kong).

Asian Wall Street Journal (Hong Kong).

Business Times (Singapore).

Export Bulletin (Philippines).

Far Eastern Economic Review (Hong Kong).

Foreign Affairs Malaysia (Malaysia).

Indonesian Development News (Jakarta).

New Nation (Singapore).

New Straits Times (Malaysia).

Philippine Development (Philippines).

Straits Times (Malaysia).

Straits Times (Singapore).

INDEX

Asian and Australasian Hotel and
Restaurant Association, 157
Asian and Pacific Council (ASPAC),
36, 37
Asian Badminton Confederation, 156
Asian Cultural Forum, 156
Asian Development Bank (ADB), 48
Asian Development Center, 156
"Asia-Pacific Triangle," 75
ASPAC (see Asian and Pacific Council)
Association of Southeast Asia (ASA),
36-37
Association of Southeast Asia Nations
(see ASEAN)
Asymmetrical interdependence, 4,
6, 29, 62
Australia: ASEAN economic ties, 48-
49, 65, 66, 167; ASEAN investment
policy with, 115, 167; and "Asia-
Pacific Triangle," 75; Indonesian
trade policy with, 74, 76; and
Malaysia, ties to, 47; Singapore's
investment policy with, 112
Australia-ASEAN Business Council,
167
automobile industry, 45, 171
automobile parts industry: Canadian
cooperation in, 115; Japanese cooperation in, 171
autonomy, political, 20-21

Bali summit (1976), 39, 41, 42, 47,
162
Bangladesh, Singapore's investments
in, 112
banking: Indonesia's development policy, 101; service organizations,
156, 162-63 (see also individual
names)
Barisian Sosialis, 110
Board of Investments (Thailand), 113,
114
British Airways, Quantas agreement,
49
Brotherhood of Asian Trade Unionists,
156
Burma, 16, 184, 185

Canada: ASEAN investment policy with,
115-16; ASEAN ties, 51, 66; lumber

imports, 163; Malaysia's investment policy with, 107; Philippine ties, 47
Canadian International Development
Agency (CIDA), 115
Capital Assistance Scheme (Singapore), 111
Caporaso, James, 2, 5, 29, 195
cartels, 16, 24
centrality (social-network theory),
145, 146, 152-53, 159
chambers of commerce (see indi-
vidual names)
China: autarky, 184, 185; dominance
of, 39; Japanese ties, 50; and
Malaysia's New Economic Policy,
106; Malaysia's trade with, 73;
Singapore's trade with, 68; socie-
ties and families, Asian influence
of, 142; Thailand's trade with, 77;
and United States relations, 69
Choucri, Nazli, 1
Christian Conference of Asia, 156
CIDA (see Canadian International
Development Agency)
COIME (see Committee on Industry,
Minerals and Energy)
"collective-bargaining force,"
ASEAN as, 51
Colombo Plan, 36
colonialism, 69, 72, 186, 189
COMECON (see Council for Mutual
Economic Assistance)
commercial associations, 156, 157,
158
Committee for ASEAN Youth Cooperation, 40
Committee on Industry, Minerals
and Energy (COIME), 168
Committee on Trade and Tourism
(COTT), 168
commodity clubs, regional, 170, 171
commodity-price-stabilization agreement (see STABEX)
Commonwealth Advisory Aeronautical Research Council, 152
Commonwealth Agricultural Bureaux,
152
communication, organizational, 142,
145, 173

Confederation of ASEAN Chambers of Commerce and Industry (ASEAN CCI or ACCI), 45, 162; committee on Banking, 163; industry and commodity clubs, 170-73; international connections, 166-67; national members, 164; ties with ASEAN governments, 168; Working Group on Industrial Complementation (WGIC), 164, 166, 170; Working Group on Trade, 164, 165-66, 170
conferences, diplomatic, 115-16
control, domestic, diversification and, 26
Cooper, Richard, 24
COTT (see Committee on Trade and Tourism)
Council for Mutual Economic Assistance (COMECON), 75
Cox, Robert, 143
customs procedures, 165

Datuk Seri Mahathir bin Mohammad, 107
debts, 27
decisional power, 29
Declaration of ASEAN Concord, 42-44, 47, 63, 65
delinkage, 20-21, 184, 185, 188, 191-92
density (social-network theory), 146, 148, 152, 157-58
dependency theory, 19-22, 29, 184; vs. dependence, 11-12, 29, 195; financial ties and, 25-26; organizational ties and, 26, 141; trade and, 20-21, 25, 62
"dialogues" (diplomatic conferences), 115-16
diesel engines, development of, 44
diplomacy, 40-41, 115-16
diversification: defined, 15-16; dependence and, 4; dependency theory of, 21-22; economic, 15-16, 64; economic nationalism and, 19; of foreign investment, 16, 97-128, 190-91; geographical, 16, 19; interdependence and, 24-25; limitations of, 30-31, 88-90, 127-28; methods of inquiry, 26-30; as political strategy,

16; of sources, 26; of trade, 25, 64-90, 186-89
domestic stability, 39
Dos Santos, Theotonio, 20

Economic Cooperation among Developing Countries (ECDC), 71, 186, 187
Economic Development Board (EDB), 111, 112
economic liberalism, 22-24, 183-85
economic nationalism, 7, 17-19, 183, 188, 190, 193; domestic controls and, 26; of Indonesia, 101; of Malaysia, 104; new vs. old forms of, 63-64; of Thailand, 114; trade diversification and, 25
economic programs: external, 47-51; internal, 42-47
economic rationality, 22
economic theory, 17-25, 183-86
EDB (see Economic Development Board)
educational groups, 156, 157
EEC (European Economic Community), 40, 183; ACCI ties, 167; ASEAN investment diversification and, 116, 117; ASEAN ties, 50, 196; and Indonesia, cooperation with, 47; Indonesia's investment policy with, 103, 126; Malaysia's trade dependence and policy with, 84; Philippine's investment policy with, 109, 126; as regional organization, 159; and Singapore, investments in, 112, 122, 127; and Singapore, trade with, 82; Thailand's investment policy with, 114; trade direction, 62, 65, 66, 75, 80
employers' associations, 157
employment, Singapore's policy on, 110
energy, 164
ESCAP (see United Nations Economic and Social Commission for Asia and the Pacific)
ethnonationalism, 37
Europe, Eastern: Indonesia's solicitation of ties with, 75, 103;

Malaysia's trade policy with, 73; Singapore's trade policy with, 68

Europe, Western: Indonesian export promotion in, 76; Indonesian trade policy with, 74; Malaysia's investment policy with, 107; Singapore's trade policy with, 68; as trade partner to balance, U.S. and Japan, 67 (see also EEC)

Export Promotion Committee (Thailand), 77

exports: commodities, 62; concentration of, 89; diversification of, 21, 89; increase of, 65, 105; lumber, 163; statistics, 4, 27 (see also trade)

FAO (see Food and Agriculture Organization)

Far Eastern Freight Conference, 163

FASC (see Federation of ASEAN Shippers' Council)

Federation of ASEAN Economics Associations, 162

Federation of ASEAN Shipowners' Association, 163

Federation of ASEAN Shippers' Council (FASC), 157, 163

Federation of Malaysian Manufacturers, 169

"Filipino First" policy, 108

finance: developing countries' trade and cooperation in, 71; Philippine control of, 109; statistics, 27

fisheries, 106

Food and Agriculture Organization (FAO), 48

Foreign Investment Committee (Malaysia), 106

Foreign Investment Committee (Thailand), 77, 114

forestry: in Indonesia, development policy, 101; in Philippines, control of, 109 (see also lumber)

France, Indonesia's investment campaign in, 103

Frasier, Malcolm, 48

free trade, 21, 42-43, 183

Fukuda, Takeo, 44

Fukuda Doctrine, 64

furniture industry: Canadian cooperation in, 115; regional coordination, 172

Galtung, Johan, 5

GDP (see gross domestic product)

General Agreement on Tariffs and Trade (GATT), 40, 65, 68, 183

Generalized System of Preferences (GSP), 65, 68

geographical diversification, 16, 19

German Historical School, 17, 18

Germany, investments, 116

Gilpin, Robert, 18

glass industry, coordination of, 45

global organizations (see organizations, global)

Goh Chok Tong, 68

Great Britain: Indonesia's investment policy with, 119; Malaysia's colonial ties with, 72; as Malaysia's investor, 104, 122; Thailand's investment dependence on, 113

Greater Malayan Confederation (see Maphilindo)

gross domestic product (GDP): of ASEAN members, 3-4; proportion of manufacturing in, 97; proportion of trade in, 62

Group of 77, 47, 78, 186

GSP (see Generalized System of Preferences)

Haas, Michael, 147

Hamilton, Alexander, 17

health, professional societies, 155

Helleiner, G. K., 142

hierarchies, organizational, 145

Hill, H. Monte, 9

Hirschman, Albert O., 5, 18, 19, 61

Hispano-Luso-American-Philippino Assembly on Tourism, 158

Hon Sui Sen, 162

Hong Kong: at ACCI conferences, 167; as Indonesia's investor in textiles, 119; Indonesia's trade policy with, 74; Philippines' investment policy with, 111, 122

hotel organizations, 156

Howell, Llewellyn, Jr., 9

Huntington, Samuel, 141, 142

IGGI (see International Group on Indonesia)

IGOs (see organizations, intergovernmental)

imports: of capital goods, ASEAN percentage, 89; diversification of, 24; statistics, 27 (see also trade)

India, Malaysia's New Economic Policy and, 106

Indonesia: ACCI relations, 168-69; ASEAN relations, 73; commodities, share of, to total exports, 62; in commodity organizations, 152; domestic economy, 74, 76; EEC ties, 47; GDP, proportion to total trade, 62; industrial projects, 44, 166; investment dependence and policy, 97, 101-4, 119, 126, 127, 128; and Japan, cooperation with, 47; and Malaysia, hostilities toward, 37, 67; membership in IGOs, 148-53; membership in NGOs, 157, 158; membership in OPEC, 148, 152; and PTA, approach to, 42-43; Singapore's investments in, 112; trade dependence and policy, 67, 74-77, 84-85, 88; urea plant development, 44

Indonesian Chambers of Commerce and Industry, 164

Indonesian National Agency for Export Development, 74, 76

industrial complementation projects, 45-46, 117; ACCI Working Group on Industrial Complementation, 164, 166, 170; Canadian, 115; EEC study on, 50; regional industry clubs, 171-73

Industrial Coordination Act (Malaysia), 107

industrialization: ASEAN, 43-45, 97; Indonesian, 102

industry clubs: national (NICs), 170; regional (RICs), 162, 170-73

influence, organizational, 145-47, 156

information sharing, 142, 145, 173

interdependence, 22-25, 29, 62; asymmetrical, 4, 6, 29, 62; investment diversification and, 100; organizational relationships and, 26, 141; trade diversification and, 25

Intergovernmental Council of Copper-Exporting Countries, 152

Intergovernmental Group on Indonesia (IGGI), 75

intergovernmental organizations (see organizations, intergovernmental)

International Association for the Study of Pain, 155

International Bauxite Organization, 152

International Chamber of Commerce, 167

International Coffee Organization, 152

International Confederation of Free Trade Unions Asian Region Organization, 156

International Islamic Organization, 156

internationalism, 183-86, 188, 193 (see also regionalism)

International Organization for Standardization, 167

international organizations (see organizations, global)

international political economy, 17-25, 183-86

International Sericultural Organization, 152

International Society of Money Box Collectors, 156

International Society of Tropical Dermatology, 155

International Tea Committee, 152

International Union of Physiological Sciences, 155

International Union of Prehistoric and Protohistoric Sciences, 155

International Youth Hostel Federation, 156

Intraco, 68

investments, foreign: ASEAN's dependence and policy, 97-101, 114-18, 167, 191; diversification of, 16, 97-128, 190-91; domestic vs. foreign interests, 99-100, 114; incentive systems for, 105, 111; Indonesia's dependence and policy, 97, 101-4, 119, 126, 127, 128; Malaysia's dependence and policy, 97, 104-8, 119-22, 126, 127, 128; Philippine's dependence and policy, 97, 108-10, 119, 122, 126, 127, 128; political concerns, 102,

103, 144; Singapore's dependence
and policy, 97, 110-12, 119, 122,
127, 128; statistical analysis, 27,
28; strategic approaches to, 25-26;
Thailand's dependence and policy,
97, 113-14, 119, 122, 126, 127-28
Islamic Conference, 153

Jacobson, Harold, 143
Jakarta riots (1974), 74
Japan: at ACCI conferences, 167;
ASEAN economic ties, 49-50, 64,
196; ASEAN investment dependence
and policy, 116-17, 189; ASEAN
trade direction with, 64, 65, 80,
82, 89, 167; "Asia-Pacific Triangle"
and, 75; China, ties with, 50; imperialism, 99; industrial projects
financial, 44; and Indonesia, cooperation with, 47; Indonesia's investment dependence and policy
with, 102-3, 104, 119, 126, 127;
Indonesia's trade policy with, 74,
75, 76, 84-85, 88; lumber imports,
ASEAN, 163; Malaysia's investment
dependence on, 122, 126; Malaysia's
trade involvement with, 84, 88;
Philippines' investment dependence
and policy with, 109, 110, 122, 126;
Philippines' trade dependence and
policy with, 69, 70, 71, 83, 84, 87;
Singapore's investment promotion
in, 112, 127; Singapore's trade policy and direction with, 82; synthetic
rubber production, 40; Thailand's
investment policy with, 114, 122,
126, 127; Thailand's trade dependence and policy with, 77-78, 85, 87
Japan Auto Parts Industrial Association, 171
Japanese Chamber of Commerce and
Industry, 167
Japanese Federation of Economic Organizations, 167
Japan Lumber Importers' Association, 163
Joint Standing Committee on Commerce
and Industry of Thailand, 164

Kampuchea, 39
Kengley, Charles, Jr., 9

Keohane, Robert, 24
Khoman, Thanat, 38
Korea (Republic): Indonesia's trade
policy with, 74; lumber imports,
ASEAN, 163
Kuala Lumpur summit (1977), 47, 162

labor-intensive projects: Indonesia's
emphasis on, 101; Malaysia's emphasis on, 105; Singapore's emphasis on, 110, 111, 112
labor unions, global organizations,
156, 157
Latin America: dependency theories
and, 19; Malaysia's trade with,
73; Philippines' organizational
ties to, 158; Singapore's export
drive in, 68; regionalism in, 159,
184; Thailand's trade with, 78
Laurel-Langley Treaties, 69, 108
Lee, Kuan Yew, 41, 47, 48, 67
leisure organizations, 156
liberalism, economic, 22, 23, 24,
183-84, 185
List, Friedrich, 17, 18
loans, 25-26
Lome Agreement, 50, 62
lumber, 163

Macapagal, Diosdado, 108
Malaysia: ACCI ties, 169; and Asia,
West, cooperation with, 47; and
Australia, cooperation with, 47;
Australia's trade protectionism
and, 48; commodities, share of,
to total exports, 62; GDP, proportion of to total trade, 62; Indonesia's hostilities, 37, 67; industrial projects and policy, 44, 166;
investment dependence and policy,
97, 104-8, 119-23, 126, 127, 128;
membership in commonwealth organizations, 152; membership in
IGOs, 147-53; membership in
NGOs, 157; membership in OPEC,
147-48; Philippines' boundary debate, 37; Singapore's investments
in, 112; Singapore's relationship
with, 67; trade dependence and policy, 72-74, 84, 88; urea plant development, 44

Malaysian Industrial Development Authority (MIDA), 105, 107, 169
Malik, Adam, 75, 103
manufacturers' associations, 156
Maphilindo, 36, 37
Marcos, Ferdinand, 69, 87, 108, 109, 110
Marxism, 183
medicine, professional societies, 155
mercantilism, 17-19, 183
MIDA (see Malaysian Industrial Development Authority)
Middle East: Indonesia's export promotion in, 76; Singapore's trade policy with, 68
mining: Indonesia's development policy, 101; Malaysia's investment policy, 106; Philippine majority control of, 109
MNCs (see multinational corporations)
Moertopo, Ali, 75
Moro National Liberation Front, 153
Morrison, Charles, 172
multilateral trade negotiations (MTNs), 49-50
multinational corporations (MNCs): as focus of studies, 1; Philippine investment policy with, 110; political effects of, 98-99; trade by developing countries, 21; transfer-price abuses, counter to, 165

Nairobi, 72
National Chamber of Commerce and Industry of Malaysia, 164
nationalism economic (see economic nationalism)
nationalization, 106-7, 191
national security, 63
neomercantilism, 17, 183
NEP (see New Economic Policy)
network theory (see social-network theory)
New Economic Policy (NEP), 106-7
New Industrial Economic Order (NIEO), 1, 16, 186
New Zealand: ASEAN ties, 66, 115; Indonesia's timber market, 76; Singapore's ties with, 47
NGOs (see organizations, nongovernmental)

NICs (see industry clubs, national)
Nitisastro, Widjojo, 104
nongovernmental organizations (see organizations, nongovernmental)
North-South Conferences, 1, 11
Nye, Joseph S., 24

O'Brien, Rita Cruise, 142
OECD (see Organization for Economic Cooperation and Development)
oil, Indonesia's policy of development, 101
oil companies, Malaysia's management sharing system with, 106
Olsen, Richard, 191
OPEC, 16, 23, 147-48, 184
Organization for Economic Cooperation and Development (OECD), 4
organizations: commodity, 152; commonwealth, 152
organizations, global: ASEAN involvement in, 142-44, 147; communication and, 142, 145, 173; intergovernmental (see organizations, intergovernmental); nongovernmental (see organizations, nongovernmental); Philippines growth in, 147; political economists' analysis of, 141; regional nongovernmental (see organizations, regional nongovernmental); security, 36; social-network theory of, 144-47; statistics, 27, 28; strategic approaches to, 26
organizations, intergovernmental (IGOs): ASEAN membership, 145-54; Asian vs. ASEAN membership, 147; commodity organizations, 152; commonwealth organizations, 152; definition, 142; developed regions' concentration in, 142; economics and, 154, 173; NGO ties, 154
organizations, nongovernmental (NGOs): ASEAN in, 40, 154-59; commerce, 156, 157, 158; definition, 142; developed regions' concentration in, 142-43; educational and youth groups, 156, 157; headquarters in ASEAN states, 155, 156, 157; IGO ties, 154; industrial,

156-57; informal networks, 142; labor, 156, 157; political, 156, 157; professional societies, 155-56; social and cultural, 156, 157; Third World participation in, 142; United Nations Economic and Social Council, ties with, 154

organizations, regional nongovernmental (RNGOs): African, 159; banking, 162-63; chambers of commerce (see Confederation of ASEAN Chambers of Commerce and Industry); cultural, 162; economic emphasis of, 159-62, 173; energy, 163-64; industry clubs, 162; professional, 159, 162; Latin American, 159; lumber services, 163; origin of, 162; shipping, 163; social, 159, 162 (see also regionalism)

Pacific Basin Economic Cooperation Council, 167
Paterno, Vincente, 71, 168
Pentland, Charles, 147
Permanent Court of Arbitration, 152
Pertamina crisis, 102
petrochemical industry, 45, 164
petroleum, 84, 89
Petroleum Development Act (Malaysia), 106
Philippine Chamber of Commerce and Industry, 164
Philippine Ministry of Trade, 71
Philippines: ACCI ties, 168; and Australia, trade protectionism against, 48; banking services, 163; Canada cooperation with, 47; commodities, share of, to total exports, 62; GDP, proportion of to total trade, 62; Group of 77 ties, 47; industrial projects and policy, 166; investment dependence and policy, 97, 108-10, 119, 126, 127, 128; and Latin America, organizational ties to, 158; and Malaysia, boundary debate, 37; martial law, effects of, 69, 108; membership in IGOs, 148-53; membership in NGOs, 157, 158; and PTA, 42-43; shipping services, 163; Singapore's investments in, 112; superphosphate development, 44; trade

dependence and policy, 69-71, 83-84, 87; and United States, cooperation with, 47
Pioneer Industries Act (Malaysia), 105
political economy, international, 17-25, 183-86
polyvinylchloride producers, 172
power, decisional vs. structural, 29
Prebisch, Paul, 61, 184
Preferential Trade Agreement (PTA), 42-43, 46, 66, 165
pressure groups, 154, 159
professional organizations, 155-56, 158, 159, 162
protectionism, 17-18, 48, 68
PTA (see Preferential Trade Agreement)

Quantas, 49

racial riots, Malaysia, 106
Rajaratnam, S., 63, 100, 114, 116
range (social-network theory), 145-46, 147-48, 157
recession, 102
recreational organizations, 156
Recto, Claro, 108
regimes, international, 24, 26, 141 (see also organizations, global)
regionalism, 9, 16, 26; defensive, 186-97; development of, in Southeast Asia, 36-37, 51; domestic stability and, 63; limitations, 30 (see also organizations, regional nongovernmental)
regional nongovernment organizations (see organizations, regional nongovernmental)
religious organizations, 156, 158
Repelita series, 76, 102, 187
RICs (see industry clubs, regional)
RNGOs (see organizations, regional nongovernmental)
Robinson, Austin, 42
rubber, 40

Schubert, James, 9, 147, 154
science, 71
SEATO (see Southeast Asia Treaty Organization)
security organizations, 36

self-reliance, 21, 62, 71; collective, 184-97
sensitivity, 28, 62
shipping, regional organizations, 163
Singapore: ACCI ties, 169; airline and tourist trade, 49; ASEAN ties, 46; commodities, share of, to total exports, 62; diesel engines, development of, 44; GDP, proportion of to total trade, 62; Indonesian trade embargo, 67; industrial projects and policy, 44, 166; investment dependence and policy, 97, 110-12, 119, 122, 127, 128; Malaysia's investment policy with, 107, 108, 122; membership in IGOs, 148-52; membership in NGOs, 157, 158; and New Zealand, ties with, 47; and PTA, 42-53; shipping services, 163; textile club, 172; trade dependence and policy, 67-68, 82-83, 87-88
Singapore Federation of Chambers of Commerce and Industry, 164
Singapore Manufacturers Association, 68, 112
Singer, Marshall, 141
Smith, Adam, 183
social anthropology, 5, 144
socialist countries: Indonesia's export promotion in, 76; Singapore's trade direction with, 83
Socialist International, 156
social-network theory, 5-6, 144-47; centrality, 145, 146, 152-53, 159; definition, 145; density, 145, 146, 148, 152, 157-58; range, 145-46, 147-48, 157
soda ash, 44
Solidium, Estrella, 9
Southeast Asia Iron and Steel Institute, 157
Southeast Asia Treaty Organization (SEATO), 36, 37, 117
South Korea (see Korea [Republic])
Soviet Union: Indonesia's investment negotiations with, 103; Malaysia's economic ties with, 71; role of, to ASEAN, 64
sports organizations, 156, 157
Sri Lanka, 112
STABEX (commodity-price-stabilization agreement), 50

statistics, analysis of, 27-28
steel clubs, 172
steel industry, 45
structural power, 29
Suharto, 37, 74
superphosphates, 44

Taiwan: as Indonesia's investor in textiles, 119; Indonesia's trade policy with, 74; lumber imports, ASEAN, 163
Tan Siew Sin, 72
Tanzania, 185
tariff barriers, 42-43, 66, 165
technology: developing countries' cooperation in, 71; Singapore's emphasis on, 110, 111
technology transfers, 20, 50, 117; dependency theory on, 26; Indonesia's policy on, 101
textile clubs, 171-72
Textile Workers' Asian Regional Organization, 156
Thailand: ACCI ties, 169; commodities, share of, to total exports, 62; and ESCAP, ties to, 47; GDP, proportion of total trade to, 62; industrial projects and policy, 44, 166; investment dependence and policy, 97, 113-14, 119, 122, 126, 127-28; membership in IGOs, 148-53; membership in NGOs, 157; and PTA, 43; Singapore's investments in 112; soda ash, 44; trade dependence and policy, 77-79, 85, 87; and UNDP, ties with, 47
Thailand-Japan Joint Study Committee on Economic Cooperation, 78
Third World trade: with Indonesia, 85; with Philippines, 71, 83, 87; with Singapore, 83, 88; with Thailand, 85, 87
tourism organizations, 156
trade: ACCI Working Group on Trade, 164, 165-66, 170; ASEAN policy and direction, 64-67, 80, 167; commodity clubs, 170, 171; Declaration of ASEAN Concord (see Declaration of ASEAN Concord); dependency and, 20-21, 25; diversification of, 25, 64-90, 186-89; economic nationalism and, 18-19, 25; EEC, 50;

expansion, 79; free trade, 21, 42–43, 183; Indonesia's dependence and policy, 74–77, 84–85, 88; interdependence and, 22–25; Japan, 49–50, 62–63, 167; Malaysia's dependence and policy, 72–74, 84, 88; New Zealand, 51; Philippines' dependence and policy, 69–71, 83–84, 87; Preferential Trade Agreement (PTA), 42–43, 46, 66, 165; protectionism, 17–18, 48, 68; Singapore's dependence and policy, 67–68, 82–83, 87–88; statistics, 27, 28, 165; tariff barriers, 42–43, 66, 165; Thailand's dependence and policy, 77–79, 85, 87; United States, 167

trade unions, global organizations, 156, 157

transport organizations, 156

UIA (see Union of International Associations)
UN (see United Nations)
UNCTAD (see United Nations Conference on Trade and Development)
UNDP (see United Nations Development Programme)
UNIDO (see United Nations Industrial Development Organization)
Union of International Associations (UIA), 154, 159
unions, trade, global organizations, 156, 157
United Kingdom (see Great Britain)
United Nations: ASEAN economic cooperation, 42; and developing countries, trade policy with, 75
United Nations Commission for Latin America, 184
United Nations Conference on Trade and Development (UNCTAD), 1, 11, 48, 65, 71, 72, 76, 184–87; Manila meeting (1979), 49, 50
United Nations Development Programme (UNDP), 47, 48
United Nations Economic and Social Commission for Asia and the Pacific (ESCAP), 36, 47, 48, 163
United Nations Economic Commission for Asia and the Far East, 36
United Nations Economic Council, 154

United Nations Industrial Development Organization (UNIDO), 48
United Nations of Yoga, 156
United States: ASEAN investment dependence and policy with, 116, 117, 167, 196; ASEAN trade relations, 64, 65, 80, 82, 167; and China, effect of opening of ties on Philippines, 69; Indonesia's investment dependence and policy with, 119; Indonesia's trade policy with, 74, 76; Philippines' investment dependence and policy with, 108, 109, 110, 122, 126–27; Philippines' trade dependence and policy with, 69, 71, 83, 84, 87; Singapore's investment promotion in, 112, 122, 127; Singapore's trade dependence and policy with, 68, 82; Thailand's investment policy with, 114; Vietnam, withdrawal from, 39

urea plants, 44

Vasuratna, Ob, 77, 78
Vietnam: reunification of, 39, 41; Singapore's trade policy with, 68

vulnerability, 6, 28, 30, 62, 187

Wallace, Michael D., 153
Walleri, R. Dan, 183
Weinstein, Franklin, 61–62
welfare state, rise of, 22
Wong, John, 61–62
World Airlines Clubs Associations, 156
World Anti-Communist League, 156
World Bank, 78
World Bridge Federation, 156
World Council on Curriculum and Instruction, 156
World Fellowship of Buddhists, 156
World Poultry Science Association, 155
World Psychiatric Association, 155

youth organizations, 156

ABOUT THE AUTHOR

DONALD K. CRONE is Assistant Professor of International Relations at James Madison College, Michigan State University. He has been a research associate at the Institute of Southeast Asian Studies, Singapore, and the Institute of International Relations, University of British Columbia.

Dr. Crone's previous articles and reviews on Southeast Asia have appeared in Asian Survey, Contemporary Southeast Asia, Pacific Affairs, and an edited volume.

Dr. Crone holds a B.S. from the University of California, Los Angeles, an M.A. from Portland State University, and a Ph.D. from the University of British Columbia.